HUSTLE GUIDE

THE PRESEASON

Hustle Guide, The Preseason by Hustle 2.0, A Public Benefit Corporation

Write us at: Hustle 2.0, 500 Westover Dr. #15672, Sanford, NC 27330
Visit our website at www.hustle20.com

Book Cover and Design by Laura Boyle.

Special thanks to the people with criminal histories who contributed their wit, wisdom, and stories to make our courses more relevant and engaging.

THE STASH

I swear to Hustle, Grind, and Invest my Time.
HUSTLE GUIDE
HUSTLE GUIDE

PROGRAM INTRODUCTION

The Rundown

◂ *Illustration by Trenton Dukes*

WELCOME TO HUSTLE 2.0!

2.0

Adjective

Commonly used in the tech world to denote a superior or more advanced version of an original concept, product, service, etc.

To us, 2.0 means a second chance; a polished version of ourselves.

We're transforming our lives and our hustles, reinventing ourselves into our 2.0 versions. We owe it to ourselves, our families, and our communities.

Most rehabilitation programs are created by people who have never walked the mainline. Our curriculum is written by men doing time, for people who are tired of doing time. We are living the struggle and walking the walk.

We call ourselves H2.0's Homies. We're the incarcerated co-authors who contribute testimonials, case studies, recipes, and more. We're up at Pelican Bay State Prison, a supermax in California that has one of the largest SHU facilities in the United States. (SHU stands for Security Housing Unit, aka the hole). Several of us served 32 consecutive years in the Pelican Bay SHU before being released to the general population. California has us on the books as some of its top gang leaders. See our bios.

Several of us served 32 consecutive years in the Pelican Bay SHU.

We write in partnership with Hustle 2.0's free staff. H2.0's founders previously created Prison Entrepreneurship Program and Defy Ventures, two nationally recognized rehabilitation programs, which have served 6,000+ incarcerated people and achieved recidivism rates of less than 8% since 2004. They've incubated 450+ businesses started by formerly incarcerated grads and helped countless people land jobs.

That's our rap sheet. Any questions?

We're not just transforming our hustle; we're flipping the script on negative lingo – just like our name. "Hustle" hasn't always had the most positive connotations, which is why that 2.0 is so important. We believe that many negative things from the past can be redeemed, transformed, and redirected for positive purposes.

"There are three types of people in this world: those who make things happen, those who watch things happen, and those who wonder what happened."

Which one are you?

You'll spot this journal icon below throughout the book, with questions for reflection.

Yes, you could be a spectator and leave the line after the icon blank. But just like cheating in a workout, you'll only hurt yourself. Tired of repeating old patterns? Take 20 seconds to write out these one-liners!

Start by declaring your choice:

☑ I'm maximizing the value of The Preseason by writing at least one word on every journal line in this book.

OR

☐ I'll chill as a spectator for now.

What's a negative thing from your past that could be redeemed (e.g., my relationship with my son, my career, the way I've looked at myself)?

My relationship with myself

OUR VISION

When it comes to freedom, that's mando. Priority #1. "I'll do anything to obtain it" – says everyone.

If we could pick a superpower, it might be flying … so we could fly the flip out of here. But until we boss up on that skill, we're stuck like Chuck … some of us permanently. We're using our time to change perceptions as we engage our leadership, our skills, our hearts, and our communities in the right way.

Hustle 2.0 is about recognizing that the old-school way of thinking has only led us to more of … this.

I, Sweet Freddy, am a grown man, but I have to ask another grown man for toilet paper so I can wipe my butt. This is no way for a man to live. If my words and leadership can stop one of you from repeating history – from insanity – from the trials I've endured – it's worth it.

Hustle 2.0 is a new vision for a new future. Because we're worth it. You're worth it. You're better than this place. Real recognizes real.

We've learned to survive a gang of years in prison—and are thriving, keeping the hope, and living with purpose and dignity. If we can do it … so can you. Soak up game from our mistakes and the wisdom we've gained along the way.

We know our voices hold weight, and we're using them to create a movement that matters. Pelican Bay has always had the label, "Worst of the Worst," but the old Pelican Bay is out. In fact, incarceration is out. It's a new day.

We're revolutionizing the self-help game. Hustle 2.0 will help you sharpen the tools (not those tools …) you'll need to better your life. We're going to help you make the key that's going open up that door to big opportunities.

Our vision is to establish the correctional industry's most comprehensive and effective rehabilitation curriculum. Our vision for the future is that any incarcerated person will have access to Hustle 2.0 to step their game up. (We're not there yet … but we're grateful to work with you.)

Ride with us!

> You're worth it. You're better than this place.
> Real recognizes real.

MY WHY

By Cecil Sagapolu
aka Sweet Candy

We all know what it's like to look over our shoulder all day. When all we know is how to sell drugs, and we've got pounds of dope in the car, and we live in a constant state of fear of getting caught … is *that* freedom?

It isn't to me anymore.

I don't want to step out of prison looking like an idiot.

I desire to function like a normal person. Normal to me means that one day, I'll walk into a store and be seen as a customer … instead of feared as someone who's going to rob it.

I'm ready to transform my hustle, and Hustle 2.0 is lacing us up on making legal money. I'm proud to become more positive. I'm ready to stop repeating history, and I hope you are too.

With a name like Hustle 2.0, it's gotta be good. This program was named by us here at the Bay, and it's being written and created by us, in partnership with outside leadership that believes in us. Everyone involved is serious about this movement. We have a great vision, and we're not here to just talk about it. It's the right time and place to push this movement.

When all we know is how to sell drugs, and we've got pounds of dope in the car, and we live in a constant state of fear of getting caught ... is *that* freedom?

I have seen a lot of success coming out of H2.0 already. I like seeing others succeed; I see the pep in their step. I want some of that for myself.

H2.0

NUMBERS DON'T LIE

92% of Mavericks say participating in Hustle 2.0 has given them more hope for the future.

93% of Mavericks say they have gotten more value out of Hustle 2.0 than they were expecting.

85% of Mavericks say their confidence has improved because of their participation in Hustle 2.0.

99% of Mavericks say Hustle 2.0 has been a valuable investment of their time.

93% of Mavericks say participating in Hustle 2.0 has helped them to create goals they're proud of.

WHAT FREEDOM MEANS TO US

Though most of us Homies are lifers, we can still obtain freedom. Our freedom comes from bringing you sweet opportunity. We are nothing if all we care about is ourselves.

Freedom is seeing people keep their freedom once they're out; not just dream about it every day in here. Freedom for us is seeing you succeed. Freedom is seeing you use your hustle legitimately.

Freedom means changing the perceptions about all of us. We realize talk is cheap. Freedom requires actions that back these words up.

REAL TALK: MY MOTIVES

By Cecil Sagapolu
aka Sweet Candy

I'm willing to lose old buddies in the process of making new positive ones. I'm ready to be called a "programmer" to live for the betterment of the fellahz.

Here's what's in it for me—why I'm participating in H2.0. Maybe you'll relate to some of my motives.

Of Cecil's motives below, check the boxes that you relate to.

- ☐ Hustle 2.0 staff asked us, "If you died today, why would your life matter?" Some of us weren't satisfied with our answers. H2.0 is a pathway to creating a new legacy.
- ☐ I want to be a positive role model for my kids. They've seen me do plenty of negative things. I want them to know me for something positive.
- ☐ I like to learn. This is part of my learning and growth process.
- ☐ We're ready to show people that we're more than our pasts. I don't like aspects of my reputation. I have been known as Monster. I want to change the way people view me. That's why I'm reppin' Sweet Candy now.
- ☐ We're launching a movement. This is one of those moments in history. We hope people will talk about the greatness that comes of it. Proving the haters wrong is invigorating.

YOUR MOTIVES

What motives do you have for participating in Hustle 2.0? Check all that apply.

- [ ] 'Cause this book's in my hands. I'm bored out of my mind!
- [ ] I'm tired of the same ol' same ol' programs.
- [ ] I'm tired of the same ol' same ol' lifestyle.
- [ ] I want to land a good job—and keep it.
- [ ] I want to believe in myself.
- [ ] I want to take responsibility for my future and freedom.
- [ ] I'm ready to show the haters that I'll amount to more than this.
- [ ] I'm want to make my family proud.
- [ ] I want to transform my hustle into a legal one.
- [ ] I want to learn from others who have been in my shoes.
- [ ] I want to stop looking over my shoulder.
- [ ] Other: ______________________________
- [ ] Other: ______________________________

Consider the question, "If you died today, why would your life matter?" What one step could you take today to live life with more purpose?

____

____

THE MAKING OF A MAVERICK

At Hustle 2.0, we don't refer to ourselves as inmates, offenders, felons, criminals, murderers, thugs, losers, the worst of the worst, low-lives, or any such nonsense. We refuse to be defined by the shackles placed upon us or to just be known by the worst thing we've done. Instead, we call ourselves Mavericks. No ifs, ands, or butts. ☺

Illustration by Jesus Jasso

MAVERICK

Noun

1. An individual who does not go along with a group or party.
2. An independent thinker who refuses to conform to the accepted views on a subject.

WHAT MAKES A MAVERICK?

Check out this list of common traits shared by Maverick leaders and entrepreneurs. Put a check next to each trait that applies to you:

- ☐ Talented; tends to outperform others
- ☐ Ambitious goal setter
- ☐ Charismatic
- ☐ Truthful to the point of bluntness
- ☐ Doesn't front to fit in
- ☐ Visionary; sees problems and fixes them with innovative solutions
- ☐ Changes up the rules - not out of spite, but because the rules haven't been working
- ☐ Makes decisions that fly in the face of "business as usual"
- ☐ Deliberately puts a new twist on old thinking, always checking for new disruptive ideas and creative people
- ☐ Willfully independent
- ☐ Challenges the status quo and insists that the company works with a strong sense of integrity
- ☐ Takes risks that conformists fear, and pushes a hard line towards what others think is "insane" or "impossible to achieve"
- ☐ Focuses on meaningful work; the work is often original, creative, and experimental
- ☐ Focuses on growth by rethinking competition, continuous innovation, reconnecting with customers, and redesigning the workplace
- ☐ Obsessed with improvement
- ☐ Highly competitive
- ☐ Questions everything
- ☐ Leaves a mark
- ☐ Does things their way
- ☐ Gets bored easily
- ☐ Seeks constant challenges; likes being as productively engaged as possible
- ☐ Understands they're a square peg in a round hole
- ☐ Recruits and hires exceptional people to work for them
- ☐ Can't be managed conventionally
- ☐ Often doesn't fully utilize talents effectively
- ☐ Often exasperates the people around them; peers feel like they can't keep up
- ☐ Often hurts others' feelings when delivering feedback in their brutally honest way
- ☐ Breaking rules and challenging systems gets them in trouble

Adapated from source: https://medium.com/@johnsonbandi/mavericks-explained-what-being-a-maverick-is-all-about-f67b50dd400b

WHY WE'RE MAVERICKS

Mavericks are individuals who prefer to do them and not do what others do. Famous entrepreneurs who are known as Mavericks include Steve Jobs (Apple) and Richard Branson (Virgin).

In the 1800s, a Texas rancher named Sam Maverick became widely known for allowing his unbranded cattle to roam wild instead of penning them in fenced-in ranges. People began referring to unbranded cattle as Mavericks. The name eventually came to mean anyone who didn't bear another's brand, or "an independent thinker who refuses to conform to the accepted views on a subject." This independent spirit describes the companies, entrepreneurs, and business leaders who are qualified as Mavericks.

At Hustle 2.0, we call ourselves Mavericks because we use our independence to challenge the status quo and make changes in our lives and environments.

We challenge negative labels about us, refusing to be defined by our felonies or worst decisions. We are challenging society's perceptions of "once a criminal, always a criminal," by committing to a new way of living that breaks down that harmful stereotype.

We're challenging the implicit bias and racial divides that permeate corrections.

We're advocating for policy reforms that will result in fairer justice systems and more humane treatment.

We're challenging gang-related violence and illegal activities, steering one another towards education and programming and pushing a positive, legal future.

We're challenging the values and beliefs that got us entrenched in criminal lifestyles. Through rigorous and uncomfortable self-examination, we're establishing new identities and purposes.

ARE MAVERICKS ABOVE THE RULES?

Mavericks are known as rule-breakers, but:

Mavericks break rules and traditions to
improve systems and businesses.

Criminals break rules and laws
for their own benefit.

Don't go confusing Mavericks with criminals.

In Hustle 2.0, being a Maverick is *never* a license for breaking rules or for being disrespectful, regardless of circumstance. To the contrary, you'll see us preaching respect and loving and forgiving our enemies. Hustle 2.0's curriculum reinforces the importance of respecting authorities, observing rules and laws, and creating and keeping peace. This is the standard we're proud to hold ourselves to.

Hustle 2.0 is about creating a *peaceful* movement.

> "The whole world loves a maverick and the whole world wants the maverick to achieve something nobler than simple rebellion!
>
> - Kevin Patterson"

HUSTLE 2.0'S VALUES

HUSTLE

Our can-do attitude, resourcefulness, curiosity, initiative, urgency, and scrappiness result in a high sense of hustle in all that we do.

HOPE

We choose positivity daily, show gratitude, and embrace a better future for us all (even in the face of unrelenting negativity).

COMPASSION

We empathize with our Mavericks' pain and distress and take daily actions to alleviate their suffering as we partner with them in the transformation of their futures.

IMPACT

We care about people and strive to leave everyone we interact with better than we found them.

CANDOR

We improve when we are constructively informed about our shortcomings. We value open and honest communication that is humble, helpful, immediate, and doesn't personalize.

OWNERSHIP

We're committed to excellence and generating positive outcomes. We're accountable for the results of our actions and trust each other to do the right thing.

GROW

When we stop growing intellectually, creatively, or professionally, that area begins to die. We pursue growth by having the guts and resolve to improve and transform.

> You will never influence the world by trying to be like it.
>
> - Unknown

WHY H2.0 IS A CUT ABOVE THE REST

What are our competitive advantages and differences with many other programs?

✓ **First-time Programmers**

Haven't been tagged as a "programmer" before? We've been looking for you. We believe in you. Don't worry, hard-core programmers: we won't short you on meat and potatoes just 'cause we're having some fun with it.

✓ **Real Talk & Lingo**

This curriculum speaks our language. It's straight-up, relatable, written in plain English, and is non-boring (which is also why we succeed with new programmers).

✓ **For Us, By Us**

H2.0 is created by us, in partnership with people who care deeply about us and have personal stakes in our rehabilitation and successful journeys. The whole curriculum is relevant and authentic. We're not just talking about the testimonials … we've intentionally designed the learning structure, topics, reflection quizzes, art, jokes, and even the test questions ("Mandos") so they're relatable and cool.

✓ **History of Success**

Our founders' programs have served 6,000+ of us with success. This stuff works.

✓ **All Around Transformation**

H2.0 is holistic. It isn't just about entrepreneurship. Or criminal thinking. Or reentry. Or job readiness. It's all of the above and more. Our 12-book program features 80+ in-depth courses.

✓ **We Crack Jokes & Sip Cokes**

We've all been in boring self-help classes that we used to get out of our cells … and could barely keep our eyes open. Who said this is how learning has to be? So, yeah, we incorporate humor, mazes, and entertainment because we believe there's power and effectiveness in bringing fun into education.

GAME PLAN: THE PRESEASON

Here's the game you'll soak up in this book. Our goal? For you to learn, love it, and want more of it!

1. **Pretest**

   Test your knowledge coming into H2.0. Check the answer key to see how much you have to learn.

2. **Crash Courses**

   In The Preseason, we're providing snippets from our other Hustle Guides. Get your feet wet with 12 crash courses that serve as tools for personal transformation. If you continue H2.0's 12-book program, we provide in-depth training in these areas.

- Entrepreneurship
- Healthy Relationships
- Leadership
- Employment
- Victim Awareness
- Character Development
- Reentry
- Criminal Thinking
- Becoming the Solution
- Purposeful Living
- Persevering
- Anger Management

3. **Self-Assessments**

   Put everything to the test, from your cupcakin' skills (how to be a good romantic partner) to your employment readiness. Mavericks have referred to many of our "No Judgment Quizzes" as mirrors. You might be in for a few wake-up calls.

4. **Entertainment**

   To have fun on the run, we packed The Preseason with mazes, sudokus, jokes, recipes, crosswords, word searches, and our own version of Mad Libs ("H2.0 Libs"). If you's a square, take a deep breath, pump yo' breaks, and learn to enjoy the ride. The farts and giggles don't take away from the hard work you'll have to put in.

5. **Awesome Artwork**

   The art comes straight from the hearts of our amazing Ink Slayers at Pelican Bay who volunteered their time and talent to make the pages pop.

6. **Inspiring Quotes**
   Get motivated by visionaries, athletes, entrepreneurs, celebrities, investors, and social change activists.

7. **Testimonials & Success Stories**
   Get inspired by incarcerated writers, and released men and women, who share a common journey.

8. **Case Studies**
   Analyze the facts from relatable, real-life situations and apply the wisdom to your life.

9. **Interesting Facts**
   Bet you didn't know most of these.

10. **Poems & Raps**
    Experience all the feels with the H2.0 Homies.

11. **Recommended Reading**
    Let your curiosity lead you to check out our best reads.

12. **Prompts for Journaling and Self-Reflection**
    "The unexamined life is not worth living" … so examine yours.

13. **A Certificate with Your Name on It**
    Oh, you want that certificate? Flip to the back to see the requirements. We'll send you (or your loved ones) a certificate that'll put a Kool-Aid smile on your face.

14. **Call to Action**
    The next step for those who gotta get more H2.0.

15. **Scholarship Application and Mail Order Form**
    Know someone who wants The Preseason? Have them mail us their completed order form or scholarship application.

Of the 12 crash courses, which one interests you most?

____

QUIZ: SICK AND TIRED?

Check off all the things that you are truly sick and tired of:

	SICK AND TIRED	I CAN LIVE WITH IT
Being away from loved ones	☐	☐
Being in a negative environment	☐	☐
Prison/jail food, or being forced to miss canteen/store	☐	☐
People having to come visit you	☐	☐
Being considered property of the state	☐	☐
Getting rejected by parole	☐	☐
Working for free (or for pennies)	☐	☐
Being told what to do every day	☐	☐
Having your loved ones feel hopeless about your situation	☐	☐

How sick and tired are you of living the way you've been living?

1	2	3	4	5	6	7	8	9	10
I love being locked up!									100% done with this sh!&

How badly do you want your freedom?

1	2	3	4	5	6	7	8	9	10
I love being locked up!									I'm 100% committed to freedom

How ready are you to change your ways?

1	2	3	4	5	6	7	8	9	10
Not changing a thing									I'm 100% game

What price you are willing to pay for your freedom?

____

Welcome to the Hustle 2.0 journey!

GAME PLAN: THE COMBINE & BEYOND

This program is called The Preseason ... because it's only the beginning of your journey with H2.0. You can purchase continued programming yourself, apply for scholarships, or advocate to your institution to get Hustle 2.0!

The Preseason is followed by:

The Combine
Hustle Guides 1-4

Game Time
Hustle Guides 5-8

The Playoffs
Hustle Guides 9-12

Each of the 12 books ("Hustle Guides") contains seven to 10 courses that come with homework that is graded by H2.0. Our evidence-based curriculum is academically rigorous. As we do in The Preseason, we hit you with a combo of serious stuff and tons of fun.

For those preparing to face a parole board, we also offer a Parole Board Readiness program with customized exercises and insight from parole commissioners.

Mavericks who complete the 12 Hustle Guides earn a university certificate from Southern Utah University in Leadership & Management!

> Mavericks who complete the 12 Hustle Guides earn a university certificate in Leadership & Management!

CHOOSE YOUR OWN ADVENTURE

One of Mavericks' favorite parts of H2.O's 12-book program: just like in college, you get to pick your majors. We offer five majors, and every Maverick double-majors. (Over-achievers can complete all five, and the Parole Board Readiness program.)

Hustle 2.O's Majors

Entrepreneurship is for the natural-born hustlers who want to learn the essentials of becoming a legit entrepreneur and start their own business. Many of your entrepreneurial skills are instinctual; align your skills with best practices in the startup world. With Hustle 2.O, you'll learn about business ideation, business models, market research, financing, sales, and marketing. We'll guide you through pulling it all together in an impressive business plan. Learn from the Sharks you hope to one day pitch your idea to: venture capitalists and angel investors.

Employment Readiness is more than just looking for a job. You'll build a solid resume—the most important financial document of your life—even if you haven't held a job outside the gates. Prepare to ace interviews and discuss your criminal history with an employer. Learn the difference between a rap sheet and a background check, and how much detail to share with employers. Write a cover letter, develop references, and create a great LinkedIn profile to build your professional social media presence. Learn networking strategies to land employment within weeks of release.

Leadership and Management is about developing your leadership skills, gaining power, and maximizing your influence. You'll learn sales and negotiation strategies from leaders who are the best at getting what they want. Learn effective communication techniques, how to become more likable, and how to manage people. Develop realistic but ambitious goals, and establish positive habits. Learn about personal finance and credit building and repair.

Healthy Relationships is about developing healthy family, platonic, and romantic relationships. Learn to write an effective profile letter to get a penpal. We'll explore parenting strategies, building and repairing broken trust (including healing from infidelity), and engaging in meaningful conversation. You'll learn about cupcakin' and how to be a better partner, parent, friend, and family member. You don't have to be in a relationship or be a parent to benefit from this major.

Reentry Planning is crucial if you'll hit the gates anytime soon. Learn to set realistic expectations for your release. Learn what you can start doing now to get on the fast track. Make a detailed plan for your freedom, outlining goals for employment, money, relationships, time management, fitness, and spirituality. Learn tips and strategies from formerly incarcerated grads who have successfully navigated the hardships that come with a criminal record.

Our 12 Hustle Guides also contain Fundamental Courses, which include:

Criminal thinking	Addiction and recovery	Relapse planning	Time management
Personal finance	Victim awareness	Anger management	Forgiveness
Meaningful apologies	Boundaries	Value remapping	Integrity
Learning to feel again	Domestic violence	Resilient grieving	Accountability
Making amends	Living with purpose	Coping skills	Etiquette

Want more Hustle 2.0? Flip to the back and complete the last four pages, which include our Call to Action.

MEET H2.0'S HOTSHOTS

Please meet Sluggo D. Sloth. He's posted up all over our Hustle Guides. You probably already know this dude. He might be your cellie … or that homie who shows up out of nowhere when the spread is done with spoon in hand, but was nowhere in sight to pitch in. Yup, you know who we're talking about. (If not, it's probably YOU.)

Being Sluggo is tough. For him, explosive diarrhea is hereditary; it runs in his genes. He likes to marinate in that bootie juice 24/7. Courtesy flushes and showers are out. Sluggo was cool on Hustle 2.0 and put up this posting, looking for some other loser to do his dirty work.

Holla at Ya Boy, Sluggo

Illustration by Trenton Dukes

HELP WANTED:

People willing to misuse their skills, smoke their chance at going home, and kick it with me & the Sloths fo'eva'eva

Major Company Benefits!!

- Free coffee-stained slingshot
- Free SlothLife tattoos (signing bonus)
- Sloth membership fo' life
- Fair-chance hiring: we accept all sloths; no questions asked; no barriers to entry
- No room for advancement or a raise
- Doesn't pay well (or at all, actually)
- I (Sluggo) take weekends and holidays off, as well as weekdays and non-holidays. You get to work every day!

Job Openings – Start Date ASAP

KITE MULE:	Transportation specialist for important messages regarding super-secret sloth bidnizz. Must be loose enough for quick export/import. Most of the messages are about how hungry and sleepy I am.
STASH HOUSE WORKER:	We (meaning me) are looking for someone who is willing to hold onto all contraband and take the fall when you get caught.
LETTER WRITER:	I talk, you write. Looking for someone with great writing skills and penmanship. Must convert the thoughts and opinions of a sloth into spicy poetry for my penpal site.
HOMEWORK SPECIALIST:	Do you like doing homework? I don't. I'll let you do it for me! Great learning opportunity for you to advance your education while I take all the credit.
NARRATOR:	War Storyteller. Need to know how to put a 10 on a two. Looking for someone to take my semi-exciting stories and turn them into a Hollywood-like epic, I'm talking Braveheart-type stuff here. Serious creatives and compulsive liars will feel right at home, getting to spin amazing tales of my heroism and bravery.

Apply today by doing absolutely nothin'

WHAT'S UP WITH THEM HONEY BADGERS?

The Honey Badger is the antithesis of Sluggo. The Honey Badger is H2.0's spirit animal because we're committed to relentlessly pursuing our best futures.

Your goal is to become a total Honey Badger. We know the odds are stacked against us and that we're fighting uphill battles to get employed, stop engaging in the criminal lifestyle, and win our families back. We're not easily deterred by predators and big challenges. Oh, and just like four-legged honey badgers, we're hungry beasts too. Like when it comes to program, we're starvin'!

Honey Badger Status, or HBS, is our elite academic status reserved for the elites, the nerds, the go-getters, the fo'real hustlers. We'll introduce a lil' competition in The Combine, but for now, you know if you're looking more like Sluggo or a Honey Badger.

Illustration by Trenton Dukes

EVERYTHING YOU WANTED TO KNOW ABOUT THE FEARLESS HONEY BADGER

Honey badgers are with the bizz; they ain't scared of nothin'. On the real, they're listed as the "world's most fearless animal" in the Guinness Book of World Records. They're named for a mop of golden hair on top; they look like skunks on steroids (but they've got chips on their shoulders 'cause they can't gas their neighbors).

They're considered the Connor McGregor/ Pacquiao/ Mayweather of the animal kingdom. They put in work to keep their reputation – just check their paperwork.

Honey badgers are hungry little bastards, and can be found darting around African and Asian soils hunting for anything and everything. They're on single cell-status, living in self-dug holes. They're skilled diggers, able to dig tunnels into hard ground in 10 minutes. Honey badgers are super smart, and are one of a few species capable of using tools.

What other mammal faces a predator 10 times its size without the slightest hint of fear or backing down? Honey badgers ain't scared of nothin' ... including the King of the Jungle. They've been known to take on lions and tigers and leopards, oh my! They fight to death rather than giving up. Honey badgers have a short-man complex and fight dirty, severing their opponent's testicles, neutralizing them in more ways than one.

They grunt loudly. They eat snakes. At chow time (which is 24/7), they'll run right up in a house of bees to get that larvae. They'll get stung a thousand times, but they don't turn down for nothin'. What other animal does that? (Almost sounds like us …)

Nobody puts honey badger in a corner. They're even known to survive bites from poisonous cobras. The poor little badgers occasionally get put on their pockets … will sag out a nap … get right back up … and then will throw that cobra in the canteen bag for the next month. Okay, maybe just the week … or just the night.

Because of the toughness and looseness of their skin, honey badgers are near-impossible to kill. Their skin is hard to penetrate, and its looseness allows them to twist and turn; they're experts at slippin' their cuffs. Their skin can even resist several machete blows. The only sure way of killing 'em, since you can't catch 'em on a head-up fade? You gotta' snake that foo'. It's going to take a blow to the skull with a club or a shot to the head with the mini-14 (the block gun won't cut it).

> "Get up, get out, and get some."
>
> - The Hungry Honey Badger

The grunt of the honey badger goes like this:

"khrya-ya-ya-ya"

(sort of like a crazy person screaming on the tier)

PRETEST

Think you got it all figured out? Test your knowledge with this tool. Don't cheat; your score doesn't impact your performance at H2.0.

Ground rules:

✓ This is a closed-book pretest. Set a timer for 25 minutes.

✓ Circle the best answer for each question. Do not record these answers on the Bubble Sheet at the end of the book.

✓ Grade your answers using the Pretest Key after you've completed the test. The more you get wrong, the more you can get pumped about the knowledge and skills you'll gain from The Preseason.

1. If an entrepreneur wants to calculate what their business really pocketed, they should look at their:
   - A. Net income
   - B. Gross profit margin
   - C. Revenue
   - D. Cash flow
2. Incarcerated people reduce their odds of recidivating by 43% by:
   - A. Wanting to change
   - B. Participating in correctional education programs
   - C. Not getting disciplinary cases
   - D. Only committing misdemeanors
3. Prosocial thinking and behavior refers to:
   - A. Acting professionally in social situations
   - B. Acting in a way that is positive and promotes social acceptance and friendship
   - C. Refining skills to act professionally
   - D. Acting in a way that leads to making friends quickly
4. One of your most important networking tools is your:
   - A. Professional hairstyle
   - B. Business card
   - C. Business attire
   - D. Smile
5. Business ideation is:
   - A. Entrepreneurs presenting their ideal business vision to investors
   - B. Monetizing ideas
   - C. Entrepreneurs' brainstorming of multiple business ideas to solve customer problems
   - D. Asking customers their ideal price for the product
6. The key to coming up with a solid business idea that works is to be:
   - A. Secretive
   - B. Innovative
   - C. Useful
   - D. Market-oriented

7. The statement, "Everything's been taken from me, so now I can take what I want" is an example of:
   A. Consumerism
   B. Criminal thinking
   C. Lying by commission
   D. A give and take economy
8. Some states have a "ban the box" law, which forbids companies from:
   A. Running background checks
   B. Hiring people who check a box disclosing a violent criminal history
   C. Rejecting people based on their criminal backgrounds
   D. Asking applicants to check a box on applications to disclose criminal records
9. Romanticized expectations from our loved ones about our release often lead to:
   A. Unnecessary pressure and failure
   B. Rekindled romance
   C. Sexual frustrations
   D. Pleasant reunions
10. In the job searching process, you should share your criminal history:
    A. Only if/when asked about it
    B. In your cover letter
    C. At the start of the interview
    D. When you are informed that the company will run a background check
11. At a professional networking event, the proper way to introduce yourself, if your name is Bobby Jones, is:
    A. Excuse the interruption of your day; my name is Bobby Jones
    B. Pardon me, Bobby Jones here
    C. Hi, I'm Bobby Jones
    D. Hello, I'm Mr. Bobby Jones
12. A competitive advantage you provide to an employer is that when they hire you within one year of release, the employer can qualify for:
    A. Criminal insurance
    B. Tax credits
    C. Awards from the Federal Felony Council
    D. Government loans
13. Research shows that a benefit of healthy relationships is:
    A. Avoiding early death
    B. More sex than when people are single
    C. A 25% reduction in divorce rates
    D. Becoming wealthy quicker
14. When an investor or customer makes a purchasing decision, the first thing they look at is if they:
    A. Like and trust you
    B. Like and trust your product or service
    C. Were already on the market for your product or service
    D. Can afford your product or service
15. The percentage of HR professionals who report that their companies have hired people with criminal histories is:
    A. 10% (one-tenth)
    B. 33% (one-third)
    C. 50% (half)
    D. 67% (two-thirds)
16. An effective strategy for not taking the bait is:
    A. Not going to sleep hungry
    B. Rising early
    C. Snapping your fingers instead of using violence
    D. Knowing your triggers

17. Even if you're boring, a key to successful networking and being perceived as a great conversationalist is:
    A. Keeping your personal introduction to less than three minutes
    B. Asking excellent questions
    C. Name dropping
    D. Asking for at least one referral to an interesting person
18. Employers claim the most important factor in hiring people with criminal histories is:
    A. That the candidate served five years or less in prison
    B. Whether or not the employer has a job opening
    C. That the candidate has a strong reference from their PO
    D. The candidate's demonstrated consistent work history
19. When someone looks for their first job after incarceration, the best advice can be summed up as:
    A. Keep looking until you land a great job with a good salary, or you're more likely to recidivate
    B. Set realistic expectations: you probably won't land a job for six months
    C. Apply for jobs even when you're not qualified; try enough times, and you'll land one
    D. Don't be picky with your first job: you're more employable when you're employed
20. A proven leadership strategy in setting "smart goals" is to make sure the goal is:
    A. Time-bound
    B. Easy to achieve
    C. Ambitious
    D. Broadly defined
21. To credibly articulate your transformation to an employer:
    A. Point to tangible ways in which you've changed your life
    B. Share that you've become a person of faith if it's true
    C. Share your plans to volunteer and give back to the community
    D. Emphasize three times in the interview that you will never get incarcerated again
22. The stress of telling a lie:
    A. Reduces life expectancy by an average of five years
    B. Leads 60% of people to overeat
    C. Leads your body to release hormones like cortisol and testosterone
    D. Leads most people to never tell that lie again
23. A common criminal thinking error is:
    A. Stealing from the victim
    B. Stalking the victim
    C. Playing the victim
    D. Ignoring the victim
24. A resume is:
    A. A listing of every job a person has held
    B. Considered by recruiters to be the most important job-hunting tool
    C. Evaluated for an average of three minutes by employers
    D. The most important financial document of most people's lives
25. Selling drugs:
    A. Is a victimless crime, if the user was planning to buy from someone else
    B. Is the most profitable trade in America
    C. Often leads to homelessness
    D. Leads innocent children to be victimized

Grade your answers using the key below. Don't trip if some of the answers are confusing; we'll break it down in The Preseason. Happy learning!

YOUR SCORE:

________ OUT OF 25 QUESTIONS

If you scored ...

25:	All-star Honey Badger!!!
21-24:	We see you, future Honey Badger!
0-20:	Get crackin' on this book. Let's hear it for the underdogs!

PRETEST KEY

1	2	3	4	5	6	7	8	9	10	11	12	13	14	15	16	17	18	19	20	21	22	23	24	25
A	B	B	D	C	C	B	D	A	C	C	B	A	A	D	D	B	D	D	A	A	C	C	D	D

THE PRESEASON CROSSWORD

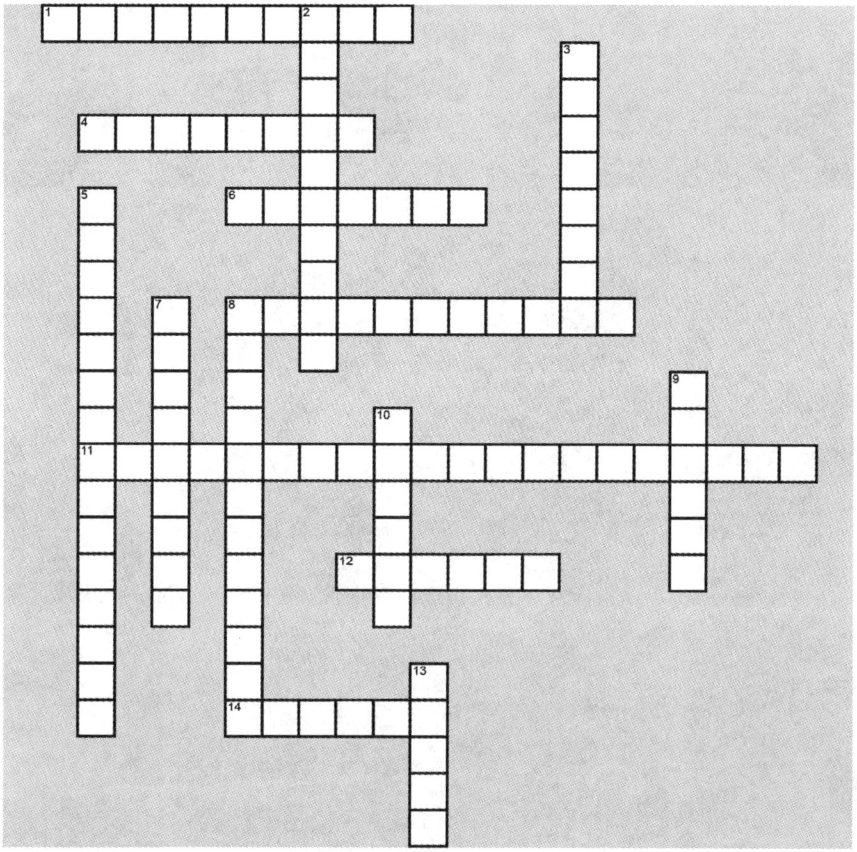

Across

1 Finish all 12 Hustle Guides to earn a certificate from a ...
4 Hereditary for Sluggo
6 Awesome stuff produced by H2.0's Ink Slayers
8 The most elite status you can earn
11 H2.0's extra program with customized exercises and insight from commissioners
12 H2.0's incarcerated authors
14 He might be your cellie

Down

2 99% of Mavs say H2.0 has been a valuable ________
3 Sluggo's transportation specialist
5 H2.0's major that teaches you to make a detailed plan for your freedom
7 We're not inmates, offenders, felons, or criminals; we're ...
8 What H2.0 calls our books
9 Pass these with 80%+ to get your Preseason certificate
10 H2.0's value that calls for honest communication
13 We crack jokes and sip these

HUSTLE 2.0

PROUD
TO BE A
MAVERICK!
HUSTLE 2.0

MEET THE HOMIES

Sweet Sugarcane

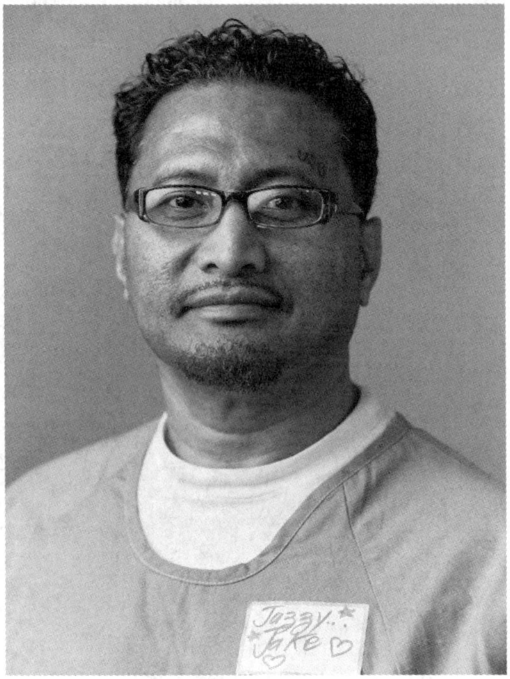

Illustration by Hung Le

JACOB AMA, formerly known as C-nut, is now called Sweet Sugarcane. He's 54 years old, and his signature raised-eyebrow, crazy-eyed stare is still intact, and though still very disturbing, it no longer scares people. Originally from Compton, he came to prison in 1987 with a sentence of 26 years to life for murder. He's spent over 13 years in the SHU. CDCR (the California Department of Corrections and Rehabilitation) validated Jacob as a member of the Park Village Compton Crip Street Gang in 1986.

Jacob says he would wish for superhuman strength, but have you seen the guns on this guy? He's got 50-inch *forearms*, so think what his biceps must look like. When he's at work as an education porter, he sings as he cleans, usually off-key, but who's gonna tell him? Not us!

Sweet Sugarcane is a nice guy once you get to know him. As a kid, his family called him 'coconut' because he was always climbing and falling out of trees.

Sweet Owl

DARRYL BACA, formerly known as Night Owl, is now known as Sweet Owl. He was sentenced to 17 years to life in 1981. He's spent 32 of his 39 years of incarceration in the SHU. He's used his time to earn his AA in Social and Behavioral Science. CDCR validated Darryl as a member of The Mexican Mafia.

Darryl is old enough to have met Charles Manson way back in 1885 … or 1985. Sweet Owl is 59 years young, but has never once worn a suit and tie. Only prison jumpsuits and handcuffs.

Sweet Owl hoots every night for the love of his life, who he's been with for more than 20 years. This just proves that he's a big softie with a kind and caring heart. He also clings to a poem from his mother (RIP), who gave it to him back in 1995.

Darryl is now using his leadership and senior citizen status to mentor young men and promote change with his brave and outspoken writings in Hustle 2.0.

Sweet Tamale

Illustration by Trenton Dukes

ARTURO CASTELLANOS was as skinny as a board growing up, so his dad called him Tablas, and the name stuck. He's now known as Sweet Tamale. Today he feels like a spring flower in bloom after spending 32 years in the SHU. He came to prison in 1980 with a 25 to life sentence for murder. CDCR validated Arturo as a member of The Mexican Mafia.

The best day of Arturo's life was the end of the 60-day hunger strike, which he celebrated by eating not one but *two* Top Ramen noodles (after so long, even a butt-naked soup tastes gourmet). Along with eating Ramen, his simple pleasures include laughing at random things and watching *Baywatch* (Why? Do you have to ask?) and *The Big Bang Theory* ("Bazinga!" exclaims Arturo … yeah. He's that guy.).

Sweet Tamale admires his dad, despite the bowl cut the man gave him when cutting his hair (this is why he opts for a bald cut now). The best gift he ever got was a visit from his mom while he was in the SHU, but he was so hungry during the visit that she began morphing into a burrito, his favorite food.

Sweet Grandpa

Illustration by Trenton Dukes

JOHN JACKSON, formerly known as Tex, is originally from San Antonio, Texas. Although he's far from being a senior citizen, we call him Sweet Grandpa because he's hip as any grandpa – his dancing skills included. He spent 18 years incarcerated, earning himself four SHU terms before coming to Pelican Bay. John earned his GED, a certificate from Baylor University, and has led networking events in prison attended by some of the world's top executives and investors.

You should know that he played the trumpet in junior high, where he specialized in making fart sounds. Sweet Grandpa proudly declares to everyone he meets that he knows all the lyrics to The Sound of Music, but no one questions him, because no one wants to hear it.

After paroling from Pelican Bay in 2019, Sweet Grandpa was hired to work for Hustle 2.0. He now spends his time writing – specializing in fart jokes – and extreme skiing (or what he calls skiing ... it's really just him cart-wheeling down the bunny slopes.) He's leveling up his leadership by participating in altMBA, an intensive online workshop created by bestselling author and entrepreneur Seth Godin.

Sweet Chewy Cookie Dough

Illustration by Trenton Dukes

JESUS MURILLO, now known as Sweet Chewy Cookie Dough, has been incarcerated for 13 years, three of which were in SHU. While in the SHU, Sweet Chewy Cookie Dough won an entrepreneurship competition with his idea of creating and selling cards, showcasing the art of incarcerated men. He amassed entrepreneurial skills from life before prison, helping his family to operate a home business that became a retail store.

Jesus grew up on a farm, where he raised animals. (His nickname should be *El Ranchero.*) He also played softball for eight whole years, even once earning an award for MVP. In his free time, Jesus likes writing poetry because it helps him to escape.

As a young boy who always wanted more presents, Sweet Chewy Cookie Dough started the tradition of leaving cookies and milk for Santa every Christmas … until last year, when his cellie made him stop. Now, instead of attempting to win Santa's favor, he shamelessly cupcakes with his wife every chance he gets.

Sweet Gummy Bear

EDDIE NAPOLES, once known as Speedy, has taken on a new handle, Sweet Gummy Bear. He's served 14 years of a life sentence for first-degree murder. He has since earned his GED and is enrolled in college, working on his AA in Business. Eddie has helped others who are incarcerated earn their GEDs and move on to higher education.

Sweet Gummy Bear tears up whenever he watches chick flicks. He also loves giving and receiving tender bear hugs, and his grandma still calls him *Fuchilas*, or "Stinky," because he used to run around with a dirty diaper.

Since Eddie joined the Hustle 2.0 Homies, he has stepped his game up and changed his dirty diaper, becoming a great writer. He has authored great testimonials on addiction and recovery and has written amazing poetry.

Buttercup

Illustration by Trenton Dukes

LITTLE JOHN PERRY, formerly known as BJ, now proudly embraces his H2.0 name, Buttercup. Hailing from South-Central LA (Athens Park), Little John is far from "little." He's 6'3", at – what *he* claims is – 300 pounds even. He's spent over 23 years in prison for murder, with eight of them going back and forth to the SHU. CDCR validated BJ as a member of the Athens Park Bloods Street Gang in 1994.

Buttercup is happily engaged to his lovely fiance. He met her by sharing some of his coursework from Hustle 2.0. This is no joke! He can't stop talking about it.

Despite his alarming size, Buttercup is actually a big softie (just don't say that to his face). He, too, like Sugarcane, enjoys motorcycles – it's just too bad they don't make sidecars that are bigger than the bike, otherwise, they would have a lot of fun. Buttercup also likes to cuddle, and since he can't do it with his lady, he has a pillow that he pretends is her (we feel sorry for that pillow …).

Sweet Pwally

Illustration by Trenton Dukes

PAUL PICHIE, formerly known as Sinister, now goes by Sweet Pwally (pronounced "Pwaaaawly"). He has spent 14 years of his life in prison, seven of which were in the SHU. He was first arrested at the age of 10 for breaking and entering.

Sweet Pwally was a talented singer, dancer, and football player in high school. The problem was he chose to combine all three and break out into a Backstreet Boys lip sync on the football field.

Somehow, Sweet Pwally graduated from high school (likely prompted by his football coach to prevent future team embarrassment on the field). He went on to serve in the military, but was kicked out for fighting.

Sweet Pwally is now enrolled in college, attends AA, and due to his outstanding work with Hustle 2.0, is a total Honey Badger! Khry-ya-ya-ya-ya! His all-time favorite activity is mentoring other Honey Badgers and Mavericks in Hustle 2.0.

Sweet Candy

Illustration by Hung Lee

CECIL SAGAPOLU, formerly known as Monster, now lives up to being Sweet Candy. He's 37 years old. He stands at 6'1" and 254 pounds, though he can't emphasize enough that he isn't "fat," he's just "big-boned." He came to prison in 2011 at age 29 for second-degree murder and got 25 to life. This is his third term; he's done about 20 years behind bars, starting at the age of 15 … and he's never been out longer than five months.

The best gift Cecil ever got was his freedom, though he must not like it very much since he keeps re-gifting it. His favorite time period was the '70s, when there was peace, love, happiness … and his mullet was actually acceptable (not very good-looking, but acceptable).

Sweet Candy likes Shrek because they look so much alike, and, like Shrek, he doesn't care how people see him; it's what's inside that counts. He also has a very intense fascination with Pocahontas, mainly because he's jealous of her hair (guess the mullet left him scarred, after all). If he could have any superpower, Sweet Candy would want to be able to fly, because, again, he's not fat … and if he wishes for something hard enough … well, maybe not.

Sweet Freddy

Illustration by Trenton Dukes

ALFRED SANDOVAL, known for most of his life as Chato, has now taken the name of Sweet Freddy. He's been incarcerated most of his life, from boys' homes to Death Row. He was five days from execution when his sentence was commuted to life without parole. He spent 32 years in the SHU, but despite all he's been through, he keeps a smile on his face. With all his experience, he wants to help the coming generations do better than the last.

Sweet Freddy loves to laugh, even if it's at himself – which is often. He's a great-grandfather, and even though he looks old and out of shape and doesn't *look* very nimble or quick on his feet or like he would enjoy exercise … he's surprisingly decent at sports.

Sweet Freddy always sings happy birthday to people on their birthdays, so we try not to let him know when ours are. Once in a while, when he makes a good play on the handball court – a very rare occasion – he does a little dance. Well, he dances when he loses too so … yeah.

Sweet Butter Pecan

Illustration by Trenton Dukes

CHRIS SUCCAW left behind his former name of EC Looney and has taken on the new moniker of Sweet Butter Pecan. He's done 16 years of a 57-to-life sentence. After five years in the SHU, Chris decided to make a change. He is now a college student and an executive member in numerous programs.

His family calls him Mookie, and for one soup, you can too.

Sweet Butter Pecan used to use his mother's old handbag as an imaginary garage for his Hot Wheels. Furthermore, his mother dressed him in an Indian skirt to go to school one day … No wonder he ended up in prison. Despite his mean mug, Sweet Butter Pecan couldn't help but shed a tear or six while watching *The Shack* – just think what would happen if he watched *The Notebook*.

Because of his journey of transformation, Sweet Butter Pecan was transferred from a maximum-security prison to a lower level prison. He misses his fellow H2.0 Homies, but is working on kicking off a Hustle 2.0 program at his new facility.

Sweet Cheeks

Illustration by Hung Lee

KUNLYNA TAUCH, formerly known by all as Uly, is now aptly named Sweet Cheeks. He's served 13 years of a life sentence. From 2010-2014, he spent March of every year going to the hole and believed he was cursed. Since then, he's spent every March either in a class or at work, so it's safe to say his curse is broken. Today, he is a co-founder of *The Pelican* newsletter, and has earned his AA in psychology.

K's mom used to call him "elephant" because he was fat. He still kinda is. (That's not entirely true – he *really* is.)

Sweet Cheeks enjoys long walks on the beach, mainly because he's from Long Beach, but also because he's a romantic at heart. He believes in love at first sight. Also love at second sight, third sight, hindsight, and out of sight. He also believes that smiles can change the world.

Sweet Cheeks is an exceptional writer and actor. He was featured in not one, but two documentaries about a theatre program at Pelican Bay State Prison.

Fuzzy Koala Bear

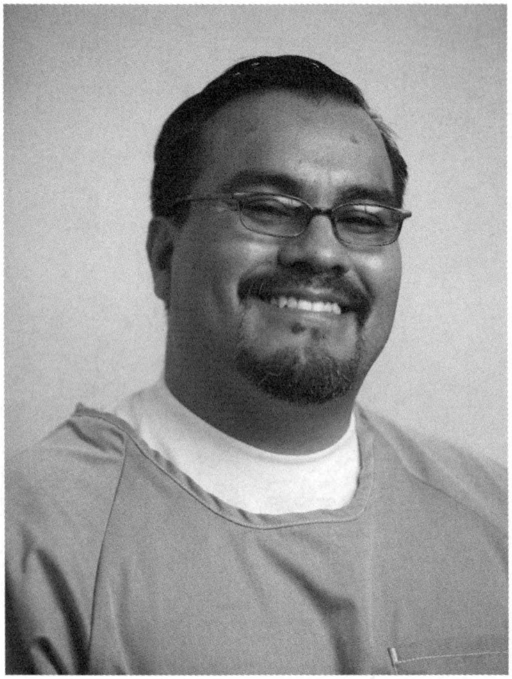

Illustration by Hung Lee

ABEL TORRES, previously known as Malo, now known as Fuzzy Koala Bear, was born and raised in Compton. At 11, he joined a gang. At 17, he was arrested for murder. He's been in Pelican Bay since 2001, spending more than 10 years in the SHU. He now has a passion for learning. He has earned an AA and is currently working on his BA.

Abel, the nerd, has a comic book collection of 150+ comics – mostly of Wonder Woman. He also plays Dungeons and Dragons whenever he can, and often loses touch with reality – he thinks he's a green dwarf right now.

Fuzzy Koala Bear organized the first-ever Cancer Walk at Pelican Bay in memory of his son who died of cancer. He helped raise more $1,200.

Fudgy

Illustration by Trenton Dukes

THABITI SALIM WILSON, who was widely known as Lil T-Way, but who is now famous as Fudgy, has been incarcerated for 21 years. He's done eight SHU terms, but refuses to let violence define him. Today he is a college student and is committed to helping others on their journeys of transformation.

Thabiti swears he's allergic to 98% of the environment – old cellies can attest to his constant sneezing for no apparent reason (maybe he's just allergic to bullspit??). He is also deathly afraid of bees. Once, he got the yard put down because he was running from a supposed bee attack, but later realized that it was just a fly.

Fudgy is really a big sap who likes to watch romance movies – he and Sweet Butter Pecan would make quite the duo (Fudgy Sweet Butter Pecan?). Fudgy is also a twin … and he's a mama's boy who melts like sweet chocolate whenever he talks to her. Grudgingly, Fudgy reveals that his mom's nickname for him is "luv bug."

ENTREPRENEUR

ENTREPRENEURSHIP

Transform Yo' Hustle

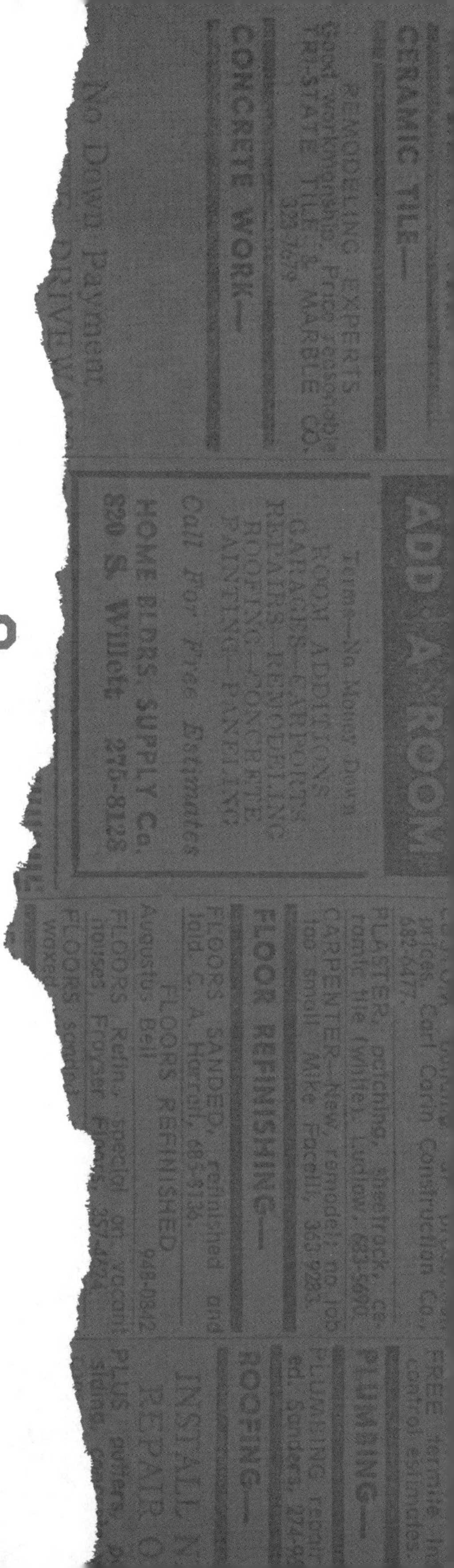

◂ *Illustration by Trenton Dukes*

LEARNING OBJECTIVES

In this crash course, you will ...

- ✓ Use our Dope Math Worksheet and learn why drug dealers still live with their mommas
- ✓ Learn why hustlers make natural entrepreneurs and have transferrable skills, and how we can transform our hustle from illegal into legal profits that will keep us free
- ✓ Learn what an entrepreneur is, study the characteristics of legal entrepreneurs, and discover if you have the mindset of an entrepreneur
- ✓ Analyze case studies of formerly incarcerated people who transformed their hustle, are crushing it, get to be their own bosses, and don't have to look over their shoulders

In Hustle Guides 1-12, take in-depth courses and gain insight into:

- ✓ Landing your first investment
- ✓ Sales and marketing
- ✓ Business finance
- ✓ Legal structuring (e.g., S-corp, LLC)
- ✓ Naming your business (and protecting the name)

DO I REALLY NEED TO CHANGE?

Yes! Period. Point blank.

What we've been doing ain't working!

Case in point: take a look at where you are today and all you've lost. We may have seen some financial "success" in the street game, but it wasn't lasting and it's definitely nothing we can feel good about. We lost whatever we had the day we were arrested.

We may be some of the strongest hustlers, but we're also some of the weakest risk management strategists. The lives most of us have been living have been full of hurt. Our actions hurt ourselves, the people we love, and the victims of our crimes. Are you ready to stop the pain?

Many of us lack an understanding of assets and liabilities. We sell ourselves short through our extremely basic view of what we consider success to be. It obviously isn't what we've thought thus far.

Something's got to give. Each and every one of us is better than this!

Take a minute to strike up a list of what illegal hustling has cost you. What have you lost or given up along the way, or after you landed in prison?

What would happen if you put the same amount of time, energy, and effort into a legal hustle?

> How has our lifestyle worked out for us so far?

How does being the CEO of your own legal business sound to you? Change can be difficult, but the hardest part is just making the decision to change. Stop telling yourself it's too hard and focus on the reasons you need to do it. Change means risking failure and venturing into untested waters. Rarely do people choose to change until their current pain outweighs the discomfort of change.

As long as you can still (even unconsciously) say, "*I can live with the way things are,*" you won't disrupt the status quo. Remember: Mavericks are those who disrupt the status quo.

So, do you really want to transform?

H2.0 believes in underdogs and second chances. You may not think you're capable of becoming a legal entrepreneur, and that's okay, for now. We don't need to be convinced. We believe in you, your skills, and your talents. We challenge you to challenge yourself and to BOSS UP!

Strike up a list of what illegal hustling has cost you. What have you lost or given up?

NOTHING CHANGES IF NOTHING CHANGES

Change begins with hope and belief. Hope is the most powerful drug in the world. Let's get high. ☺ We have to believe in our ability to change. If we can't see it, it won't happen. Imagine yourself as the person you want to become.

- What does a successful you look like?
- Describe the way you're fitted, the car you're driving, how you spend your time, your hobbies, your career, etc.

Visualize your success.

____

____

____

____

ENTREPRENEUR

Noun

A person who organizes and manages any enterprise, especially a business, usually with considerable initiative and risk.

NACHOS TOPOS LOCOS

By Richard Garcia

Ingredients:

2 Cactus Annie tortilla chips
1 San Miguel salsa verde/green sauce
1/2 Velveeta Mexican cheese block
1 Brushy Creek salami stick with beef and chicken
1 Chilorio de Pollo
2 Pickles
1 tsp of Cilantro leaves
1 tsp of Lime juice mix
1/2 bag of Cactus Annie pork rinds
1/2 of Onion or minced dried onion
2 pouches of Hot chili beans!

How to assemble:

- ☐ Put chilorio de pollo, salami stick, and bag of pork rinds in a bag and heat up to let all the flavors marinate.
- ☐ While that's going, cut up pickles to pieces and mix in a small bowl with cilantro leaves and lime juice mix and add a little cold water.
- ☐ Cut up the onion (if available).
- ☐ Put the 1/2 block of Mexican cheese in a small bag and melt.
- ☐ Heat up chili with beans ... make it hot!
- ☐ In a bowl, add some tortilla chips, then some chili with beans. On top of that, add some meat mixture. Melt cheese on top of that; then add the pickle mixture and onion or minced dried onion.
- ☐ Final touch: add the salsa verde.
- ☐ For some kick, add sliced jalapeño.

MONEY OVER EVERYTHING ... ?

By Jesus Murillo

aka Sweet Chewy Cookie Dough

"Money over everything!"

How many times have you heard this?

I know too well how this motto is utilized and circulated in today's culture. I also gravitated towards it. I enjoyed coming home after a day's work of hustling in the 'hood and counting the money I made.

Night after night, this was a little ritual of mine. I don't know what I was saving for, but I was raking in all I could from whoever had it.

I didn't know this at the time, but my values were out of order. I let money drive me. I let it be my motivation. I think back to the people I sold to and can't help but feel ashamed of the teenager I used to be. These people had a problem with addiction, and I didn't care about it. I exploited it to my advantage. I just wanted their money and it didn't matter where it came from: government checks, robberies, or stolen items.

Addiction drove my clients, and money drove me, so we met in the middle and both "won." But some of these people were my own family, struggling with addiction.

As long as money was my top priority, my behavior remained corrupt. My criminal mindset ruled my life, because after all, it was "money over everything." I wasn't taught exceptions to the rule; it was the lifestyle to live.

I now see this motto doesn't apply to a healthy lifestyle. We all need money to pay bills and live a sustainable life ... but this should never come at the cost of freedom, good values, and others' well-being, whether directly or indirectly.

What motto would sum up your life's actions?

____

"Money over everything?"
Hold up ... I think I got it twisted and conflicted.
I thought you wanted *freedom* more than anything?

I thought you said you'd pay
all the money in the world
to get your freedom back?

Maybe it's time to flip yo' script to:
"freedom over everything"

Because Honey Badgers don't do captivity.

Ain't that real?
How are you going to rearrange your priorities
to finally get
what you say you really want?

- The Honey Badger

SELF-ASSESSMENT: BEEN AN ENTREPRENEUR?

In the past, we, the H2.O Homies, did anything (well ... almost anything) to earn a dollar. We've been transforming our hustles, but to take inventory of our entrepreneurial skills, let's start by recognizing when we used our hustle for illicit gain while incarcerated.

Check off the illegal hustles you've used to profit at any point while incarcerated:

- [ ] Been the commissioner of a fantasy football, basketball, or NASCAR league
- [ ] Had greeting cards mailed in to resell for a profit
- [ ] Made and sold custom rings, bracelets, and necklaces made of string or beads
- [ ] Made and sold picture frames and jewelry boxes out of chip bags and color paper
- [ ] Sold tacos and burritos
- [ ] Ran a bootleg liquor store out of your cell
- [ ] Sold roses made out of toilet paper and Kool-Aid
- [ ] Broke down a jar of coffee to sell shots on the tier
- [ ] Sold candy bars for a profit
- [ ] Organized raffles for coffee, drawings, CDs, etc.
- [ ] Ran a weekly football pool
- [ ] Ordered pictures for stamps to resell on the tier for food
- [ ] Drew and sold portraits and greeting cards
- [ ] Sold used chewing tobacco to smokers
- [ ] Had a waiting list for cellies who wanted to get tatted
- [ ] Ran a barbershop out of the dayroom

Point is, most of us are not only entrepreneurs at heart ... we also have years of experience and creativity. We're ultra resourceful. What if we transferred our experience to legal enterprises?

List three skills you gained through illegal hustling that might serve you well as an entrepreneur.

____

> A person who sees a problem is a human being; a person who finds a solution is a visionary; and the person who goes out and does something about it is an entrepreneur.
>
> \- Naveen Jain

ENTREPRENEUR

Chinese Traditional	qǐyè jiā
French	entrepreneur
German	Unternehmer
Portuguese	empreendedor
Spanish	empresario
Swahili	mwekezaji

WHY DRUG DEALERS LIVE WITH THEIR MOMMAS

In their book, *Freakonomics: A Rogue Economist Explores the Hidden Side of Everything*, authors Steven D. Levitt and Stephen J. Dubner explore the economics of drug dealing.

Levitt and Dubner wondered: If drug dealing is so profitable, why do so many drug dealers live with their moms?

Gang operations are similar to many businesses – but mostly businesses like McDonald's.

The answer isn't because drug dealers are mommas' boys and can't cook for themselves.

A University of Chicago graduate student, Sudhir Venkatesh, set out to answer the question by befriending a gang leader and living with him and the gang for six years so he could conduct a study. He was given access to their books and analyzed the gang's hierarchy and financial transactions.

The study concluded that gang operations are similar to many businesses – but mostly businesses like McDonald's. If you checked out the org charts for McDonald's and a gang, you might not know the difference.

This gang was one of about 100 branches ("franchises") of the larger organization. They had a leader who reported to a board of directors. Depending on the season, they had 25 to 75 foot soldiers. They had up to 200 rank-and-file associates who weren't employees, but paid dues, hoping to one day qualify as foot soldiers.

The gang had total revenues of $32K/month. Not counting wages, it cost $14K/month to operate, including $5K/month for the wholesale purchase of drugs, plus $5K/month in taxes to the board of directors.

The leader paid himself $8,500 a month ($100K annually). That might sound solid. But … is it? Especially when you could earn the same paper in a legal hustle, and not have a life sentence (or a fatal threat) hanging over your head?

There were about 100 other leaders (of the other branches) like this one in the gang who raked in about $100K/year. The 20 or so board members each made $500K/year. So … the top 120 guys in the entire gang made bank. (But how long did that last before they got locked up?)

Summarized concepts from an LA Times article, April 24, 2005, by Steven D. Levitt and Stephen J. Dubner https://www.latimes.com/archives/la-xpm-2005-apr-24-oe-dubner24-story.html

How well did the rest of the associates make out?

- The Foot Soldiers: There were about 5,300 foot soldiers working for those 120 bosses. They averaged **$7 an hour**—or $14,560 annually — well below minimum wage.
- The Rank and File Associates: There were 20,000 unpaid rank-and-file associates, who just wanted a shot at becoming a foot soldier. How much does that job pay? About **$3.30 an hour**.

If you really like stacking paper, analyze these numbers and odds:

	# People Involved in a Gang's Activities	% of Gang Associates	Annual Income	Average Hourly Wage
Board of Directors/ Top Brass	20	0.08%	$500,000	$240.00
Gang Leaders/ Captains	100	0.39%	$100,000	$48.00
Soldiers	5,300	20.85%	$14,560	$7.00
Rank and File Associates	20,000	78.68%	$6,864	$3.30
# People Who Don't Value Freedom	**25,420**			

They put their lives and futures on the line every day ... for what? $3.30 an hour!?

99% of drug dealers are not only idiots — they're broke idiots — making less than minimum wage

Just because you might have acted like an idiot in your past, doesn't mean you have to keep on keepin' on. Recognize your losses and transform your hustle.

We all know the big dogs eat first. The top brass—representing less than 1% of those putting in all the work—sit back and reap all the benefits, while the rest curb-serve for pennies.

Is this rubbing you the wrong way? If so, we're getting our message across. The reality of our past sucks.

No doubt, the thought of making $100K or $500K a year appeals to all of us. But if we can make that money legally, and never be incarcerated again, why would we go back to the game?

Only a fool would keep playing these odds.

Where did you fit in on the chart above with your take-home pay?

Ohhhhh, you think you're an exception to the rule, 'cause you were counting racks "every night"? Check out the math on this:

> Say you brought home $1,500 in one day.
>
> How many of those days did you really have?
>
> Like maybe two a month?
>
> For how many consecutive months did you have of sales of that magnitude?
>
> Even if you brought home $1.5K twice a month, every single month …
>
> That's still …
>
> Just $3K a month, or $36K a year.

We looooove telling war stories about the good times. Many of us seem to only remember our highest grossing night and talk about it on repeat. You know how we merge all the "good" memories into one war story and play like that happened every single day.

It's romanticized thinking and storytelling like this that will keep us broke, recidivating, and not living up to our potential.

Yeah …

Those times our cars broke down and we didn't have money to fix 'em.

Or when we were chased and lost our entire sacks to the cops. Or when we had to cough up more than we could afford to pay the lawyers. Or the nights we had no place to lay our heads. Or … you know.

DOPE MATH: BOOKKEEPING 101

Use this worksheet to do some bookkeeping. No one's collecting this. Do yourself a favor and don't lie to yourself.

Dope Math Worksheet		
Revenue on a "big day" in drug sales	A)	$ ________ /day
# of those big days that you had per month	B)	# ________ big days
Your revenue in a big month of drug sales *(multiply A x B to get the answer)*	C)	$ ________ /month
# of months that you pulled those big numbers in a 12-month period	D)	# ________ months
Your annual dope revenue in a good year *(multiply C x D)*	E)	$ ________ /year

Even if you had those big days every now and then ... we all know there were plenty of days when we made next to nothing, or just lost money.

Is that annual number what you call "ballin"?

Some of us didn't take accounting classes and confused "revenue" with "net income." There's a big difference, and our pockets know it. Keep working those numbers in the Net Take-Home Worksheet to figure out what you really made.

If you want accurate accounting on your profit and hourly wage, you have to factor in all of your related expenses. If you forget some expenses, you'll overstate your profit (which is a common error made by entrepreneurs), and you'll wonder why you're so broke.

Expenses to include on the next page (check all that applied to your business):

- ☐ Cost of buying dope (typically at least 50% of your revenue number on Line E above)
- ☐ Cutting supplies
- ☐ Packaging
- ☐ Gas for deliveries
- ☐ Guns for protection
- ☐ Hotel rooms
- ☐ Car mileage and depreciation of your car for deliveries
- ☐ Rent for your business
- ☐ Comped dope
- ☐ Legal fees (retainers + legal representation once you got busted)
- ☐ Anything that was repossessed when you got busted (cash, car, etc.)

Net Take-Home Worksheet			
Your annual dope revenue: ***(answer for E from above)***	**E)**	**$ ______**	**/year**
Cost of buying the year's supply of dope from my dealer:	F)	$ ______	/year
For G through O, label your expense categories in the left-hand column and enter the corresponding $ amounts on the right.			
Expense Category:	G)	$ ______	/year
Expense Category:	H)	$ ______	/year
Expense Category:	I)	$ ______	/year
Expense Category:	J)	$ ______	/year
Expense Category:	K)	$ ______	/year
Expense Category:	L)	$ ______	/year
Expense Category:	M)	$ ______	/year
Expense Category:	N)	$ ______	/year
Expense Category:	O)	$ ______	/year
Your total annual dope expenses: ***(add up all your answers for F through O)***	**P)**	**$ ______**	**/year**
Your net take-home income: ***(E - P = Q)***	**Q)**	**$ ______**	**/year**
Your estimated hourly wage: ***(Q ÷ 2000 = R)****	**R)**	**$ ______**	**/year**

**To calculate your hourly rate, estimate the number of hours you did anything associated with drug sales (driving, phone calls, packaging, looking out, etc.). If you averaged 8 hours/day, that's 40 hours/week X 52 weeks/year = 2,080 hours/year. To make the math simple, we used 2,000 hours for this calculation.*

Many of us prided ourselves in hustling 24/7 ... so if you worked 16 hours/day, you would actually divide by 4,000 instead of 2,000.

20 YEARS IN PRISON = LOSING NEARLY $1 MILLION

What was your net take-home in your biggest year? $ ________

Now divide that number by the number of years you've done: $ ________

Regardless of what you did or didn't rake in ... what's the math on the wages you lost by being locked up? Say you went legit and earned only minimum wage. In Los Angeles in 2019, that was $14.25/hour, or about $30K/year.

Years you've been incarcerated	Lost Wages (at $14.25/hour)
5	$148K
10	$296K
15	$445K
20	$593K

Hmmm, what could you have done with that HALF A MILLION DOLLARS if you had kept your freedom for 20 years (or hadn't wasted it being a junkie)? And hold up – that's if you never once got promoted and stayed at minimum wage for 20 straight years.

Say you committed to a legit career and moved up the food chain like average people do. Let's lowball it ... imagine you make an average of $20/hour ($42K/year):

Years you've been incarcerated	Lost Wages (at $20/hour)
5	$208K
10	$416K
15	$624K
20	$832K

Most of us are capable of a lot more than $20/hour, if we hustle, grind, and invest our time.

For example, H2.O's free staff recently got a message from a grad who's only been out nine months after doing 18 years on a murder charge. He'd never held a legal job before his current one, and he just got a raise in his base salary to $70K plus up to $30K in sales commissions.

Bringing in $100K legally is a lot more realistic than getting to that 1% top brass in the gang world ... and you get to spend that $100K on steak, your partner and kids, sleep soundly at night, stay alive ... and stay the frick out of this place.

HUSTLE SMARTER

By Chris Succaw

aka Sweet Butter Pecan

So you're too good for a job
But not too good for a prison cell
You're too cool for school
But you'll stand in front of a judge with a smiling face
like all is well

Gambling with your life like it's a game of dice
Willing to pay the ultimate price
For material things you find nice

An' through these things you claim you earn validation
As if the level of your accumulation is authentication
Of your manhood and its maturation

Playing big me's and little you's
As if you're better than those who use
So blinded by your naiveté
That you fail to see that you're both equally confused

Equally lost!
Equally trapped!
The truth of the matter is
That you're blind to these facts
Fortunately, ignorance is a sleep you can wake from

Hustle harder
Hustle smarter
Hustle 2.0!

SO, HOMIE ... WAS IT WORTH IT?

Only you can answer that.

Sometimes seeing the math can lead us to transform.

Oh … and those are just some of the financial costs.

What's the cost to you of:

- Becoming "property of the state" and being told what to do every day?
- Not getting a visit from your family for years, or losing them altogether?
- Not being there for your loved ones when they need you?
- Missing your loved ones' funerals, graduations, weddings, and birthdays?
- Breaking your mother's heart and watching her cry at visit?
- Letting down all the good people who believed in you?

To beat a dead horse, say you're one of the 1% who really was ballin' and you think prison time was worth the financial and emotional costs:

- Have you thought about where your cousins and brothers fit in these equations?
- What about your kids? How will they fare?
- You want any of your family being lured into $3.30 an hour so they can one day also be fed through a tray slot?

> For every 20 members whose pockets really are swoll, 25,000 other people get caught up in the game. That's 25,000 misguided kids who are prison-bound ... all for the benefit of 20 "top brass" members.

If the economics aren't making it obvious enough, think about this:

- How many thousands of drug user's lives are lost – or destroyed—because we're willing to sell to whoever's buying?
- How many of these drug user's kids didn't get to eat that night because you gave their parent a "sweet deal"?
- How many parents' souls were crushed as they desperately pursued rehabilitation and intervention for their beloved drug-addicted kids?

Maybe you justified your actions by saying, "If someone's going to get their money, it might as well be me."

What if you had to answer this:

If you died today, why would your life matter?

Would you be pleased with your answer? Would "because I had the best dope on the block" do it for you?

ARENT WE BETTER THAN THIS???!!

Gangs operate similarly to standard businesses … but we all know that slangin' dope is dangerous and costly. Just look around you at all the incarcerated people who forfeited their freedom in pursuit of a dollar … (okay, more than a dollar: $3.30 an hour!!) … That's cray-cray.

Why were we so naïve to fall into the trap? Are we over this yet?

Let's Summarize:

- Selling drugs is the most dangerous job in America.
- 99% of the time, it pays less than minimum wage.
- It leads us to become property of the state.

What did you learn about your criminal lifestyle from this case study?

____

After running the numbers, was your lifestyle worth it? Why or why not?

____

What is one positive action you will take as a result of completing this case study?

____

HERE TO HUSTLE

By Gabriel Arce

Pre-verse:

I ain't just playin'
They're payin' just what I'm sayin'
I'm making outrageous digits
That'll leave you feelin' fainted
I'm not famous but I'm 'boutta be
Making money like a celebrity's salary
Never paid attention to what the haters tellin' me
And now I'm shining like it wasn't even challenging
Wasn't challenging
I got a felony
But that ain't stopping nothin, no boundaries
Still money-makin' every day, counting green
And not a single thing changes when I'm sound asleep
Now I'm out my sleep

Verse 1

My aggression propelled me to focus my mind on a hustle
I'm allowing my struggle to motivate these words I mumble
From the ghetto where the rubble of the wicked reside
Our intelligence was developed bound to be recognized
From terrorizing to righteously utilizing my mind
Million-dollar businesses are now the plans I devise
It was an uphill battle, but I reached out for the sky
With diligence now realizing all the stars I see in my sight

If you think small
Best believe you're gonna be small
It's no wonder why they keep calling me King Kong
I'm a real hustler and I'm coming strong
I'm 'boutta run this show like it's a marathon
It's Hustle-Two-Point-O and we're coming on strong
We about run this show like it's a marathon

Hook/chorus
My pockets on swoll
Steady makin' money like people don't know
Whether in the rain, sunshine, or in the snow
Ima get my grind on and that's just the way it goes
If your pockets lookin' small but my pockets on swoll
You should grab a pen and paper and start taking notes
It's time for me to shine so Ima let it show
Even if I wanted to, I couldn't keep it on the low
Why?
Bcuz I hustle and watch my money double
Everybody lookin' at me like if I came to bring trouble
But I'm just here to hustle and watch my money double
Everybody lookin' at me like if I came to bring trouble

Verse 2
Have I been gifted by the father bcuz they been tellin' me I'm blessed
King Kong hustlin' strong while I keep beating on my chest
I'm not easily impressed with big pockets or how you dress
I got my mind upon the best like tryna purchase a jet
I suggest if you're hoping to see me fail, don't hold your breath

Bcuz I be spittin' so fresh like I'm brushin' my teeth with Crest
They lovin' the way I be going about my business when I rap
Started with nothing without really knowing I'll get it right and now's my chance
I'm makin' money the righteous way, make no mistake, it's time to get paid
Every single day I wake I'm tryna increase what's in the bank
And now my pockets so fat I think they need lipo
Everybody keep callin' my name like it's Mike Jones
In the Bay but I'm shining like I'm white gold
So bright you can see me with eyes closed
Hustle-Two-Point-O in the building
Real hustlers like us we make a killing

Repeat hook 2x here

A PH.D. IN CONSEQUENCES

By Chris Succaw
aka Sweet Butter Pecan

Most of us have made moves to fill our pockets with illegal money. Like most, for me it was just supposed to be a quick come-up. A means to an end.

Somewhere along the way, it became much more. It became a career. The lifestyle became just as important as the money.

"Easy come, easy go"—that's the motto, right? Well I got that fast money, and that's exactly how I spent it too. Selling drugs was my niche, and I quickly learned that I was exceptionally good at it. I started off corner hustling. Huggin' the block and slangin' rocks. It was part-time tedious and full-time risky. The most dangerous traps are often the most profitable, so the risk of ending up in cuffs—or worse—is ever present. Just not enough to get me and most others to give up on that fast money. For many of us, the allure of that fast dollar was just too strong to ignore.

I was serious about my grind and quickly elevated from slangin' rocks on the block to moving weight O.T. (out of town/state, where the product sold for much higher prices). Long gone was the plan to make a quick buck and get out of the game.

I can easily speak on the women, the whips, and the ice. All of the turnin' up, shining, and ballin'—but I'm not about to do that. Nah. Instead, I'm going to give you the flipside of the game … the side of the game that few, if any, ever speak out about.

What gives me the authority to speak on it, you might ask?

Well, I got a Ph.D. in consequences. Consequences of what those of you still asleep consider a "game." Listen up and get woke, homie. I'm certified! I'm 16 years in

All that remains are the inevitable consequences of my decisions and actions.

on a 57-years-to-life sentence for attempted murder, drug sales, and drug and weapons possession. The whips are gone. The women are gone. The ice is gone. Family and friends are gone. And yea, that money is gone, too. All that remains are the inevitable consequences of my decisions and actions. Decisions and actions that I know harmed and destroyed the lives of so many. When we attempt to secure the bag by illegal means, we fail to acknowledge the pain and destruction we leave in our wake.

Life is an extremely precious and priceless thing, and I'm consciously aware of the fact that I've single-handedly negatively impacted many. I take full responsibility for the decisions and my actions, and I deeply regret them. There isn't a single day that I don't think about the people I've harmed by selling them drugs: mothers, fathers, sisters, and brothers. I carelessly put poison in their hands. The households, communities, and the lives I destroyed …

I sit inside of a small closet-sized cell and relive sitting in the courtroom, facing the victim of my crime and his family, listening to their candid and emotional testimony of how my actions harmed them. And I think about my own family and how my decisions and actions have negatively impacted them.

Nothing about this is a game.

Ultimately, the price you pay is your life, and the lives of others. Whatever your hustle, if it's an illegal one, trust and believe it's a short-lived thing. It's not worth it. It's a lose-lose that guarantees one, some, or all of the following:

Prison
Regret
Guilt
Pain
Loss
Sorrow
Shame
Death

The good news is this: there is a better way. A legal way. A much more fulfilling and sustainable way. It's called entrepreneurship.

Entrepreneurs embody the hustler's mind and spirit. Many of the skills you already possess are critical for being a successful entrepreneur. In fact, you may already have a leg up on the competition. Don't repeat the same mistakes that countless others and I have made.

Transform your hustle, homie. Hustle 2.0!

> I carelessly put poison in their hands … Nothing about this is a game. The price you pay is your life, and the lives of others.

SUDOKU

Complete the puzzle by filling in the numbers 1-9 in each row, each column, and each 3x3 grid without repeating a number in any row, column, or 3x3 grid.

		9				8		
	4		1	6	3	9		
				4		1		6
						6	5	
	5	1		7				
	9			5	1		3	4
8	7					4		9
		3	7					2
	2	5			4			

CASE STUDY: THE ART OF GETTIN' IT

What I Learned from H2.0's Business Ideation Process

By Chris Succaw
aka Sweet Butter Pecan

"Be useful. Solve a problem and **GET PAID FOR IT!**" This is platinum game from the battle-tried, tested, and proven entrepreneur Seth Godin. Yea, this dude is official like a referee with a whistle! In a nutshell, this is the Business Ideation Process. At Hustle 2.0, we define it as, "Brainstorming that allows entrepreneurs to generate multiple business ideas to solve customer problems." I just like to think of it as "The Art of Gettin' It."

Growing up in poverty, I've always been an innovative thinker and natural-born hustler. I mean, doing without was the ultimate motivator for me. I had to go out and get it. Thinking outside of the box has always been my "modus operandi." This worked wonders for me throughout the business ideation process. My experience in the streets had equipped me with a unique set of skills that were easily transferable to legal entrepreneurship, once I had the game on how to do so and what to look fo'. The ideation process laced yo' boy up real nice and got me game-tight. I learned how to identify customers' problems, identify competitive advantages, find my target customers, list and address realistic barriers, and detail relevant skills, credentials, experience, and passions that outline my qualifications.

Learning to be useful—not original—was the concept that helped me most. Initially, I was stuck. I had a lot of ideas, but in my mind, they were all basic. Those who know me know I don't do basic. I'm also really competitive. So I'm all in my head like; "Man, you gotta do it big. You gotta go hard and stunt on them with something new. Something they ain't seen before."

> Learning to be useful—not original—was the concept that helped me most.

This just isn't the case. I can't stress this enough. Being original is cool. But the thing that is going to secure the bag is being useful. People pay problem solvers. Identify customer needs, address them, and the probability of your success rises expeditiously. I earned second place in a pitch competition in one of the closest votes ever. This process is what got me there.

> Entrepreneurship is bossin' up fo'real.

Through entrepreneurship, we can take control of our own destiny. Entrepreneurship is bossin' up fo'real. I strongly recommend that you're serious about gettin' it. Act like a sponge and soak it up, homie.

CASE STUDY: HONEY BADGER HUSTLING 24/7

Silverio Strong, Founder & CEO
SHAP Cleaning and Maintenance, Inc.

After 20 years in prison, Silverio Strong has defined what it means to be a Honey Badger.

Seven months after incorporating his business, Silverio has five employees. His business became profitable in his fourth month. He's now served more than 180 customers in the Sacramento area.

When asked why he started his business, Silverio stated, "I've been hustling all my life, sweeping floors at the laundromat, cleaning out the lint traps, and cutting lawns … and then as I got older, selling drugs."

Silverio didn't let his incarceration stop him from conducting market research. He shared what he did to set himself up for success while at Pelican Bay:

1. Went to c/o's to ask about his competition.
2. Went to the law library to read up on health codes relevant to his business.
3. Picked up books and magazines that guys were throwing away (e.g., Inc., Fast Company). He wrote companies featured in the ads, asking for resources, inquiring about their services, and how much they charged.
4. Asked homies on the phone if they would ask their families to do research for him.

Now that's some Honey Badger Hustle! Silverio said about his early days after his release, "I had fears about whether I had what

Silverio returned to Pelican Bay to mentor Mavericks a year after his release.

it took and about my ability to connect with customers, so to overcome that I went door-to-door, conducting market research."

It wasn't easy, and Silverio had to overcome his fear of failure. "I was knocking on 40 doors a day to get customers, and only around 22 of them were opening. Out of the 22 that opened, 22 were a no."

"Instead of giving up, I used this as an opportunity to do some qualitative research. When they said no, I asked if they had already received this service somewhere else, how often, and when."

Silverio came back to Pelican Bay in July of 2019, a little over a year after his release. This is not just someone you hear about on the tier. This is someone who walked that tier with us and used every resource that is currently at your disposal.

Shout out to Silverio Strong!
Khrya-yaaa-yaaa!!!

> Instead of expectations, have a plan ... and have a backup plan to that plan ... because once you're out, you'll see that even with the best market research, life will throw things at you that were not in your research. Then the voices in your head will say, 'Look, I tried, and I failed.'
>
> - Silverio Strong

What did you learn from Chris Succaw's advice about business ideation?

Silverio wrote about turning rejection into an opportunity. What action can this inspire you to the next time you fail?

HEALTHY RELATIONSHIPS

Cupcakin' 101

LEARNING OBJECTIVES

In this crash course, you will ...

- ✓ Learn benefits of healthy relationships, including living a longer life with less stress
- ✓ Brush up on the art of cupcakin' to improve your relationship with your special someone, including ways to ask more thoughtful questions and engage in meaningful conversation
- ✓ Take a quiz to determine what you have to offer in a relationship and whether you're ready for a healthy one ... and how to get right before you get left
- ✓ Learn why you might want to lose your type and start choosing character over characteristics
- ✓ Learn guidelines for writing an effective penpal intro to gain new healthy relationships, and learn creative penmanship tips for letters and communicating meaningfully

In Hustle Guides 1-12, take in-depth courses and gain insight into:

- ✓ Finding and developing healthy relationships
- ✓ Parenting from behind bars and after incarceration
- ✓ Making a romantic partnership work
- ✓ Building and re-building trust
- ✓ Healthy boundaries and necessary endings

THE BENEFITS OF A HEALTHY RELATIONSHIP

A healthy relationship can be shared between any two people who love, support, encourage, and help each other practically as well as emotionally. When we reference "relationships," think about your friendships, professional relationships, family ... and romantic relationships.

People in healthy relationships tend to:

- Listen to each other
- Communicate openly and without judgment
- Trust and respect each other
- Consistently make time for each other
- Remember details about each other's lives
- Engage in healthy activities together

Benefits of healthy relationships include:

1. **Less Stress**
   Being in a committed relationship is linked to less production of cortisol, a stress hormone. Married or paired people are less responsive to psychological stress, and the emotional support from a partner can be a great buffer against stress. There's evidence to suggest that couples who cohabitate are happier than those who don't.

2. **Better Healing**
   Whether your partner reminds you to take your medicine, or helps take your mind off pain, studies show that married people who have undergone heart surgery are three times more likely to survive the first three months after surgery than single patients.

3. **Healthier Behaviors**
   A healthy relationship can set the tone for a healthy lifestyle. If loved ones encourage eating a healthy diet, exercising, not smoking, etc., you're likely to follow in their footsteps.

4. **Greater Sense of Purpose**
   It's natural to want to feel needed and like we're part of something bigger. We often strive to do something good for someone and the world. Being in a loving relationship, no matter what kind, can give us a sense of well-being and purpose. Having a sense of purpose can actually add years to your life.

5. **Longer Life**
   Research suggests that healthy social relationships help to avoid early death. One study even suggests that a lack of social relationships has the same effect on health as smoking 15 cigarettes a day.

If you enjoy being alone, that's okay, but nurturing a couple close relationships could mean noticeable benefits to your mental and physical health.

CUPCAKING OR CUPCAKIN'

Verb

1. Making a small cake, the size of an individual portion.
2. When a person leaves his or her friends to flirt with someone. It comes from the sweetness of cupcakes and the phrase "being sweet on someone."
3. Being hugged up with a person you like or are in a relationship wit' even tho you around yo' patnaz.
4. The act of farting into your cupped hand, trapping it, and moving the confined stench to a victim's nose or mouth to cause nausea and discomfort. (Do not try this one with yo' girl.)

Source: Adapted from Urban Dictionary

Cupcakin' at H2.0 ain't about baking or farting. It's about building and maintaining healthy relationships with your loved ones or someone you may want to be in love with.

NO JUDGMENT QUIZ: CUPCAKIN'

		AGREE	DISAGREE
1.	I've made a sincere effort to develop and nurture healthy relationships in the past six months.	☐	☐
2.	When I write a letter to that special someone, I struggle to find the right words.	☐	☐
3.	It's been more than six months since I was in a romantic relationship.	☐	☐
4.	My loved ones have not come to visit me in more than one year.	☐	☐
5.	Love hurts.	☐	☐
6.	I've had a serious argument with a loved one recently.	☐	☐
7.	It's difficult to empathize with my loved one's emotions.	☐	☐
8.	I've hurt a loved one in the past.	☐	☐
9.	I've been hurt by a loved one in the past.	☐	☐
10.	I am prepared to be my best self as a romantic partner.	☐	☐
11.	I've written a cheesy love letter.	☐	☐
12.	I would be a better version of myself if I had healthy relationships.	☐	☐
13.	I've written 10-page letters and received a half-hearted, half-page response.	☐	☐
14.	I desire the benefits that come from a healthy relationship.	☐	☐
15.	When I use the phone, it's often to ask someone to order my package, or to ask for money.	☐	☐
16.	When I call or write, more than half of the conversation is about me, me, me ... what I want, what I'm interested in, or what I'm going through.	☐	☐

	AGREE	DISAGREE
17. I shouldn’t have to tell my family I love them; they already know.	☐	☐
18. When I talk on the phone or at visit, I am just waiting for an opening so I can start talking.	☐	☐
19. I don’t feel very lovable.	☐	☐
20. I love myself.	☐	☐
21. I’ve given up on love.	☐	☐
22. I’ve been in here so long, I wouldn’t even know how to love someone properly.	☐	☐
23. I’m not living as the best version of myself and don’t feel ready for a relationship.	☐	☐
24. I have at least one close friend I can tell anything to.	☐	☐
25. I feel all alone.	☐	☐
26. I’m in an unhealthy relationship or friendship that I would be better off ending.	☐	☐
27. When I’m in a relationship or friendship, I do most of the giving.	☐	☐
28. When I’m in a relationship or friendship, I do most of the taking or receiving.	☐	☐
29. If I were someone else, I would want to be with me; I have a lot to offer.	☐	☐
30. I wish I had someone special to cupcake with.	☐	☐

Which of your answers stand out to you the most? Circle the three that feel most like wake-up calls.

Write one thing you’re realizing from this quiz.

____

GET RIGHT BEFORE YOU GET LEFT

Illustration by Trenton Dukes

Many people look to relationships to "fix" them. When we feel a void (e.g., we feel lonely or sad from a rejection or breakup), it's easy to think that someone new can come along and make us feel whole. The early stages of a relationship *can* provide a welcomed distraction from pain … but if we're not healthy, our neediness and unrealistic expectations (e.g., that a partner will heal us) nearly always destroy a relationship that could have been good.

Instead of jumping into a relationship, what if you dedicated time to work on yourself, heal, and find fulfillment … and then offered the healthier you in a relationship?

SELF-ASSESSMENT: ARE YOU READY FOR A HEALTHY RELATIONSHIP?

		AGREE	DISAGREE
1.	I am confident.	☐	☐
2.	I'm open-minded and accept change.	☐	☐
3.	I am comfortable in my own skin.	☐	☐
4.	I have a strong understanding of myself: my strengths, weaknesses, likes, and dislikes.	☐	☐
5.	I don't need a relationship to feel happy and worthy (I may desire to share my life with someone, but I don't need this to feel complete).	☐	☐
6.	I don't need to be "fixed" or "saved"; I don't feel broken.	☐	☐
7.	I'm not afraid to be alone; I'm okay being single.	☐	☐
8.	I don't constantly seek distractions.	☐	☐
9.	I build memories, not walls.	☐	☐
10.	I've gotten rid of my crazy expectations and am ready to be giving in a relationship.	☐	☐
11.	I value character over characteristics.	☐	☐
12.	I'm happy and I smile a lot.	☐	☐
13.	I'm healed from my last relationship and am no longer entangled in it. I've forgiven my ex and am not weighed down with resentment or constant thoughts of my ex.	☐	☐
14.	I'm willing to take a risk; fear doesn't run my life. I'm willing to make myself vulnerable with love.	☐	☐
15.	I don't have any current addictions.	☐	☐
16.	I've done significant introspection and/or therapy and have obtained healing.	☐	☐

KEY - # times you checked the Agree box:
16: You're ready!
10-15: Pay attention to the statements where you checked the Disagree box. These things could lead you to sabotage your next relationship.
0-9: Do some work on yourself before engaging in a new romantic relationship. Pursue healthy friendships and mentors first. We've all been there. You can do it.

LOSE YOUR TYPE

Ask yourself: how's your "type" been working out for you? When it comes to romance, unless you're happily coupled with someone who fits your type, the answer for the rest of us is:

Not so well.

In his book, *How to Find a Date Worth Keeping*, Henry Cloud writes about the importance of losing our types. Typically, we have expectations for a partner that include surface requirements (characteristics), like:

- Physical appearance/ attractiveness
- Age
- Race/ethnicity
- Salary/money
- Career
- Kids (or lack thereof)
- If they're homegirls or squares
- If they're from the 'hood

Character over Characteristics

Why is it so rare that our "type" consists of character requirements? Think about your past relationships. Many of us make statements like, "All my exes are crazy." Instead, could it be that you consistently choose crazy partners, because you have a poor "people picker"?

What if you scrapped your entire list of requirements — like, *everything* from the surface requirements we listed — and instead, set a different standard for your relationships, like, I will only engage with someone who demonstrates:

- Generosity
- Respect
- Kindness
- Emotional maturity
- Trust

Watch out: it's easy to make a list of higher standards than we hold ourselves to, so ask yourself if you embody your own list of character requirements. If you want someone who is trusting, are you trusting? Or are you always one step away from an accusation? Like, the first time they don't answer

Could it be that you consistently choose crazy partners, because you have a poor "people picker"?

the phone, they're subject to interrogation ("Where were you? Who were you with??").

Ask yourself what your relationships would look like if you screened for character instead of fleeting, surface requirements.

Character usually lasts a lifetime. Everything else, like looks, money, circumstances, etc., changes. We can all think back to when we were in love with someone who was "so hot"—but that love faded quickly when we discovered their character defects.

Conversely, if we engage in healthy friendships with people with strong character, we might not be initially attracted to them, because they might not fit our physical types

> It's amazing how beautiful strong character is.

... but it's amazing how beautiful strong character is. Healthy relationships are made of matching values, beliefs, strong character, emotional maturity, giving spirits, loyalty, and commitment.

> When you stop expecting people to be perfect, you can like them for who they are.
>
> - Donald Miller

What are three characteristics (surface requirements) you have consistently looked for in relationships?

____

Going forward, I will only engage in relationships with people who exhibit these three *character* traits:

____

CRAY

CHEESIEST BREAKUP LINES

1. Want to know a joke? Our relationship.
2. I regret having held in even a single fart for you.
3. Our relationship is like a fat guy, it's not working out.
4. I treated this relationship like my diet, one cheat day a week.
5. Is it hot in here or is this relationship suffocating me?
6. Sorry you didn't meet my ridiculously low standards.

CHEESIEST CLEAN CUPCAKIN' LINES

1. You may fall from the sky, you may fall from a tree, but the best way to fall ... is in love with me.
2. Can I tie your shoe? Because I can't have you fall for anyone else.
3. Your hand looks heavy. Let me hold it for you.
4. Know what's on the menu? Me-n-u.
5. Guess what I'm wearing? The smile you gave me.
6. Me without you is like a nerd without braces, shoes without laces, a sentence without spaces.
7. Is there a science room nearby, or am I just sensing the chemistry between us?
8. Are you a parking ticket? Because you've got FINE written all over you.

CRAY

SELF-ASSESSMENT: WHAT DO I HAVE TO OFFER?

		AGREE	DISAGREE
1.	I have plenty of time to write on a regular basis.	☐	☐
2.	I can call nearly every day.	☐	☐
3.	I'm a great listener.	☐	☐
4.	I've got good cupcaking game and can make a partner feel cherished.	☐	☐
5.	I'm a great conversationalist and am good at asking interesting questions.	☐	☐
6.	I'm dependable; you can count on me. When I say I will call or write, I do so.	☐	☐
7.	I'm thoughtful and love to surprise my partner with little things like letters, art, and cards.	☐	☐
8.	I will respect my partner and value their opinions, and will give consideration to their opinions as I make decisions.	☐	☐
9.	I will defend my partner's honor and not allow anyone to speak disrespectfully of them.	☐	☐
10.	I'm funny and will keep my partner laughing.	☐	☐
11.	I'm upbeat and positive and see the good in tough situations. I'll cheer my partner up.	☐	☐
12.	I have strong values of family and loyalty, and have a track record of faithfulness.	☐	☐
13.	I'm conscientious and am great at remembering special occasions like birthdays and anniversaries.	☐	☐
14.	I'm trusting and am not jealous or possessive. I'm encouraging of my partner having friends, hobbies, and a life of their own.	☐	☐
15.	I engage in difficult and intense discussions about topics that are important to my partner and me.	☐	☐

		AGREE	DISAGREE
16.	I give great advice.	☐	☐
17.	I know the difference when a friend is looking for a solution to a problem vs. just venting.	☐	☐
18.	When my partner is going through a tough time, I've got broad shoulders and know what it's like to struggle.	☐	☐
19.	I know what it's like to mess up badly. I will not judge my partner for their past.	☐	☐
20.	I understand that I might not be the center of my partner's life.	☐	☐

Which statement that you agreed with do you like the most about yourself? Why?

BE A GIVER

If you are looking for a relationship because you "need" something from it, you're setting the relationship up for failure. Wait until you're ready to offer something meaningful to a partner: a healthy you.

It could be easy to think that because we're incarcerated, we don't have much to offer, but this isn't true. Check out all the statements in the quiz above you agreed with! *Now circle the three statements that represent the best offerings you have for a current or potential partner.*

> People are lonely because they build walls instead of bridges.
>
> - Joseph F. Newton

TIPS FOR WRITING AN EFFECTIVE PENPAL INTRO

If you are using that same old game to write your intro letter, don't be surprised if you don't get a hit.

There are thousands of profiles running the same old drag. If you are looking to gain a *quality* friendship, focus on what you offer your new potential friends.

1. **Give a snapshot of who you are, what you have to offer, and the relationship you are seeking.**

   Start your profile by describing your most positive character traits. Are you funny? Outgoing? Creative? Loyal? Affectionate? Intellectually curious? Choose three or four adjectives that describe your personality. If you're at a loss, ask your friends for help. How would they describe you to someone they were setting you up with?

   Instead of going with the, "I love puppies" bit, talk about what you're passionate about. Share an insight into what drives you as a person and what that looks like in your life.

   Be straight up about what you are looking for. If you're not looking for a committed relationship, don't put that you are.

2. **Focus on the character, not the characteristics.**

   Don't list the characteristics (hobbies, height, body type) you are looking for. Remember, looks fade away; character endures. If this was your ideal partner, what character would you like them to have?

   Example: instead of saying that you are looking for someone fit who works out, say that you are looking for someone with the character trait of "valuing health and fitness."

   Also very important: when writing about yourself, write about your character, not your characteristics!

3. **Don't just talk about it, be about it.**

   Writing about your life and what it looks like on a daily basis in a few words isn't easy. Providing specifics is important to attract the right people your way.

   Every profile says, "I'm loyal." What does this look like in action? Give a tangible example of how you exhibit the values in your life. "Paint the picture" with words.

4. **Don't be a Negative Nancy.**

   You only have so many words available; why waste them on being negative, writing about what you're *not* looking for?

   If you say you're "tired of the games and drama," others will assume that your life is full of games and drama, which means you don't have the self-awareness to see how much of it you create!

Too hard for the yard ... and for any penpal site!

5. Decide the story you want to tell.

Your intro is a story, so, what is your story, and how does it capture who you are? Is it a story of a resilient person who is making a difference in the world, or of a person who is fed up with the drama because they have had so much of it in their life and they're looking to be rescued from it?

Your story will determine who is attracted to you. If you are telling a story about what is unique and attractive to the person you are looking for, there is a good chance you'll get your name called at mail time.

6. Make your profile others-centered.

Most profiles are all about what that person wants to get out of a relationship. They scream, "Me, me, me, me, me! I'm all about what I want!" Instead, look at our quizzes and write about what you have to offer a penpal.

7. Check your spelling and grammar and cut words that don't matter.

We don't all have the best spelling and grammar. Before you send out that intro, ask someone with the skills to make corrections. Ask a homie in the computer class to type it up to use spellcheck and propose corrections.

Also, most profiles are filled with redundant words. If you want your profile to stand out, analyze every word and ask, "Does this convey new or pertinent information?" If not, cut the crap!

8. A picture's worth 1,000 words.

You get what you put out. If you're looking for the rando penpal and more crazy relationships, keep posting your same thug mug photos. Just stop complaining about unhealthy relationships and realize you're choosing brokenness, and usually, you're advertising for it.

If you're ready for a healthy relationship, submit photos you would want your potential long-term partner to see. If you want them to see you as a kind, respectful, humble, honest person, try putting a smile (and a shirt!) on.

It is more effective to focus on attracting the right people than repelling the wrong ones.

HONEY BADGER'S PENMANSHIP POINTS FOR PERFECT PENPAL WRITING

Instead of This ...	Do This ...
Starting off a letter like a kite (e.g., "Respects to you and your cellie")	Set a romantic tone: I'm writing to remind you how much I love and care for you; how you're always on my mind and in my heart.
Having your thug mug on while you write your letter	Drop your guard and get vulnerable, and share your feelings and emotions, e.g., "I feel so grateful to be loved by you and feel connected to you when I write to you to tell you how much I love you."
Being the Average Joe or Plain Jane	Spice it up. For example, "I love gazing into your beautiful brown eyes. My favorite memories are of us waking up together and holding each other. I feel so safe and loved in those times with you."
Just writing about your own day (e.g., what you're cooking)	Tell your partner when they popped into your head. Paint a picture that helps them imagine your future together. For example, "Today I was working out and I thought of all the time we spent at the park."
Writing to ask about your quarterly package or Jpay	Ask about their interests and affirm the things you appreciate about them, e.g., "I love how compassionate you are and the dedication you put into personal growth. It's one of the things I admire the most about you."

Instead of This ...	Do This ...
Just having words on paper	Draw stars, hearts, and smiley faces.
Writing a 10-page letter and expecting one back; writing passive-aggressive statements like, "You sure must be busy out there because I haven't heard from you in months" or, "Man, I ain't got a package in two quarters."	Ask about their communication preferences. For example, "I know you don't have as much time as I do, and I don't want to flood you with letters that could lead you to feel guilty about not writing back. So how long would you like my letters to be, and how often would you enjoy writing?" (Make sure that writing feels fun and exciting — and doesn't become an obligatory or guilt-inducing activity).
Always using the same paper and pens	Invest in different colors, shapes, and sizes of paper and cards so your letters feel like a new treat every time. Use different colored pens.
Writing one-for-one letters	Drop extra love, out-of-the-blue letters, poems, and drawings. For example, send a half-colored drawing to your loved one to finish coloring. This is especially great with kids!
Writing with sloppy or hard-to-read handwriting	Invest in your penmanship. Make your letters a joy to read and look at. Show that you took time and pleasure in writing them.

10 TIPS FOR RESPECTFULLY ADDRESSING A PARTNER

1. **Be a great listener.**

   If you are the only one talking during an entire conversation, that will get old fast. Learn to ask interesting questions. Instead of just nodding your head and smiling, listen intently and display body language that says, "I care about you and what you are saying." Don't check your watch or talk to other homies on the tier while you're on the phone.

2. **Be a loyal friend. Keep your word.**

   No one trusts a gossip. When a friend tells you something, be a vault and keep your mouth shut.

3. **Take pride in your appearance and physical fitness.**

   Don't be a sloth. Work out and eat healthy. Incarceration is not a free pass to skip showers and laundry. Keep your clothes clean and your appearance sharp.

4. **Maintain a sense of humor.**

   Don't take yourself too seriously; laugh at yourself and life's mishaps.

5. **Don't sweat the small stuff. Keep your cool.**

   Pettiness isn't a good look for anyone. Forgive. We've all made mistakes and our pasts aren't the prettiest. And when you're wrong, admit it and ask for forgiveness.

6. **Share some secrets.**

   Trust is built when both partners share secrets about themselves.

7. **Don't swear. Watch your language.**

   Express yourself without using foul and offensive language. It sounds uneducated and immature.

8. **Say "please" and "thank you" often.**

9. **Find your purpose.**

   If you know what your purpose is in life, others who are going in the same direction will be drawn to you, and you to them. Connect around shared purpose and values.

10. **Be clear about what you want.**

    Don't put out there that you're "just looking for a friend" when you're really looking for romance or vice versa. Know what you want and be straight up about it.

HEALTHY RELATIONSHIPS

Q R C O V P T E K D L B
S P U H T N F R A Q K N J N J W
L M U K M U L L Z S J X K L O K F E W A
J J O W C A L S Y Z Z O K H A A F C Z F C I R R
P R P V F W Y N T V Y F X M D W N F F C L F R P R H
I M B I B E I H E A L T H Y X L K C O R R J S W K I P P F I
I M I H I Z T K T Z P E S I E A J F E V J Q W B A P M E Q F A
V Z Z S L V P B N E E U H T M G M N F H V P H T H A E N J Y X
A Q W N O B H U Q H C H I A U O I P Q G D Z K A V A Y P L U I
H F G O O X X R O Y W U W K R X P H U D I G I E C H O A Q J W
Y B Z I F H U E H J I I G C H D X O T Y H B R S U O M L A D O
K W G T B I D G U V N P W J W N E G P B N I L Q L O Q K C C I
A J A V D R D S N R N F L Y D W R Q H C K H J F K U U R O
X I L T C H A T I H Z Q X Z U J A Y K K M S V G X P Y I S
A D E J P R B L Y W L D V O N O D Q A X Y C V X C K Y C E
H R S D F Y E O J T C B I N S C I F F Q H B A B P I X
X Z M R N E O H O E P A R T N E R Z K N Z K A H T F H
E X A M N V S F I H Y S B U G I B O M I B R S O L
X S K H O M F P Q M O Q B U I L K Z N J D I T M F
R W D H T M V H X Q W J S X L Q G Q S R K V X
A Q Z U E T T X E V L V I C H Z J E J O A
G C S Z D O U C F S S F M F Z T T O C
D F I S E L M N R X S Y N W C V K R N
C Y H U S S A R E P Z V A K Z T O
N P Z T Y M F C R P R I S Y C
K B P S O N D E A X S N Z
I Z P R S B H Y V Q Q
Y W H C I D P
V L E Z A
M E K
I

CHARACTERISTICS
CRIMEY
CUPCAKING
FRIEND
HEALTHY
HONEY BADGER
HUSTLE
HUSTLE HARDER
LOVE
MAVERICK
PARTNER
PENPAL
RELATIONSHIP
ROMANCE
SLOTH

30 DEEP THOUGHTFUL QUESTIONS

How well do you really know your loved one? How many answers do you know (for sure) about your partner?

If communication is becoming the same-old, same-old, spice it with these questions. Ask a couple in every letter (or discuss them by phone).

These questions aren't just great for romantic cupcaking. Try these questions with your children, cellie, mom, or cousins!

Circle three questions you'll ask loved ones in the next week.

1. What would constitute a "perfect" day for you?
2. If you were able to live to the age of 90 and retain either the mind or body of a 30-year-old for the last 60 years of your life, which would you want, and why?
3. Name three things you and your partner have in common.
4. For what do you feel most grateful?
5. If you could change anything about the way you were raised, what would it be?
6. Take four minutes and tell your partner your life story in as much detail as possible.
7. If you could wake up tomorrow having gained any one quality or ability, what would it be?
8. If a crystal ball could tell you the truth about yourself, your life, the future, or anything else, what would you want to know?
9. Is there something you've dreamed of doing for a long time? Why haven't you done it?
10. What is the greatest accomplishment of your life?
11. What do you value most in a friendship?
12. What is your most treasured memory?
13. What is your most terrible memory?
14. If you knew that in one year you would die suddenly, would you change anything about the way you are now living? Why?
15. What does friendship mean to you?
16. What roles do love and affection play in your life?
17. How close and warm is your family? Do you feel your childhood was happier than most other people's?
18. How do you feel about your relationship with your mother and father?
19. What is the greatest gift or talent you have to offer the world?

20. What does friendship mean to you?
21. What roles do love and affection play in your life?
22. Alternate sharing something you consider a positive characteristic of your partner. Share a total of five items.
23. Make three true "we" statements each. For instance, "We are both in this room feeling ... "
24. Complete this sentence: "I wish I had someone with whom I could share ... "
25. If you were going to become a close friend with your partner, please share what would be important for him or her to know.
26. Tell your partner what you like about them; be very honest this time, saying things that you might not say to someone you've just met.
27. Share with your partner an embarrassing moment in your life.
28. What, if anything, is too serious to be joked about?
29. If you were to die this evening with no opportunity to communicate with anyone, what would you most regret not having told someone? Why haven't you told them yet?
30. Share a personal problem and ask your partner's advice on how he or she might handle it. Also, ask your partner to reflect to you how you seem to be feeling about the problem you have chosen.

Source: Adapted from http://36questionsinlove.com/

PASSPORT

LOVE

Chinese Traditional	ài
French	amour
German	Liebe
Portuguese	amor
Spanish	amor
Swahili	upendo

CRAY

Pt. 1: Before Marriage

He: Ah ... At last. I can hardly wait!!

She: Do you want me to leave?

He: No! Don't even think about it!

She: Do you love me??

He: Of course! Always have, always will.

She: Have you ever cheated on me??

He: No! Why are you asking?

She: Will you kiss me??

He: Every chance I get.

She: Will you hit me?

He: Hell no! Are you crazy?

She: Can I trust you??

He: Yes!

She: Darling ...

Pt. 2: After Marriage

(Read from the bottom back up to the top)

CRAY

CUPCAKE DELIGHT

By Jesus Murillo

aka Sweet Chewy Cookie Dough

Makes Two Cupcake Delights

Ingredients:

2 Honey Buns
1 pack of Peanut Butter
2 Nutrageous candy bars
1 pack of M&Ms

How to assemble:

- [ ] Flatten the honey buns with your hand while still in the wrapper.
- [ ] Warm up the peanut butter and pour it over the honey buns.
- [ ] Crush candy bars while in wrapper and sprinkle on top of honey buns.
- [ ] Crush M&Ms and sprinkle on top.
- [ ] Fold each honey bun in half like a taco.
- [ ] Enjoy the sweet sugar rush of Cupcake Delight.

H2.O
MARVELOUS MAVERICK
H2.O

LEADERSHIP

Runnin' Point

◂ *Illustration by Trenton Dukes*

LEARNING OBJECTIVES

In this crash course, you will ...

- ✓ Pinpoint why you get nervous when it comes to networking, and know you're not alone
- ✓ Learn networking basics: how to be interesting, tips to be a bomb conversationalist, and how to introduce yourself in a professional setting
- ✓ Discover how to gain trust and get people to invest time and money in you to get what you want
- ✓ Take an assessment to determine how successful you've been with setting realistic goals
- ✓ Learn the SMART goal planning framework and use it to set an achievable, realistic goal
- ✓ Take quizzes to determine if you're a leader and to rate your leadership qualities
- ✓ Learn about leaders vs. followers, and get inspired by a case study about transforming influence

In Hustle Guides 1-12, take in-depth courses and gain insight into:

- ✓ Public speaking
- ✓ Power: why some people have it and others don't
- ✓ Personal finance
- ✓ Managing people
- ✓ Finding and keeping a mentor

DEFINING YOURSELF

Let's kick off our leadership training with networking. If you want to lead, you need to learn to connect with people and convince them that you're worth following.

When someone doesn't know who they are, doesn't know what they love, and doesn't know what they want to do … they come across as BORING. People might want to tell them, "I wish you the best of luck with … nothing!"

To improve your networking skills, answer these questions:

Five things I'm passionate about:

Five of my biggest achievements:

Five of my most valuable skills:

Five things I have to offer:

NETWORKING 101: NERVOUS, ANYONE?

Check off all the reasons you might be nervous about legit networking:

	AGREE	DISAGREE
I'm insecure about my physical appearance.	☐	☐
I'm shy.	☐	☐
I'm socially awkward.	☐	☐
I haven't spoken with people on the outside in a hot minute.	☐	☐
I've been in solitary and am not used to being around people, period.	☐	☐
I experience fear of rejection.	☐	☐
I feel like I'm not good enough.	☐	☐
I'm scared of making a fool of myself.	☐	☐
I lack meaningful conversation skills.	☐	☐
I fear people will judge me for my past.	☐	☐
I just don't know how to network.	☐	☐
I get nervous about meeting new people.	☐	☐
I've never been one to mingle.	☐	☐
I'm a little shook up about public speaking.	☐	☐

Studies show that 90% of people are uncomfortable in a group setting! You're not alone.

WINNING THEM OVER

What do you think people invest in first:

You or your product?

They invest in you first.
We buy from people we like.
We like people we trust.

We tend to trust people who are like us.

One of the best ways to make a connection is to establish common ground. If you find things in common that are generic (e.g., "we both like money"), the connection won't "stick" or be genuine. If you want to bond with someone, share values and meaningful experiences. Be passionate!

If you don't come off with a little confidence, we can work on that (a little is good; too much confidence is … usually arrogance).

If you're a lil' low key, you might need to push yourself to talk to people and be more social. Take a shot of coffee beforehand (then brush your grill; don't be networking with stank breath using all the "h" words like hhhhhhhhhello, hhhhhow you doin'?).

If you've got a resting thug mug … you might need to take a little off to keep from intimidating people. Practice flexing your cheek muscles (your smile … not the other cheeks).

You don't have to enjoy networking to be good at it. If you like getting what you want, then you'll practice networking.

If you've made negative statements about yourself or labeled yourself with things like:

- I'm not social
- People don't like me
- I'm shy

… It's time to change the narrative. You are a Maverick. Congratulations, you are also now a networker, and you're going to get good at it!

HOW TO BE INTERESTING

If you could talk about these things with confidence, *check them off:*

- ☐ You have dreams and passions
- ☐ You have (legal) skills
- ☐ You have a generous hustle (a way of giving back that makes your world a better place; a cause/non-profit that you contribute to)
- ☐ You have hobbies
- ☐ You have educational pursuits
- ☐ You wrote a book or published something
- ☐ You have future business plans

Two Secrets

1. Even if you're boring, others will perceive you as a great conversationalist (and will like you) if you just ask excellent questions.
2. Even if you're the most interesting person on the planet, if you don't ask questions during networking, you are likely to be perceived either as boring ... or arrogant.

"You've got to find yourself first. Everything else'll follow.

- Charles de Lint"

10 TIPS FOR BEING A BOMB CONVERSATIONALIST

1. Make them feel important.
2. Listen more than you speak (you've got two ears; one mouth).
3. Turn your full body toward them.
4. Smile. A lot. In a non-creepy way. Your smile is more important than a fancy business card or suit.
5. Give them your full attention (when you own a phone, put it away while networking).
6. Ask questions and follow-up questions.
7. Don't think of what you'll say next. Stay in the moment.
8. Nod to show agreement and acceptance.
9. After they reveal something interesting, say, "Tell me more about that." Go deeper.
10. Limit your fidgeting. Fidgeting, looking away, and playing with your face can make it look like you're lying.

At a professional networking event, the proper way to introduce yourself is to simply say, "Hi, I'm {First Name} {Last Name}. Nice to meet you."

QUIZ: AM I A LEADER?

		AGREE	DISAGREE
1.	I can name people who follow my ways and are influenced by me.	☐	☐
2.	When something needs to be done, I'm the first to take the initiative to get it done.	☐	☐
3.	I clearly know my values and beliefs and live them out every day.	☐	☐
4.	I use my leadership skills to create positive change in prison.	☐	☐
5.	Those around me experience the impact of my values and beliefs in action. I could point to multiple examples of my impact on others in the past 48 hours.	☐	☐
6.	People tell me they learn from me.	☐	☐
7.	People come to me for advice.	☐	☐
8.	I take initiative in group projects.	☐	☐
9.	I love to serve others and lead by example.	☐	☐
10.	I speak my mind and am known to practice what I preach.	☐	☐
11.	I generously praise others when I see positive qualities in them.	☐	☐
12.	I break large goals into smaller ones and regularly hit my goals.	☐	☐

KEY
Add up the number of times you checked "Agree."
Less than 3: Work on developing leadership qualities
4 to 6: You have clear leadership qualities and potential
7 to 9: You're a leader
10 to 12: Apply your leadership in the right direction, and you'll change the world

NATURAL BORN LEADERS

When things get tough, do homies look to you for a solution? While everyone else is standing around waiting for things to happen, do you take action?

LEAD

Verb

To show (someone or something) the way to a destination by going in front of or beside them.

WHAT MAKES A GREAT LEADER

Check out these 10 qualities of great leaders. Note that resilience is often listed as the #1 quality of a great leader!

1. Resilience

"There's so much change afoot in the workplace today and when change occurs, individuals who have resilience generally are also resourceful and agile. They have the ability to take on change and adapt to what's happening around them and to them as the workplace changes. Individuals who have resilience/grit are able to take good risks and are open to change." - *Kimberly Rath, Chairman & Co-Founder of Talent Plus, Inc.*

2. Open-minded

"Leaders cannot work in a vacuum. They may take on larger, seemingly more important roles in an organization, but this does not exclude them from asking for and using feedback. In fact, a leader arguably needs feedback more so than anyone else. It's what helps a leader respond appropriately to events in pursuit of successful outcomes." - *Jack Canfield, world record holder for having seven books on the New York Times Best Sellers list at once*

3. Diplomacy

"Tact is the ability to step on a man's toes without messing up the shine on his shoes." - *Harry S. Truman, 33rd President of the United States*

4. Initiative for action

"No task is beneath you (even menial tasks). Just because you are a high up executive does not mean that you are above cleaning the extra dishes in the sink, or clearing off the table after lunch. Take the initiative to do small tasks around the office– lead by example." - *Zvi Band, Co-Founder of Contactually*

5. Humility

"Humility is not thinking less of yourself, it's thinking of yourself less." - *C.S. Lewis*

6. Purpose

"Good leaders organize and align people around what the team needs to do. Great leaders motivate and inspire people with why they're doing it. That's purpose. And that's the key to achieving something truly transformational." - *Marillyn Hewson, CEO of Lockheed Martin*

7. Vision

"Great leaders are able to help their team members understand the big picture so they can connect their success back to the success of the business. The vision should be big enough to inspire and broad enough to be inclusive. Doing so allows everyone in the organization to understand the importance of the role they play in bringing that vision to reality." - *Steven Benson, CEO of Badger Maps*

8. Integrity

"A great leader is someone who does the right thing, even when it's unpopular or extremely tough to do so. You have to find something to care deeply about in your business and in each individual that touches your business. Do what you love in the service of people who love what you do." - *Steve Farber, President of Extreme Leadership*

9. Listening

"Effective leaders take the time to listen deeply to every person related to the business, group or organization. Often overlooked, creating and modeling a culture of listening in one's company is the key to connecting with customers and employees, making each person feel valued as a person as well as a member of the team. I've seen listening grow businesses, make money, and build relationships and it's the key ingredient to being an effective leader." - *Marilyn Shannon, Founder of Women's Empower Networking LLC*

10. Ownership

"When a team, and especially a leader, takes ownership of its problems, the problem gets solved. It is true on the battlefield, it is true in business, and it is true in life." - *Jocko Willink, podcaster, author, and retired Navy SEAL*

Adapted from: 21 Most Compelling Qualities of Great Leaders
https://transparency.kununu.com/compelling-qualities-of-great-leaders

RATE YOUR LEADERSHIP QUALITIES

Below are 21 common leadership qualities. Take an honest look in the mirror and rate each quality according to this scale:

1 = Not one of my strengths
2 = I have room for improvement in this area
3 = This is one of my strengths

	1	2	3
Resilience	☐	☐	☐
Transparency	☐	☐	☐
Emotional Intelligence	☐	☐	☐
Passion	☐	☐	☐
Empathy	☐	☐	☐
Empowerment	☐	☐	☐
Open -minded	☐	☐	☐
Patience	☐	☐	☐
Diplomacy	☐	☐	☐
Initiative	☐	☐	☐

	1	2	3
Humility	☐	☐	☐
Influence	☐	☐	☐
Purpose	☐	☐	☐
Vision	☐	☐	☐
Trust	☐	☐	☐
Integrity	☐	☐	☐
Problem-solving	☐	☐	☐
Perspective	☐	☐	☐
Listening	☐	☐	☐
Ownership	☐	☐	☐
Motivation	☐	☐	☐

How many 3's did you give yourself? ______________________

Of this list, which is your:

Strongest leadership quality?

____

Weakest leadership quality?

____

LEADERS VS. FOLLOWERS

> Those who can make you believe absurdities, can make you commit atrocities.
>
> - Voltaire

Unless you were the founder of the Crips, if you became a Crip, you're a follower, and same goes for every other gang. 100% of us were followers, and all of us are *still* followers.

Following under the right circumstance is a positive thing. For example, prosocial people follow the laws of society.

Honey Badgers stand on their own two feet and don't allow the gang mentality to dictate their actions. They follow prison rules, and when they get out, they follow the law.

Following For The Wrong Reasons

People who join gangs are followers of criminal thinking and criminal behavior. Gang members follow protocol that perpetuates the cycle of violence, drugs, and incarceration. They are not followers of *prosocial* ways.

Followers follow protocols established by leaders and ask the leader what to do in unclear circumstances, largely so they will never "be wrong." When someone else makes the decision, the follower often shirks responsibility. They get to play the victim. "I had to do it" is what an unhealthy follower tells themselves.

A leader takes personal responsibility, because they make decisions for themselves. They make the choice to follow the rules, or to follow another inspirational leader ... or to break the rules. Whatever the outcome, it's on them.

Nearly all of us ended up incarcerated because we followed someone into criminal behavior. We saw criminal behavior modeled for us, and we followed suit. Then we earned our keep behind bars because we continued to *follow* criminal thinking. We followed gang rules, and prioritized criminal conduct over our free will and our freedom.

Herd mentality—and being susceptible to peer pressure—will lead us to continually forfeit our freedom.

If you've been a gang member, how do you stop being a follower?

You become your own leader. You make decisions that are in line with prosocial values, not that are in line with criminal values. If someone asks you to do something against prosocial values, you refuse to compromise your values. You might not be left with many friends, but you will transform, go home, and get to be with your family.

TRANSFORMING MY INFLUENCE

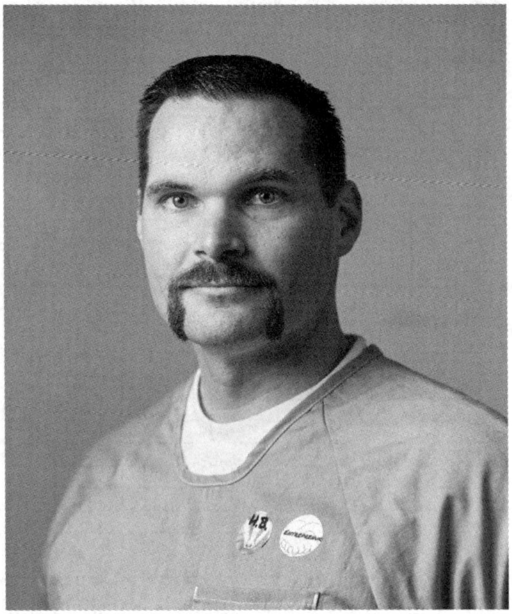

By Paul Pichie
aka Sweet Pwally

When I came to prison, I wasn't inclined to do anything positive. Even more, I had the utmost disdain for anyone who did and considered them cowards. I thought anyone who wanted to act like a gangster on the streets should act like one in prison. It wasn't until Hustle 2.0 that I started to think differently.

I served nearly all of my first term in county jail, with only three months left to do in prison. I could have minded my own business and gone home.

Instead, the first time I went to yard, I contributed to an incident in which another person had his face and neck sliced open. When I was transferred to a new prison, my first order of business was to cut a knife out of my desk or locker. I encouraged others to do the same. I used my influence to normalize criminal behaviors for myself and others. People emulated my attitude and committed violence, often resulting in SHU terms and life sentences.

Leadership has always come naturally to me, and prison was no different. I feel strongly about leading by example. I am contemptuous of people who ask others to do what they are not willing to do themselves. I thought I was being a good leader, paving the way for others to follow down the same path of destruction. I was wrong. I did not stop to consider that I was misusing my leadership ability.

I'm on my third term now, and my sentence is for another five years. I gave up on my positive potential long ago, after becoming estranged from my family. I grew up in a group home until the age of five, and after my grandma came and got me, I got in more trouble and had to move away. As I got older and continued down this path of destruction, I lost all contact with family. I felt worthless. My mother and grandmother died, and I knew with my record, it would be hard to find a job after my release. I experienced hopelessness. Therefore, I accepted death in prison as the likely outcome, even though I never had a life sentence.

My perspective began changing a few years ago when I saw people I respected doing positive things. I started questioning my values and outlook on life.

It took a long time for me to see how my actions affected others. It took experience and maturity to realize it is harder to do something positive than to do something negative. Any idiot can waste hours sliding a piece of metal back and forth on their locker to cut a knife out, with the result being pride in destroying another life. It is far more rewarding to spend hour after hour reading and writing your way to a college degree or learning to transform your illegal hustle into a legal one.

I took a chance on Hustle 2.0. People told me they believe in me and think I'm smart. I got back in touch with family. I finally started leaning into my positive leadership potential.

I've learned that doing something positive doesn't make you a coward; rather, it takes courage and commitment, two traits that deserve admiration.

I can't change the negative contributions I've made to the world, but I can devote myself to living amends. I am proud to now steer others away from destroying their lives. For example, I recently discouraged someone from committing an act of violence that could've resulted in them taking another life and possibly spending the rest of theirs in prison. This is in stark contrast to what I promoted in the past. I now encourage people to enroll in college because of the benefits I have received from college myself.

Seeing the success of Hustle 2.0 graduates and participants, I feel a sense of pride that I, in some small way, have contributed to building this movement. Today, I can see how my leadership is creating positive change every day. People come to me for advice, and I use what I've learned in Hustle 2.0 to steer them in the right direction.

> It takes nothing to join the crowd. It takes everything to stand alone.
>
> – Hans Hansen

> It takes a great deal of bravery to stand up to our enemies, but just as much to stand up to our friends.
>
> -J.K. Rowling

> Never underestimate the influence you have on others.
>
> - Laurie Buchanan

> I will do nothing because of public opinion, but everything because of conscience.
>
> - Seneca

QUIZ: READY. SET. GOAL.

	AGREE	DISAGREE
I often fail at reaching my goals.	☐	☐
I feel demoralized; what's the point of goals?	☐	☐
Having detailed and well-thought-out goals will help me succeed.	☐	☐
Setting goals is unnecessary. I just make it happen.	☐	☐
Setting goals is a recipe for disappointment.	☐	☐
Goal setting is investing in future success.	☐	☐
I feel one step closer to securing the bag when I make SMART goals.	☐	☐
I set goals with every intention of meeting them.	☐	☐
My goals are often too ambitious.	☐	☐
I'm a Honey Badger and am ready to set SMART goals.	☐	☐
I've studied or have received instruction on goal setting.	☐	☐

What stands out to you about your answers to this quiz?

____

GOAL INVENTORY

3 things that matter to me (e.g., physical health, family, reading)

1. ______
2. ______
3. ______

3 things I'm good at (e.g., writing, having meaningful conversations, working out)

1. ______
2. ______
3. ______

3 things I'd like to improve (e.g., following through on commitments, reading, trying new things)

1. ______
2. ______
3. ______

> The moment you put a deadline on a dream, it becomes a goal.
>
> - Stephen Kellogg

SETTING OURSELVES UP FOR FAILURE

Let's be real. At one point or another, we have all set ourselves up for failure by setting lofty goals, and then quickly told ourselves, "Yeah right, maybe in another lifetime."

"I want to play in the NBA."

"I want to hold the #1 spot on the Billboard Charts."

"I want to be a millionaire in the next year."

This isn't to say that you shouldn't dream big. If any of the statements above are included in your life goals, get it …

However, many of us have experienced the negativity that comes after failing to hit a lofty goal. We set expectations too high; we don't think through how we're going to make it happen; we don't give ourselves enough time. We don't give ourselves a chance to succeed.

Our actions tell us a story about ourselves. If we consistently set unrealistic goals and fail, we more easily will consider ourselves to be failures.

If we are consistently setting realistic, attainable goals, we will consider ourselves worthy and capable of greater things in our lives. We will build momentum to achieve more.

It's important to think about why we set goals and how we're going to achieve them. It's important to remember the impact our goal setting will have on our self-esteem.

The reality is that we cannot always achieve the goals we set. It's important to realize our limitations. Perseverance is important, but if you're giving it your all and it's not working out; if you're feeling tired, frustrated, and discouraged, it may be time to try something else.

Trying something else is not the same as quitting. A quitter doesn't give a full effort, but throws in the towel and gives up when things get tough. That's not what a Honey Badger does.

Honey Badgers adapt and discover different strategies and frameworks.

Achieving a large goal is *not* a quick, straight path.

You are not measured by how big you dream, but rather, by the actions you take.

Unrealistic:

LARGE GOAL SET → LARGE GOAL ACHIEVED

Large goals take time. They are the accumulation of reaching many, many small goals.

Realistic:

LARGE GOAL SET → SMALL GOALS ACHIEVED → SMALL GOALS ACHIEVED → SMALL GOALS ACHIEVED → LARGE GOAL ACHIEVED

It's better to set and achieve a small and attainable goal than to set a large goal and drop the ball.

The problem with dreamers is they usually get stuck in their dreams. Honey Badgers are go-getters. We set goals and work proactively toward them.

When was the last time you set a goal of any size? Did you achieve it? When you achieved it, did you feel ready to take on the world?

Write down a goal that you achieved in the past year, regardless of size:
e.g., I read a book, I signed up for a GED class

How did it make you feel?
e.g., good for a moment, amazing, proud of myself

Did you fail at something within the past year? If so, what happened to your self-esteem?
e.g., felt bad about myself, I stopped trying, I gave up

Don't worry—we've all had experiences with both.

Often, when we reflect on a past goal, the size didn't matter; what did matter was whether we accomplished it.

A NEW APPROACH

Only 8% of people achieve their New Year's goals. So ... 92% (including Sluggo D. Sloth) smoked it.

Entrepreneur and author Lewis Howes shows the impact of goal setting. He's an advocate for thinking small. Meaning, he believes that we should set and achieve many small goals to prove to ourselves that we can accomplish what we say we are going to. He says, build self-esteem first, and then start to set larger goals.

Lewis gives two examples of how we usually think about setting goals:

1. We set a BIG goal (usually the same goal we've been promising ourselves for years). Often, these goals stem from resolutions, promises, and short-term excitement.
2. We tell ourselves, "I just need to get more motivated" or, "I've really gotta want it this time." Essentially, if I just try harder this time then I'll make it happen.
3. We map out what we need to do in our minds.
4. We take a couple steps ...
5. And then SPLAT! We face our first trial or miss our first deadline, spiral off course, and throw in the towel (like Sluggo does!).

We've all been there.
Let's see how we can change our mindset to avoid this scenario.

1. Review the goals you've set in the recent past but did not accomplish.
2. Identify ONE goal from that list that you'd still like to accomplish.
3. Boil it down to a smaller goal – one that you can accomplish in three to seven days. Instead of saying, "I will lose 10 pounds this month," change that goal to a smaller one like, "I will not eat cookies tomorrow."
4. Walk the walk and complete it.
5. Pick another small goal.
6. Get it done.
7. Do this until you've got three to five completed goals under your belt ... each of which are a little bigger than the one before it.
8. Go after your big goal.

REACH YOUR GOALS THE SMART WAY

S

M

A

R

T

SPECIFIC: The more detailed the better. Spell out the what, where, when, and with whom for your goal.

MEASURABLE: Decide how you'll know when you've met your goal. If it's measurable, you can answer, "How much?" or "How many?".

ATTAINABLE: Determine what needs to be in place to reach your goal (e.g., adjusting your routine, developing skills, or adopting a certain attitude).

REALISTIC: Make sure you can achieve your goal. If it seems unachievable, break it into smaller goals to make it realistic.

TIME-BOUND: Put a timeframe on your goal. How long will you give yourself to achieve it? The timeframe should be long enough to achieve it, but not so long that you risk putting it off.

Now go back to the Goal Inventory and pick one thing you said you want to improve. Turn it into a SMART goal:

Specific: ______________________________

Measurable: ______________________________

Attainable: ______________________________

Realistic: ______________________________

Time-bound: ______________________________

LEADERSHIP

Chinese Traditional	lǐngdǎo
French	direction
German	Führung
Portuguese	Liderança
Spanish	liderazgo
Swahili	uongozi

CRIMINAL THINKING

It Wasn't Me

LEARNING OBJECTIVES

In this crash course, you will ...

- ✓ Take a quiz to see if you think like a criminal ... and if you're aware of your criminal thinking
- ✓ Evaluate the origins of your criminal thinking; identify values that shaped your beliefs; determine if you're addicted to criminal thinking
- ✓ Learn the top 10 criminal thinking errors and determine their role in your choices
- ✓ Analyze how gang violence is similar to genocide
- ✓ Determine how far you would go when it comes to violence, and if this is what you signed up for

In Hustle Guides 1-12, take in-depth courses and gain insight into:

- ✓ Understanding your preconviction history
- ✓ Your causative factors
- ✓ Addressing gang involvement
- ✓ Creating empathy
- ✓ Intro to Cognitive Behavioral Therapy (CBT)

POP QUIZ: CRIMINAL THINKING

To assess your current level of criminal thinking, choose the answer that best represents what you would actually do ... and not what you think is the "right thing" to do.

1. Walking home, you notice a parked car with its window open. As you get closer, you see an iPhone on the driver's seat. You ...
   - A. Take the phone. No one will know it was you.
   - B. Knock on the door of the house where the car is parked and notify the owner.
   - C. Keep walking. It's not your problem.
2. While shopping for canteen, you get an extra case of soups you didn't pay for. You ...
   - A. Accept the come-up and don't say anything.
   - B. Return the soups
   - C. Pass them out to your friends so everyone can eat.
3. Your cellie brings in a cup of white lightning and offers you half, even though you decided to quit drinking. You ...
   - A. Pound it so it hits you harder and faster.
   - B. Stick to your commitment and stay sober.
   - C. Take a sip because you've been stressed out.
4. The parole board asks about a riot you were involved in last year. What do you say?
   - A. I didn't start it. I was in the wrong place at the wrong time.
   - B. I made a poor decision. I got involved, but I didn't start it.
   - C. If I didn't get involved, I would've been in hot water.
5. A c/o searches your cell, finds contraband, and writes you up for it. What do you do?
   - A. Confront the c/o because he's targeting you.
   - B. Accept responsibility for the contraband and keep your cell clean in the future.
   - C. Ask your cellie to take the rap because you are short to the house.

KEY

If you got mostly ...

A's: If you want to get free and keep your freedom, take a deep dive into this course or you'll die in prison.

B's: You're making conscious decisions to change your life.

C's: Criminal thoughts lead to criminal actions, which lead to prison. You've got work to do.

WHAT'S YOURS IS MINE

Imagine we're meeting for the first time and we sit down to a delicious meal at a five-star restaurant. You order a sizzling ribeye steak. I get fish.

After a few bites of mine, without asking, I start digging into your plate. At first, you're a little taken aback and think I must be joking. You don't want to be rude, and don't know what to do. As I keep shoveling your food down, you find yourself speechless and see that your steak is half-gone. Now imagine I spit a bite back into the middle of your plate. Then I take a sip of your drink, gargle it, and spit it back into your cup, and set your cup back down.

What are you feeling as you sit there?

Your values are calling this behavior unacceptable and disrespectful.

If I have no problem disrespecting you, there is something inside of me—some values—that lead me to think this behavior is acceptable. I might even realize that there could be consequences, but I obviously have a disregard for them.

What values allowed me to cross boundaries and justify this behavior to myself?

Value	**Justification to Myself**
Envy	Your food looked better than mine, and I want it, so I can take it.
Disregard	Your rights, opinions, personal space, and property don't matter. I can ignore your feelings.
Short-Sightedness	I don't care about the future; I don't even care or think about one minute after your food is in my belly. All I know is I see good food, and I'm going for it.
Thrill-Seeking	If I think gangstering your food is rude or naughty, I'll get a thrill out of watching you get angry. If you let me, I'll get a thrill from getting over on you.
Entitlement	I deserve your food and have a right to it.
Greed	I have an intense and selfish desire for your food, and I want it more than you do.

All of these values come down to two things:

1. Selfishness
2. A lack of empathy

SELFISH

Adjective

1. Lacking consideration for others
2. Concerned chiefly with one's own personal profit or pleasure

Without empathy, I don't care or even consider how you feel, or if you will suffer.

It's all about me, me, me, me, me.

Many of our actions came from this criminal thought:

Everything's been taken from me, so now I can take anything I want.

We may not have been aware of this belief or our other underlying values as children, but now as adults, it's time for us to analyze and recognize why we made our choices.

VALUES THAT LEAD TO CRIMINAL THINKING

The example of taking your food might seem ridiculous and unacceptable. But to most people outside these gates, the things we've done are far more outrageous and unacceptable. They cannot fathom doing such a thing or understand how we could have possibly done what we've done. We are called monsters, animals, and sociopaths because they believe we have no regard for anyone.

What made you think it:

- Was okay to pull a gun on someone?
- Was okay to steal people's things?
- Was okay to lie?

Imagine telling your grandma or mom this in your next visit or phone call:

> *"Today, someone got stabbed on the yard. It wasn't even a good one. They barely even beat the dude up. I can't believe they got the yard recalled early for that crap. If you're going to ruin my yard, make it worth it. They better be covered in blood."*

No one would ever tell a gory story like this to their mom or grandma, because we know that violence like this is unacceptable in society. When did it become acceptable to us?

At some point—maybe when you were five, or younger—violence was unacceptable to you. You were innocent, and seeing people get hurt felt wrong.

When did violence become your norm?

When did your values change and when did you start thinking it was okay to hurt someone "as a form of discipline"?

Can you separate yourself from the criminal lifestyle for a split second and realize that this is savage thinking? These violent values are completely void of empathy.

We were raised with certain values or formed values and beliefs as a result of our experiences. We then acted in accordance with our values and beliefs. We often hear the phrase, "My momma raised me better than that." Did she? Or did you choose to ignore the values instilled in you at a young age?

For example, if one of your values was "empathy," you would have had a really hard time committing a crime against someone, because you would feel the future victim's pain so deeply that you couldn't imagine creating another victim. If one of your values was "respect," you would not take what didn't belong to you.

If we're ready for a new set of values, it means looking at the ugly ones that led us to where we are today and not making excuses for them or our actions. In our Character Development crash course, we'll explore our values in more depth.

> Your beliefs become your thoughts,
> Your thoughts become your words,
> Your words become your actions,
> Your actions become your habits,
> Your habits become your values,
> Your values become your destiny.
>
> - Gandhi

NO JUDGMENT QUIZ: CRIMINAL THINKING

	AGREE	DISAGREE
1. I feel like I'll always be a criminal. Why try to change?	☐	☐
2. I don't think like a criminal. I think like a survivalist.	☐	☐
3. Thoughts can't be criminal, only actions.	☐	☐
4. My crimes were a means to a necessary end.	☐	☐
5. I always look out for myself first.	☐	☐
6. I've done the hard work and identified the factors that led to my criminal behavior.	☐	☐
7. Criminal thinking will lead to criminal behavior.	☐	☐
8. I feel remorse for the crimes I've committed (including those I haven't been caught for).	☐	☐
9. I believe everything happens for a reason; I was meant to be where I am now.	☐	☐
10. I have no control over my thoughts, only my actions.	☐	☐

Which of your criminal thoughts have had the most negative impact?

____

FROM THE JUMP

We have a lot in common.

1. We're all in here.
2. Not one of us was born a criminal.

When did your thoughts make it easy to commit crimes?

> At some point, we developed thinking patterns that led to our criminal lifestyle. Have you ever stopped to think about how we got here?

When did you begin to glorify, justify, or minimize your harmful actions?

Although many of us faced injustice or were unfairly sentenced, we will never grow or change our patterns until we accept our part in what brought us here.

What caused you to take those steps in your life?

How old were you when you were arrested for the first time? How did you feel that first time?

Maybe you jacked school supplies because there was no adult in your life who could (or would) buy them for you. Maybe you stole a neighbor's bike simply because you wanted it. Doin' dirt may seem innocent for children, but it quickly becomes arrestable behavior.

> Let's keep it 100: most of us didn't catch a raw deal. We took many small, premeditated steps to get where we are.

When was the first time you consciously decided to break the rules? Why did you do it?

____

____

TOP 10 CRIMINAL THINKING ERRORS

Samuel Yochelson and Stanton Samenow co-authored a three-volume book called, The Criminal Personality, based on 16 years spent studying people who committed crimes at St. Elizabeth's Hospital in Washington, DC. Here are the top 10 criminal thinking errors they identified.

Error	Description of Error	Correction in Thinking
1. CLOSED CHANNEL THINKING	Not teachable. Doesn't accept feedback (but good at giving it). No self-criticism. Lies by omission.	Good active listening. Healthy self-awareness and self-criticism. Operates with full and complete disclosure.
2. PLAYING THE VICTIM	Places the blame on others and considers themselves to be the innocent victim.	Accepts responsibility for actions and consequences.
3. VIEWING YOURSELF AS A GOOD PERSON	Paints themselves as the hero. Only acknowledges the positive aspects of their personality. Ignores negative or destructive behavior. Makes themselves look better at the expense of others.	Healthy, truthful understanding of own strengths and weaknesses. Humility.
4. LACK OF EFFORT	Will not engage in something boring or unpleasant. Says, "I can't" when they really mean, "I won't."	Drive and self-motivation. Pushes themselves to complete tasks even when they are difficult or undesirable.
5. LACK OF INTEREST IN RESPONSIBLE PERFORMANCE	Fails to learn from the past. Makes ill-informed decisions based on own assumptions and prejudices, instead of on facts. Demands that others respond immediately to desires.	Uses the past as a learning tool. Sets and accomplishes goals.

Error	Description of Error	Correction in Thinking
6. LACK OF TIME PERSPECTIVE	Fails to learn from the past. Doesn't acknowledge cause and effect. Doesn't consider future consequences of actions.	Delays gratification. Uses the past as a learning tool. Sets and accomplishes goals.
7. FEAR OF FEAR	Unwilling to admit fears. Deeply afraid of losing respect and of failure. When held accountable for actions, they experience "zero state" in which they feel worthless and ashamed.	Lets fear guide them. Chooses to engage with the fear instead of letting it paralyze them. Believes positive self-affirmation.
8. POWER THRUST	Need for absolute control. Manipulates others. Uses independence and deception to exert control.	Empathy. Puts themselves in another's shoes.
9. UNIQUENESS	Considers themselves special and better than others. Holds themselves to a different (often lower) standard than others. Shuts down at the possibility of failure out of fear.	Connection. Vulnerability. Appreciates their own gifts and unique qualities, and those of others.
10. OWNERSHIP ATTITUDE	Views objects and people as possessions. Does not acknowledge the rights of others. Yields sex as an aggressive tool for power and control instead of love and intimacy.	Acknowledges the many harmful effects of possessive behaviors. Recognizes the rights of others. Has respect for others and objects.

Which of these 10 criminal thinking errors has been most prevalent in your past? Give an example.

CRIMINALITY IS A CHOICE

By Darryl Baca
aka Sweet Owl

Living in a world of ignorance doesn't mean you have to continue a pattern of manipulative behavior. If you really believe that you must participate and engage in criminal activity to be accepted, your perception is flawed. Stop believing the stories from 10, 20, and 30 years ago.

When you continue pursuing criminal activity, you send a message that you don't care about what happens to you or to those who mean the most to you. When you get caught up in the game (because it'll definitely catch up to you; believe me), don't go blaming it on outside influences like drugs or claiming, "The homies made me do it."

No one will drag you into a conversation you don't want to be in, or force you to drink that cup of white lightning, or stick a needle in your arm. If you allow these things to happen, it's because you want it.

Like the old saying goes: if you want to run with the big dogs, you're gonna get fleas, boy!

If you were doing things you needed to do to be a better version of yourself, like educating yourself in school and minding your own business, the homies would recognize that, support that, and simply pay you no mind.

We are living in a new era. The narrative has shifted. I want to do things from a different perspective, because I now view life from a different lens. I will not continue to live in the past. For personal growth to occur, I need to think and act differently.

What I am saying to all you youngsters is this: stand up on your own two feet and live a meaningful life of purpose. Show and prove that you're serious about going home by not getting yourself involved in all the dumb sh**!

People will accept you for the person you are, and never for the fake person you are trying to be.

Think about the legacy you want to leave behind; set some goals, achieve greatness, and thrive. We each need to decide what it is that we are willing to devote our futures to.

And for you knuckleheads who choose to continue with the criminal activity and dumb sh**: own your choice. And also own the five, 10, or 15-year denial that you will certainly get from the parole board.

CRIMINAL VS. PURE HEART

Have you ever been shocked when someone acted out of character—maybe it was someone you considered a saint? Even the most virtuous humans give in to temptation and make bad decisions. We all act inconsistently with our own values at times, which makes it easy for any human to feel double-minded.

Everyone engages in criminal thinking at times. A classic criminal thought is:

> *"Rules and laws are made for others. I have my own way of doing things."*

Is there a human who hasn't intentionally sped while driving? The point isn't to find technicalities. It's to establish that even the squarest still engage in criminal thinking.

Criminal thinking wouldn't be as much of an issue if it didn't materialize into criminality. The problem is, criminal thinking *nearly always* turns into criminal behaviors.

The more immersed we are in an environment of criminal thinking and criminality, the more likely our minds and hearts take on a "criminal identity." We are all products of our environment.

THE MAN IN THE GLASS

By Peter Dale Wimbrow Sr.

Published in The American Magazine in 1934

When you get what you want in your struggle for self
And the world makes you king for a day
Just go to the mirror and look at yourself
And see what that man has to say.
For it isn't your father, or mother, or wife
Whose judgment upon you must pass
The fellow whose verdict counts most in your life
Is the one staring back from the glass.
He's the fellow to please – never mind all the rest
For he's with you, clear to the end
And you've passed your most difficult, dangerous test
If the man in the glass is your friend.
You may fool the whole world down the pathway of years
And get pats on the back as you pass
But your final reward will be heartache and tears
If you've cheated the man in the glass.

THE ADDICTION OF CRIMINAL THINKING

By Darryl Baca
aka Sweet Owl

It's important to start talking about criminal thinking and criminal behavior as an addiction, the same way we speak of drugs and alcohol as an addiction.

Just like alcoholics and drug addicts fall off the wagon and relapse, the same argument can be made for acts of criminal behavior. We know our criminal acts are wrong, yet it's a choice we've all made. It's an addiction.

Most of us were introduced to criminal thinking at a very young age, before we were introduced to drugs and alcohol. By the time we were teenagers, breaking away from our parents' ideas and philosophies while trying to form our own identities, we automatically embraced what we had known for most of our young lives: criminal thinking and behavior. When our values were reinforced by other like-minded youngsters, the detrimental impact was compounded.

Realizing we were victimized by generational criminal thinking as youngsters isn't an excuse for past behaviors, but it helps us to understand our causative factors. A causative factor that many of us might share is "the normalizing of criminal thinking and criminal behaviors" in our childhoods.

Committing violence can't be blamed on addiction. Committing crimes in society or in prison is a choice; a bad choice with consequences.

Personal accountability trumps all. Just like a relapsing alcoholic or drug addict needs to attend more meetings, we need to do more work on ourselves.

Our past behaviors don't define who we are today. I like to think of my change as a process that never ends. It's important to learn something new and different every day. After years of study and increments of change, I'm still at it. I've learned that after decades of addiction to criminal thinking, transformation doesn't occur overnight. We must dedicate years of discipline and commitment to mold better versions of ourselves.

> A criminal only thinks of himself. When he does, it's short-sighted thinking. A criminal will eventually be arrested. When he is, he suffers in silence. So do his children, friends, family. The victims might suffer for the rest of their lives. Everyone is affected and pays a price because of one selfish individual.
>
> \- Darryl Baca

GOOD VS. EVIL

By Jesus Murillo

aka Sweet Chewy Cookie Dough

I'm fighting the demons inside,
Will I win the struggle or be led to demise?
Day after day the conflict continues,
Some days I strive, some days I get the blues.

THE QUESTIONS IS:
Why do you fight?
What's wrong with being desensitized?
Who cares about these lies?

I DO! I make my own way,
I seize the chance to one day dance with freedom.
Can you blame my will?
Can you offer something better than a cell,
Visits from family, and stressing over mail?
This ain't the dream I had,
It's all bad.
You took me down a messed up path,
Now, you gonna feel the wrath,
Of who I can be.
No more pain,
No more insane,
No more throwing my life down the drain.

O, so you think you got it good,
Gonna move out of the 'hood, dressed all Mr. Hollywood.
And forget I exist, yeah! I'll be there when you get that itch,
When you get pissed and clench your first.
Who taught you how to have fun,

Get spun and pull a gun,
For the cash when you were broke
Stealing stereos out the dash. Yeeaah!

I admit, it's a thrill,
But what fun when I'm on the run,
Can't go home 'cause the cops are busting felony stops,
Looking for me, and I'm out of money,
And forget about honey,
I'm arrested and straight to county,
You think this is who I wanna be?

Hey, this is the life of a G,
Nobody said it was easy.
But I been riding with you from the start
And now you wanna have some kind of heart-to-heart,
Man you're falling apart.

I knew you couldn't understand.
How I plan to rebrand
Myself and build wealth with knowledge
I learn thru Hustle 2.0 College.
You're stuck in yesteryear, full of anger,
Trying to throw gang signs with one in the chamber.
That's a path to destruction,
So listen here to my instruction:
I'm my own man, that can stand,
For what I believe and if you don't like it you could leave.
I wasted too many years
And watched my family shed too many tears.
My pain is theirs,
And seems like I'm the only one that cares ...
And you're just the evil in my mind, so it's time,
To leave you behind.

SEGREGATING OURSELVES

By Thabiti Salim Wilson
aka Fudgy

Segregation ended a long time ago, but in our communities, we tend to self-segregate. Blacks over here, whites over there, Mexicans over there, and so on. This self-segregation breeds mistrust. When we don't know someone, we are less likely to trust them. We can also become indifferent to others' feelings because of the disconnect.

Gangs do the same thing. I grew up in a Blood neighborhood, and before I ever saw a Crip, I was programmed to view any Crip as the enemy. I was just a kid, but I would listen to the conversations my brothers had with the homies, and I would pick up their language and make it my own. By the time I started gang-banging, Crips were not even human to me. They were just Crips; the enemy. I committed violent acts against Crips and thought nothing of it; it really didn't seem wrong to me.

When I got locked up, my views remained the same. I always viewed them collectively.

I didn't begin to see Crips as individuals till I did my first SHU term.

I was sent to the hole with nothing but a pair of boxers. The first person to look out for me was an older Crip. He sent me some food, hygiene products, clothes, and something to read. When we would go to the cages on the yard, he would talk to me and lace me up. I had not had too many of my own older homies take the time he took to get my mind right.

How could I continue to see this man as my enemy?

This had a profound impact on me and led to me viewing Crips and other groups in a human light—something I had never done before.

Describe a time when one of your "enemies" treated you with humanity.

THE RWANDAN GENOCIDE

In April 1994, the hatred, fear, and violence between Hutus and Tutsis erupted. A plane carrying the president of Rwanda was shot down, and Hutus blamed a Tutsi rebel group for the president's assassination. Extremist Hutus seized power and encouraged a systematic extermination of all Tutsis and moderate Hutus.

Over the course of the next 100 days, 800,000 men, women, and children were slaughtered.

Think about that for a minute. Almost one *million* people, killed in about three months.

> Unchecked hate can make people do unthinkable things.

Most of the killing was not committed by soldiers, but by ordinary citizens who murdered their neighbors with machetes. In addition, an estimated 250,000-500,000 women were raped and then killed, or left with the thought that they would "die of sadness."

Unchecked hate can make people do unthinkable things.

Journalist Philip Gourevitch traveled to Rwanda a year after the massacre. The italicized passages on the following pages in this crash course are from his account, "After the Genocide," published in *The New Yorker* on December 18, 1995.

> *Hutus in Rwanda had been massacring Tutsis on and off since the waning days of Belgian colonial rule, in the late fifties.*
>
> *These state-sanctioned killings were generally referred to as "work," or "clearing the bush."*

Does using terms to justify and minimize atrocities sound familiar?

Think of the terms we use today. When someone goes on a mission, we say they're "putting in work," or "handling their business." When we commit an act of violence, we tell ourselves, "I did what I had to do."

What terms have you used?

Why did you use these words or phrases to describe violence?

Hutus referred to Tutsis as "cockroaches" to dehumanize them. It's easier to kill someone whom you don't see as human. This is a form of psychological warfare in which you objectify your enemy to make it easier to hurt them.

> *Following the militias' example, Hutus young and old rose to the task. Neighbors hacked neighbors to death in their homes, and colleagues hacked colleagues to death in their workplaces. Priests killed their parishioners, and elementary-school teachers killed their students. Many of the largest massacres occurred in churches and stadiums where Tutsis had sought refuge—often at the invitation of local authorities, who then oversaw their execution.*
>
> *In mid-April, at least 5,000 Tutsis were packed in the Gatwaro Stadium, in the western city of Kibuye; as the massacre there began, gunmen in the bleachers shot zig zag waves of bullets and tossed grenades to make the victims stampede back and forth before militiamen waded in to finish the job with machetes.*
>
> *Throughout Rwanda, mass rape and looting accompanied the slaughter.*

Militia bands, fortified with potent banana beer and assorted drugs, were bused from massacre to massacre. Hutu prisoners were organized in work details to clear cadavers. Radio announcers reminded listeners to take special care to disembowel pregnant victims. As an added incentive to the killers, Tutsis' belongings were parceled out in advance—the radio, the couch, the goat, the opportunity to rape a young girl. A councilwoman in one Kigali neighborhood was reported to have offered 50 Rwandese francs apiece (about 30 cents at the time) for severed heads, a practice known as "selling cabbages."

During the genocide, the work of the killers was not regarded as a crime in Rwanda; it was effectively the law of the land, and every citizen was responsible for its administration.

Think of three names an enemy has called you.

____

Now think of three names you have called your enemy (to their face or behind their back).

____

IS THIS WHAT I SIGNED UP FOR?

Did you ever imagine you would see or commit the violence and crime you have? Was there ever a time when you thought, "I didn't sign up for *this*!"? When was that? Who was involved? How did it end?

Or maybe you got so caught up in the moment that you weren't thinking straight. When was a time when you got carried away?

When did violence become "normal?" When did you become desensitized to violence?

Think of all the names of loved ones you have lost due to gang violence, or violence in general. Who were they? How did losing them make you feel? How did you deal with it?

Who has been harmed at your hands? You probably don't know the names of all of the victims—but mentally list the people who have been hurt (physically or emotionally) due to your actions. Think of the trauma you've caused, ranging from the first responders (e.g., 911 operator, medical staff, witnesses, innocent bystanders) to your victims' families, to c/o's, to taxpayers.

Have you ever considered the other victims of your crimes? Have you thought about the parents who lost their child? The pregnant wife who lost her young husband? The child whose father was murdered by you or your people?

To transform, we must demonstrate a deep understanding of the harm we've caused and show empathy for all of the victims.

When was a time you got carried away?

When did violence become normal?

Write down the names of those you've lost to gang violence.

How did you deal with your loss?

HOW FAR WOULD WE GO?

If the things you did with your homies became legal, what would happen? Would you keep repeating your past if you could get away with it?

What if things got as bad as they did in Rwanda? What would you do? Would you kill and rape women and children if there were no consequences? Is it hard to imagine that this could happen in other places, like where your family lives?

At Nyarubuye, in the province of Kibungo, near the Tanzanian border, more than a thousand Tutsis were rounded up in the church. Hutus killed with machetes all day, and at night they hobbled the survivors by severing their Achilles tendons; then they went off to eat and sleep and returned in the morning to kill again.

The killers at Nyarubuye "had become mad," the sergeant said. "They weren't human beings anymore."

But Dr. Richard Mollica, the director of Harvard's Program in Refugee Trauma, believes that mass political violence cannot simply be written off as madness. "It is one of the great human questions," he told me. "Why, in these situations, is there always the extra sadism to achieve the political goal? You achieve your political power, why do you have to flay some guy alive like a piece of lox and then hang him out to suffocate in the sun? What does a guy get from raping a woman? One five-minute rape can destroy an entire family for a generation. Five minutes. Now we're talking about a whole country, and my opinion is that the psychology of young people is not that complicated, and most of the people who commit atrocities in most of these situations are young males. Young males are really the most dangerous people on the planet, because they easily respond to authority and they want approval. They are given the rewards for getting into the hierarchical system, and they're given to believe they're building heaven on earth. In most atrocities, there's a big utopian dream—a cleaner society, or purer society. Young people are very idealistic, and the powers prey on the young people by appealing to their more idealistic nature."

Mollica also challenges the "presupposition in modern Western society that people who commit a murder will live to regret it or that it will sicken their lives." He said, "I haven't seen it, to tell you the truth." In fact, he told me, "people who commit murder find it very easy to rationalize it and to come to terms with it," and this is particularly so "when it's being condoned by the state."

Reflect on the Rwandan Case Study

Dr. Richard Mollica says, "Young males are really the most dangerous people on the planet, because they easily respond to authority and they want approval."

He also says, "People who commit murder find it very easy to rationalize it and to come to terms with it," and this is particularly so "when it's being condoned by the state."

Do you think it's easy to rationalize and come to terms with murder when a gang condones it; when it's referred to as, "taking care of business"?

What's your gut reaction as you read about the brutality in Rwanda? How does it make you feel?

If the things you did with your homies became legal, what would happen?

Would you keep repeating your past if you could get away with it? Why or why not?

We all fought, and some died, for a city or street that would never be ours.

- Alfred Sandoval

One survivor recounted the fear that he and his neighbors lived in: "I had accepted death," he said. "At a certain moment, this happens. One hopes not to die cruelly, but one expects to die anyway. Not death by machete, one hopes, but with a bullet. If you were willing to pay for it, you could often ask for a bullet. Death was more or less normal, a resignation. You lose the will to fight. There were four thousand Tutsis killed here at Kacyiru"—a neighborhood of Kigali. "The soldiers brought them here and told them to sit down because they were going to throw grenades. And they sat."

"Rwandan culture is a culture of fear," Nkongoli went on ... "When you're that resigned and oppressed, you're already dead. It shows the genocide was prepared for too long. I detest this fear. These victims of genocide were being killed for so long that they were already dead."

GENOCIDE IN COMPTON

By Jacob Ama
aka Sweet Sugarcane

My family immigrated to the US when I was four. The "American dream" didn't turn out as we expected. We moved to the housing projects called "Park Village" in Compton. At 11, I was a full-fledged West Side Park Village Crip. Representing my neighborhood was all that mattered.

I wish I knew then where gang-banging would take me. I didn't understand the destruction it would rain on my life, family, and loved ones.

After doing hard time, I realized that genocide is very much alive in gangs. It wasn't just happening in places like Rwanda or Cambodia; it was happening right there in the streets of Compton.

When I was 12, one of my Samoan gang members was killed by a rival. My enemy was Samoan as well, from a gang called West Side Piru. I remember standing at my friend's grave during his funeral. The anger I felt was demonic. My tears couldn't disguise my pain and anger. I vowed that our retaliation would be remembered forever.

After the funeral, the homies and I drove to their neighborhood. I hung out the window and "went to work." We got word that those guys were severely hurt, but no one died. Some Pirus retaliated against us, and my homeboys were stabbed and hospitalized.

Today, I'm happy lives weren't lost, but at the time, I felt like we failed our mission. It's sad to think of how carelessly I played the game of life, like it was a video game.

Revenge played a big role in our community and perpetuated the cycle of violence. I'd get jumped, my anger grew, I retaliated … and it would start all over again.

So many lives are lost and sacrificed to gangs' vendettas; death after death: Samoans killing Samoans; blacks killing blacks, Mexicans killing Mexicans … just because we're from different neighborhoods. Tell me how this isn't genocide?

Now 33 years into incarceration, I'm spending what's left of it trying to help the younger generations navigate this world to find meaning and fulfillment. I challenge all of you to help us build a better world.

CRIMINAL THINKING ERRORS CROSSWORD

To come up with the answers to the clues below, refer to the 10 Criminal Thinking Errors.

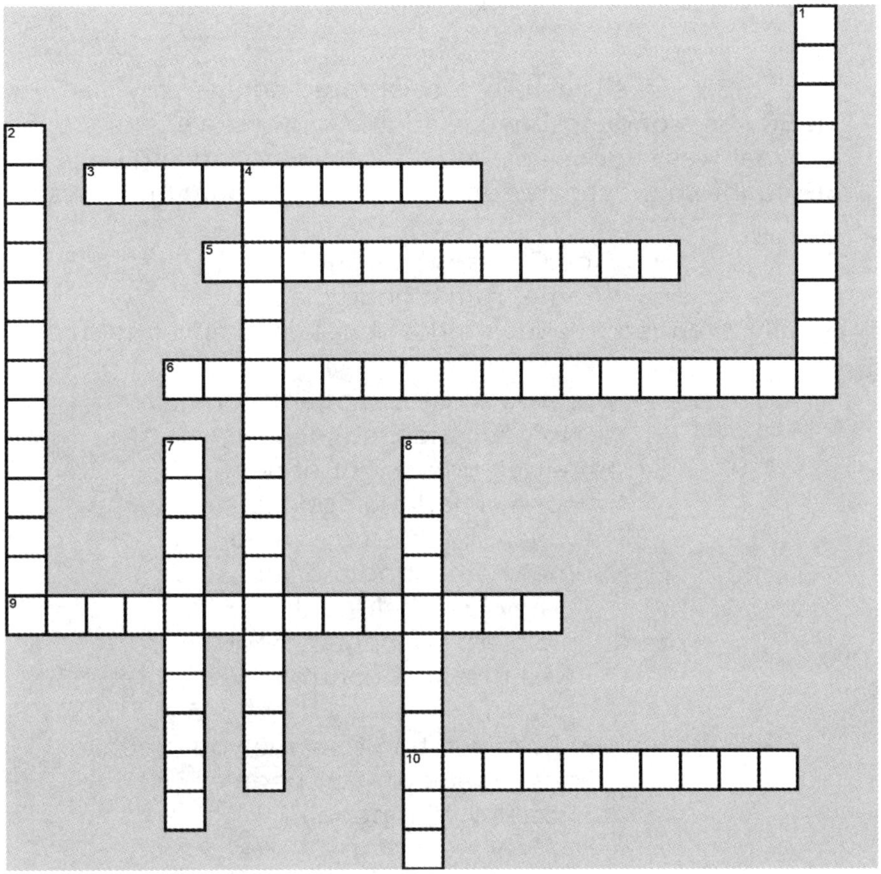

Across

3 I'm not in jail for being a bad person – I'm a victim of my environment

5 Sorry, bro, I just can't help you

6 I always wanted that car. Since I didn't have no funds, I just jacked it

9 There's way too much work involved, so I'm not going to do it

10 I don't have to follow rules; rules are for suckas and I'm not a sucka'

Down

1 I'm still young and dumb; change will come when I'm older

2 That dude's a bum ... I know way more than he does, so I don't have to listen to him

4 I wouldn't have to slide cash out the register if my boss paid me better wages

7 Everything's fine; nothing will go wrong; I'm not worried

8 That guy disrespected me, so I'm going to have to confront him

CAN WE MOVE IT FORWARD?

By Thabiti Salim Wilson
aka Fudgy

50 years is usually a celebrated anniversary
But 50 years of gang-bangin' sounds more like a curse to me
What was supposed to be about protection and unity
Brought about separation and destroyed our community

The G's had the right idea
Came from a good place
They fully intended to educate the people and empower the race

But poverty proved to be stronger than their will
No education, no jobs
Committed crimes out of need
As money filled their pockets
They were infected by greed
Somewhere along the line
They lost their goal
The people were no longer important
And they lost control

How do you go from wanting to serve your people
To serving crack to your people
Dope to your people?

Killing the will of your people
In the communities we rep
Killing each other for reppin' different sets
And we talk about respect

Respect what?!
We haven't done anything to earn that
Respect would be putting those ill-gotten gains to goodwill
Instead of poor investments in shiny rims and big wheels

We say we care about the people
And love our communities
So why do we influence the youth
To go through the same adversity?
When we should invest in the youth and send them off to a university

50 years and we are no better
Still trippin' over red and blue
Killin' a man over colors
When he is just like you

Can we move it forward?

So much potential, seemingly wasted
But it's not too late
We can still change it
Rearrange it
Mobilize and be useful

Instead of rallying up to cause mischief
We can come together and clean up the district
Instead of meeting in the streets and catchin' court cases
We can meet in the boardroom, come up with ways to earn big faces
This is not a dream
But something we can do
Just another obstacle that we can get through

With will, determination, and focus on elevation
We can begin to make a difference and enjoy a celebration
This is my vision
For the next generation
New Bloods
New Crips
Progressin'
No more stagnation

Can we move it forward?

Keepin it 100
HUSTLE GUIDE
with employers

EMPLOYMENT

Gettin' Laced Up for Work

◂ *Illustration by Trenton Dukes*

LEARNING OBJECTIVES

In this crash course, you will ...

- ✓ Take quizzes to learn if you have the know-how to succeed with a job hunt
- ✓ Learn to put yourself in the employers' shoes: would you hire yourself?
- ✓ Identify the best jobs and types of companies for people with criminal histories
- ✓ Learn the keys to landing your first job out
- ✓ Hear it directly from HR professionals: when it comes to hiring people with criminal histories, learn how many of them do it, and exactly what they look for
- ✓ Master the nine advantages to having a rap sheet, and learn to sell yourself at your interview
- ✓ Understand the most commonly asked interview question, and the best way to answer it
- ✓ Learn to credibly articulate your criminal history and transformation to an employer
- ✓ Learn the real purpose of a resume
- ✓ Analyze case studies on formerly incarcerated people who overcame obstacles while job seeking

In Hustle Guides 1-12, take in-depth courses and gain insight into:

- ✓ References, background checks, and rap sheets
- ✓ Building your social media profile
- ✓ Making a job-hunting plan
- ✓ Acing the interview
- ✓ Interview and workplace etiquette

POP QUIZ: EMPLOYMENT READINESS

	TRUE	FALSE
1. For most people, a resume is the most important financial document of their lives.	☐	☐
2. The purpose of a resume is to get a job.	☐	☐
3. A great resume is "one-size-fits-all" and can be used for all your job applications.	☐	☐
4. References should be listed on a resume.	☐	☐
5. At the bottom of your resume, write, "References available upon request."	☐	☐
6. It's best to put makeup over facial tattoos for interviews.	☐	☐
7. Employers often scan resumes and make decisions about candidates in seven seconds or less.	☐	☐
8. The most important thing your resume communicates to employers is how you will save time and make them money.	☐	☐
9. A resume is primarily used to sell yourself to employers.	☐	☐
10. If you have a teardrop tattoo, tell the boss it's because you're sad that you haven't landed a job yet.	☐	☐
11. It's good to list jobs you held in prison or jail on your resume.	☐	☐
12. If you held a job for six months, list it on your resume.	☐	☐
13. It's best to use a functional (instead of a chronological) resume format to hide your missing time in the workforce.	☐	☐
14. For many employers, your LinkedIn profile is as or more important than your resume.	☐	☐
15. To save money on interview attire, it's fine to wear the fly get-up you wear to the club.	☐	☐

KEY
True: 1, 7, 8, 9, 11, 14
False: 2, 3, 4, 5, 6, 10, 12, 13, 15
Tally your score: ______
Your Correct Answers:
15: *Want to help write our employment courses?*
13-14: *Keep learning; you're doing something right.*
0-12: *You better get those Hustle Guides ASAP.*

YOU DON'T KNOW WHAT YOU DON'T KNOW

Feeling stumped over the answers to the pop quiz, like we made some errors? In our 12-book series, we debunk job searching myths and lace you up in the best and latest strategies.

It would be easy to think, "The employer rejected me because of my criminal history," when in reality, it was because you weren't schooled properly in resume creation, interview etiquette, and the job-hunting process. Get smart training—this affects the rest of your life!

We won't leave you hanging too much, so we'll give you quick insights into the pop quiz answers.

Your resume will be the most important financial document of your life; it's your key to landing a job. However, the purpose of your resume isn't to land the job; it's to land an interview! Big difference. What you share on the resume vs. in the interview matters. A lot. You should always customize your resume to the job. Never list references, or write that they're available, on your resume (employers know they're available)! Instead, list your references on a separate sheet of paper and have it ready to hand over at the interview.

You don't put makeup on tattoos or hide your past. The key is to speak credibly about your past, taking full ownership, and demonstrating your transformation while having excellent people skills and body language—all things we'll cover in the Hustle Guides.

Don't trip if you've never had a job outside. In the 12-book program, we'll teach you to truthfully list your jobs while incarcerated—without using the words like prison, jail, or incarceration, on your resume. Don't include jobs that lasted six months, because it makes you look undependable. Most employers hate functional formats; they know you're hiding something. They don't have time for all that.

FYI, LinkedIn is the industry standard for recruiters. Nine out of 10 expect you to have it; it's the most widely used professional social media site. It's not only essential for landing a job, but for networking to find one. In the Hustle Guides, we devote an entire course to your LinkedIn profile because it's so critical to your future.

What's the most important lesson you learned from the employment pop quiz?

____

Resoomay

Sluggo D. Sloth

123 palm tree blvd
Bum city, CA
#chillin@gmail.com

Skillzzz

- Enthusiastic sleeper
- Eats well
- Very focused on nothing
- Hangin' and bangin'
- Disorganized
- Expert at chillin'

Education

- Self-edumacated
- Readin', Ritin', and Rithmatic

Xperience

- Chillin' since day one
- Hangin' since day one
- Eatin' since day one

Interests

- Mainly just chillin'
- Ladies
- Hangin'
- TV, TV, and some mo' TV!

They say nothing is impossible, but how can that be true when I do nothing all day.

NO JUDGMENT QUIZ: MY EMPLOYABILITY

	TRUE	FALSE
1. I've had a legal job in the past.	☐	☐
2. I've held a legal job for more than a year.	☐	☐
3. My criminal history will keep employers from wanting to hire me.	☐	☐
4. I feel ashamed of my past.	☐	☐
5. I'm tempted to lie about my past.	☐	☐
6. I feel uncomfortable sharing my past with strangers (e.g., employers) who will make judgments about my future.	☐	☐
7. I fear rejection and not being good enough.	☐	☐
8. I've been rejected for a job I applied to in the past, and now with this conviction, landing employment will only be harder.	☐	☐
9. The thought of preparing and applying for jobs feels overwhelming.	☐	☐
10. The thought of being vulnerable in an interview while discussing my failures and criminal past freaks me out.	☐	☐
11. If I don't get a legal job on the outside, I will likely go back to a criminal lifestyle.	☐	☐
12. I've been promoted in a job.	☐	☐
13. I've held a job while incarcerated.	☐	☐
14. I have professional or vocational accomplishments that make me proud and am prepared to discuss my strengths in an interview.	☐	☐
15. Despite my past, I KNOW I've got enough confidence to sell myself and articulate my transformation in a way that creates trust.	☐	☐
16. If I owned a company, I would want to hire me.	☐	☐
17. I have a resume and feel confident that it's great.	☐	☐

Circle the questions that led you to feel the most overwhelmed or concerned.

My biggest fear about employment is ...

____

JOBS TO CONSIDER

You can land a high-paying job without a degree or advanced training. Many of these roles have entry-level opportunities and are well-suited for people with criminal histories.

Put checkmarks next to the five jobs that interest you most:

- ☐ Welding
- ☐ Electrician
- ☐ HVAC Technician
- ☐ Case Clerk
- ☐ Help Desk Support
- ☐ Project Assistant
- ☐ Carpenter
- ☐ Sales Rep
- ☐ Customer Service Rep
- ☐ Paralegal
- ☐ Military Service
- ☐ Oilfield Jobs
- ☐ Wind Energy Technician
- ☐ Network Support Specialist
- ☐ Marketer
- ☐ Freelance Writer
- ☐ Graphic Designer
- ☐ Administrative Assistant
- ☐ Mobile App Developer
- ☐ Web Designer or Developer
- ☐ Commercial Driver
- ☐ Plumber
- ☐ Film or Video Editor
- ☐ Commercial Truck Driver
- ☐ Painter
- ☐ Auto Mechanic
- ☐ Construction Laborer
- ☐ Shipping and Receiving Clerk
- ☐ Delivery Driver
- ☐ Electrician
- ☐ Commercial Driver
- ☐ Landscaping
- ☐ Barber
- ☐ Cook

Sources: https://helpforfelons.org/high-paying-jobs-for-felons/https://www.trade-schools.net/articles/jobs-for-felons.asp

Note that heavily-regulated industries, like finance and healthcare, tend to have more limitations and present more challenges when it comes to our backgrounds.

Being interested is one thing; having the skills and experience is another. For example, if you checked the mobile app developer job, but don't have coding experience, don't apply.

Circle three jobs that you are best qualified for (you have the required skills and experience). Of these three, which interests you most, and why?

____

LANDING THAT FIRST JOB

It would be ideal to land a job in the field of your choice, but if this is not possible, take what you can get. A job is a job.

This doesn't mean you have to give up on your dream job; just work harder to get there. Get real with yourself, what you really want, and if you want to push for it. You may discover other passions you never knew you had.

> **You're more employable when you're already employed.**

You might need to take a less appealing, entry-level job to put food on the table. But once you're in that job, you automatically become more appealing to future employers.

Know your strengths. Apply for jobs where you know you will do well. If you're good with your hands, go for jobs that involve manual labor. If you're good with computers, apply for jobs that require your expertise.

Do your homework on the companies where you want to work. Understand their culture, what they're looking for, and what you can do to be their "go-to" employee. If you don't work well in an office setting, don't apply for an office job. Don't waste an employer's time—or yours—if you know you're not the right fit.

It's not rocket science to find out what the hiring manager wants. They spell it out in the job description, so study that! And know that hiring managers want to:

- Succeed and make more money
- Make a good hire, so they protect their jobs and look good
- Find someone who works hard and is dependable, so they don't have to rehire a week later
- Save time
- Delegate and know that you'll be up for the responsibility.

The more you understand what a hiring manager wants, the more you can sell directly into these points and get to YES!

What job would be the easiest for you to land quickly after your release to make you more employable?

WORD ON THE STREET

The Society for Human Resource Management and Charles Koch Institute conducted a survey of 540 managers and 1,228 human resources (HR) professionals.

Put a check next to statements that are news to you!

- ☐ Two-thirds of HR professionals report that their company has hired people with criminal histories.
- ☐ 80% of managers and two-thirds of HR professionals report that people with criminal histories bring as much or greater value to the company than people without criminal histories.
- ☐ 75% of managers and HR professionals report the cost of hiring people with criminal histories is equal to or less than hiring people without criminal histories.
- ☐ Most people said they were willing to work with people with criminal histories.
- ☐ The greatest factor in hiring people with criminal histories was their "demonstrated consistent work history."
- ☐ Other top factors for hiring people with criminal histories are: "Desire to hire the best candidate for the job regardless of criminal history, making the community a better place, and giving individuals a second chance."

Source: SHRM/CKI Workers with Criminal Records Survey (SHRM, 2018)

EMPLOYER SURVEYS

In 2009, The IPS Employment Center at The Rockville Institute Expert Employment Specialist Group conducted 128 employer surveys. We've summarized their research. Employers' answers are italicized, quoted directly from the survey.

42% of employers said the #1 reason they hired a person with a felony was because the applicant demonstrated experience, skills, and or training. The person was qualified to do the job.

- *"He had the skills that were necessary to do the job."*
- *"I hired these two because one knew how to weld and the other had 10 years machining experience."*

22% of employers cited the interview as the reason they hired someone with a criminal history. They were particularly struck by the person's good interview skills, excitement for the job, appropriate attire, and follow up.

- *"Initially, I didn't know. But the resume looked good and the person demonstrated that he was willing to do whatever was needed to get hired by showing prompt phone call and email responses, was more than ready for interviews and showed enthusiasm for the job during the interview."*
- *"When I get a stack of 200 applications, a person with a criminal record doesn't have a chance unless they make a personal connection. They need to make a personal appearance ... approach the hiring manager."*

18% of employers cited a referral from someone they trusted as the reason they hired someone with a criminal history.

- *"I knew his parole officer and talked to him personally. The person did his time, paid his dues and was upfront—talked about it."*
- *"The person seemed like a good person who sincerely wanted to work. He had an employment specialist working with him with whom I had a prior relationship. I have hired people with felony backgrounds before, but it helped having someone who knew the person and was willing to back him."*

15% of employers would risk hiring someone with a criminal history because they believed in their transformation and wanted to give them a second chance. A compelling 2.0 story of transformation is key.

- *"This person was very convincing when he told me he had lost most of what he really cared about because of some very poor choices. He told me he needed to work so he could feel normal again. He asked me to take a chance on him."*

- *"I was sure the person had changed his life for the better. He took responsibility for what he had done and was adamant about wanting to have a chance to prove himself."*
- *"He was willing to prove that he could do the job and that he would be the most dependable employee that I had."*
- *"Have the person tell in his own words why the employer should take a chance on him or her. The person better come across as believable.""Provide some sort of proof that they have made changes to their life; that they are less likely to commit another crime and are less likely to have a negative impact on the business."*
- *"Talk about the steps that he or she is taking to better their lives."*

Over 50% of employers said the applicant's crime matters. They were most hesitant to hire people with theft and financial crimes, sex offenses, violent crimes, and crimes against children.

47% of employers were more likely to consider people with criminal histories for some positions over others.

- *"I'm more likely to hire a person with a felony for the dock area (loading and unloading trucks)."*
- *"A person with a record would be considered for the courtesy clerk position (grocery) but not a cash handling position."*

Even employers suggest leaving your crime off your resume, but share it at the first opportunity in the interview. Don't lie (directly or by omission).

- *"The person needs to be honest about their record. I run background checks and I had to let someone go because they had lied about convictions on their application. This person was one of our best workers. I had to let him go due to company policy, even though I would have hired him despite the conviction if he had been honest with us."*

Source: https://ipsworks.org/wp-content/uploads/2017/08/employer-survey-legal-history.pdf

Employers value honesty, upfront disclosure, and ownership.

1. Honest and upfront disclosure is the most important thing to employers.
2. Take responsibility for your past.
3. Show your transformation. Share your 2.0 story.
4. Speak face-to-face with a hiring manager or decision-maker.

Illustration by Trenton Dukes

THE ADVANTAGES OF A RAP SHEET

What do you have to offer an employer that is unique? If you answer "nothing," you'll stay unemployed. Discover the competitive advantages that come from doing time!

Check the advantages that apply to you … and memorize them, so you're ready to sell!

☑	The Advantage	Mavericks (even those with long rap sheets!)	Other Entry-level Job Applicants
☐	**Attitude of gratitude**	"Show me the money! I'll take it!" After making pennies, entry-level wages are looking good. I'll prove my worth.	"That's it? How am I going to live off of that?"
☐	**Work ethic**	"Can't stop, won't stop." For years, we've shown up on time to assigned jobs. We worked our butts off when we didn't have to. We're stronger and faster than the rest. Duh, we're Mavericks.	After a couple of days on the job: "I'm not feelin' this." Many flake or take jobs for granted and struggle with dependability.
☐	**Low-maintenance**	We roll up our sleeves and get it done, even in unglamorous conditions.	Many whine and complain and act ungrateful.
☐	**Parole/probation accountability**	We pee in a cup every month. PO's provide free accountability. We have a lot riding on staying sober and legal.	Many struggle with substance abuse and have less motivation to stay sober.
☐	**Federal tax benefits**	Employers can actually MAKE money by hiring us! The Work Opportunity Tax Credit (WOTC) saves up to $2,400 on taxes for hiring us!	So sad: the employer forfeits the WOTC if they don't hire someone with a rap sheet
☐	**Free federal bonding**	The government offers employers six months of free federal bonding for hiring us. Scared we'll rob you? Chill, boss; you get protection for free.	Even sadder: the employer doesn't get this protection for hiring the Average Joe.
☐	**Loyalty**	We know a thing or two about loyalty.	We know all-too-well how the world is filled with flakes and snakes. So do employers.
☐	**Proven experience**	Most of us are proven hustlers with backgrounds in sales, customer service, management, and more.	Many others lack our hustle and extensive money-making background/skills.
☐	**Workforce diversity**	Some employers struggle with recruiting a diverse workforce, and this doesn't just mean skin color. We bring diversity.	Companies don't score points in the diversity category for hiring privileged people.

WHO GETS HIRED

Do you know what employers look for when they make hiring decisions?

"I will only hire someone to work directly for me if I would work for that person."

- Mark Zuckerberg, CEO of Facebook

"When you have really good people, you don't have to baby them. By expecting them to do great things, you can get them to do great things. A-plus players like to work together, and they don't like it if you tolerate B-grade work."

- Steve Jobs, former CEO of Apple

"The world no longer cares how much you know, but it cares how much you can do with what you know."

- Tony Wagner, author of Creating Innovators and The Global Achievement Gap

"Engagement is crucial in the workplace. Employers don't want to hire people who just clock their hours. They want people who are deeply engaged in their work ... Companies hiring (the growing ones) don't have job descriptions as much as a buffet of problems. They don't like hiring new graduates because "They expect us to tell them what to do." These employers want people who take ownership and just dive into solving important problems."

- Zach First, Senior Managing Director at the Drucker Institute

"What employers want and need from graduates and people they hire: grit, rigor, polish, impact, curiosity, teamwork, and ownership."

- Kristen Hamilton, CEO of Koru

YOUR 2.0 STORY

Getting job-ready takes a lot of effort, but it's worth it. For now, we're jumping into the part of the job process that takes the most courage: sharing you criminal past in a way that leads a hiring manager to understand that you're no longer the same person you used to be. We call this your "2.0 Story."

We're diving into your 2.0 Story now, because we want you to be prepared to answer the most commonly asked question in an interview, which is:

"So tell me about yourself."

If you learn to tell a compelling story with confidence, you can convince people of your value and transformation, *regardless of your criminal history*.

Do you have a lifelong history of crime and violence? It'll take more hustle; you'll have to plow through more rejection than someone who just did a few years on a drug-dealing charge – but you too can land a job. We see it happen every day. Get yo' Honey Badger on.

Here's how:

- You need to be credible.
- Keep it 100; take ownership and accountability for your past.
- Clearly articulate your transformation – and that you're no longer the same person.
- Point to specific examples of transformed actions (participating in H2.0 is a great example).

Imagine these two interview scenarios for Johnny, a charismatic 32-year-old who just touched down after doing 12-years for robbery. He's interviewing with Juan, a hiring manager.

Scenario #1

Johnny nails the 30-minute interview. Although he has no solid experience on his resume, Juan is impressed with Johnny's attitude. Johnny doesn't have visible tattoos, and Juan has no idea that Johnny did time. Johnny's too nervous to bring it up … so he doesn't. At the end of the interview:

Juan: "Anything else I should know about you?"
Johnny: "No sir!"
Juan: "Thank you for coming in. We'll be in touch …"
Juan is excited and is sure he's filled the position … until later in the day when he runs Johnny's background and sees the robbery conviction.

Scenario #2

Johnny walks into the interview, shakes Juan's hand, and sits down. Juan starts with the #1 most commonly asked interview question.

Juan: "So tell me about yourself, Johnny."

Johnny: "I've earned an associate degree, have two years of work experience, and have completed a 12-month management training program called Hustle 2.0. I'm grateful to have this opportunity to interview with you; working for your company is a dream for me. I also believe in taking accountability and being honest, so I'm going to share something difficult with you. As a teenager, I turned to gangs and drugs after I lost my father. When I was 20 years old, I made a terrible decision and committed armed robbery. I deeply regret my decision and have spent the past 12 years in a correctional facility, reflecting on my poor choices every day. I had the opportunity to become a better person, to reflect every day on who I am and want to be. {And from here, Johnny shares tangible examples of his transformation.}

Juan gulps. Armed robbery is a heavy charge. But he's also not going to escort Johnny out after three minutes. So … he keeps interviewing Johnny. And now that they've gotten the hard part out of the way, they spend the remaining 27 minutes speaking about Johnny's strengths.

Put yourself in Juan's shoes (this is having *empathy* for Juan and his predicament). Juan is 40 years old and has been a hiring manager at his company for five years. It's his duty to protect his company and the staff and to hire well.

If you're in Juan's position, in scenario #1, are you questioning Johnny's truthfulness when you discover that Johnny was convicted of armed robbery, but failed to tell you about it? Why do you feel this way?

What scenario is more compelling to you if you're an employer: #1 or #2? Why?

CHOOSING UPFRONT DISCLOSURE

We know that sharing our imperfect pasts is never easy. It's that voice in our heads that keeps saying, "You're not good enough. You're a bum."

But you have a choice.

We respect it when people are courageous and vulnerable enough to share the truth. We respect it when someone puts themselves out there. It makes us want to have their courage.

We also know how it feels when someone lies, deceives, or hides something important. We get angry. We feel played. Nobody likes that.

Tell your story – the good, the bad, and the ugly. Tell it on your terms. You get to write the ending of your story. You get to tell your future employer how much you've transformed, what you've learned from your mistakes, and that you take ownership. Home court advantage is only useful if you use it.

Some people will still reject you and judge you for your past. You can't control that. But you can keep pushing until you find someone who believes in you and sees that taking a chance on you is worth it.

The key to success: Choose "upfront disclosure."

> You either walk inside your story and own it, or you stand outside your story and hustle for your worthiness.
>
> - Brené Brown

6 TIPS FOR TELLING YOUR 2.0 STORY

1. Tell your 2.0 Story early in your interview - ideally, at the beginning, so you have the rest of the interview to talk about positive stuff. Share your past upfront so you don't get discovered/caught later; no one will feel bait-and-switched by you.
2. Highlight your strengths and accomplishments and the value you'll bring to the company.
3. Keep it short. Share just enough, but don't overshare, no gory details. Take ownership and accountability. And never brag about your criminal past.
4. Share what you've learned, and how you've transformed. You are not the same kid you used to be, and your future employer needs to see this.
5. Demonstrate sincere empathy for your future employer and the choice they are making; show them why they should hire you.
6. By the end, shoot yo' shot: ask the hiring manager to make you a job offer!

In The Combine, we'll detail 10 steps to telling your 2.0 Story. For now, we've provided sample statements. These aren't the "full" 2.0 Story examples - but they demonstrate transformation.

If you go into the interview well-prepared and on point, you're gonna be like a bag of rocks (which sells itself). ☺

Getting Specific About Your Transformation

Share the following:

- What caused your transformation
- How long ago you began your transformation process (unless it started yesterday; then leave it out)
- What your transformation meant
- The positive behaviors that emerged from your transformation
- The negative behaviors you stopped engaging in as a result of your transformation

For many Mavericks, their faith helped with their transformation. Most people will respect this - so long as you can point to the changes that your spiritual transformation led to. What doesn't work so well is when people rely on religion as a crutch.

To be credible, you must point to the tangible ways in which you have changed your life because of your faith or discipline.

SAMPLE STATEMENTS OF TRANSFORMATION

- Five years ago, I picked up the bible for the first time. I read it cover to cover, and allowed the words to sink in. My new faith led to changes. For example, for the past three years, I no longer curse; I lead a bible study, and we hold each other accountable to written goals; and I have given away 10% of my income to people who are less fortunate. I volunteer at a soup kitchen weekly.

- When I came to prison at the age of 30, I realized the pain I not only caused to the victim's family, but the plight I left my three-year old son in. The pain I felt for the first time led to a complete transformation. I became accountable so my son would have a role model. I've read 10 books on parenting. I write my son a letter every day, and in the visitation room, I help him with his homework. I started a group for young incarcerated parents, and we meet weekly to share parenting wisdom.

- While incarcerated, I learned that my mother was dying of cancer. I felt helpless. When I realized that I was not acting like the person she raised me to be, a lightbulb went off, and it changed everything. From that day forward, I disassociated from negative influences. I stopped engaging in criminal activity. I pursued my education – at first, by reading every book I could get my hands on – and then by enrolling in college and earning a 3.7 GPA. I also completed this awesome program called Hustle 2.0. ☺

If you were an employer, which of these three statements would best demonstrate transformation?

CRAY

A man goes into a job interview
and presents himself well.

"Wow, you have an incredible resume,
and present yourself fantastically,
but you seem to be missing 5 years
on this part of your resume.

What happened there?"

The man replied, "Oh, that's
when I went to Yale."

The employer is even more impressed.
"That's great, you're hired!"

The man is super happy and says
"Yay, I got a yob!"

CRAY

CASE STUDY:
THE FIRST INTERVIEW OF MY LIFE
By Ceasar Rodarte

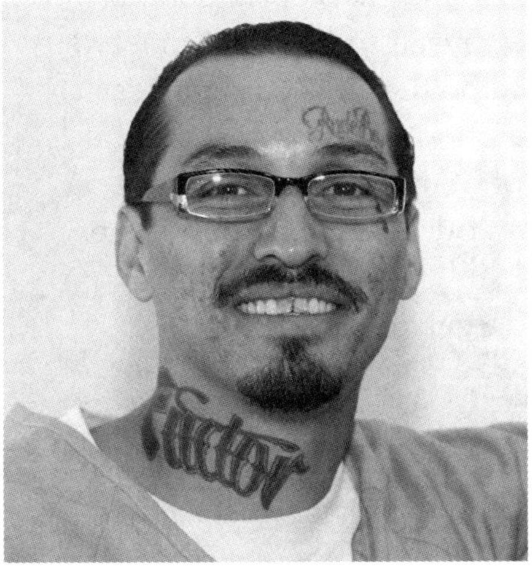

The first thing I learn as I start looking for a job is that it's a pain in the butt. Even with certifications, so many job descriptions make me feel unqualified. I come across jobs that look like easy pickings, yet they require a bachelor's degree. I see others where I'd think I would have no shot, give me just that.

The easy part is done; I submitted my resume online. Now I just have to apply to more and see where things go.

I submitted my resume today at 4:45 a.m. It's now 9 a.m., and I receive an email from the job website saying my resume has been viewed by a sales and marketing company three times in the past few hours, and that this only happens with 7% of the resumes on their site.

There's no better feeling than standing out—for the right reasons. I feel great! I don't know why this company is looking at my application, but elf it ... I'm looking good to somebody.

It's now 1 p.m. I get a call to interview over the phone. I nail it. The lady says that she loves my energy and can't wait to meet me. I say, "Great, I look forward to seeing you, too!"

The doubts set in. What will I wear?? I don't have a suit. How happy will she be when I walk in and she sees all the ink on my face??? Well what choice do I have anyways ... I just landed the first job interview of my life! Now it's the morning of the interview. I wake up and Frankenstein a suit ... Or as I later learn from a friend, "It's not a suit if the pants and jacket aren't a matching pair." (Whatevs, homegirl!) I'm looking fresh in my SUIT.

If you know me, you know that I don't lack for confidence, and this day is like any other. I know what I bring to the table, whether or not they give me the job ... and I'm going to appreciate this moment for all it's worth.

I just got done doing 13 years, and a sales and marketing company is interested in *my* resume. I refuse to allow myself to be discriminated against by me. How easy would it be to assume that this company isn't going to give me a shot, based on my background? If I have that mentality, why would any company hire me??? A lot of us take ourselves out of the running long before we ever even submit our resumes. But not me.

I refuse to allow myself to be discriminated against by me.

I send a picture of me all fresh to everyone I know to be rooting for my success and let the Love Bombs come in ... Up until this morning, it was my little secret that I landed an interview.

I'd be lying if I said there isn't an inkling of a doubt that this company isn't going to hire me because of the way I look. All I can really think about are the tattoos on my face. (Aside from those, I'm GQ material ... Shishkabob, I could still be in GQ anyway! I'm just sayin', stop hatin'.)

If I'm keeping it one-hunnid, my conflicting emotions make me feel two very real things. One is that I feel like a fraud ... that I don't belong in this "suit." The other is that I've been selling myself short my entire life, because if anyone belongs in a suit, it's me.

I look up the commute to my interview: 37 minutes via trolley and bus. To be on the safe side, I leave 90 minutes early.

As we all know, things don't always go the way we plan.

The bus is delayed; like, really delayed. I cringe as I realize I'm probably

I've been selling myself short my entire life.

going to be late, so I do the only reasonable thing: I call to let the receptionist know I'll be arriving late. I get an answering machine. I don't want to leave a message; will they even get it? I make myself leave a message anyway; it's the proper thing to do. Another five minutes tick by, and what does Honey Badger do? Call back again, so Honey Badger gets what Honey Badger wants. This time, I get the receptionist and tell her I'll be late. She says she received my voicemail, asks me how late I'll be, and thanks me for being so considerate of their time.

Phew.

I arrive five minutes late.

I get to the office, and there are maybe 10 people there applying for my job. I'm greeted and take my seat. I ear hustle as my competitors talk about the colleges they went to. I would be discouraged if they didn't look so nervous. Jeepers, one is even sweating ... about WHAT?! It's just a job interview.

They call my name.

The interview isn't nearly as painful as I anticipated. Maybe the tattoos are a big deal; maybe they're not?? Maybe all anyone really cares about is whether you can get the job done? I'm not going to wait to find out the hard way, so I take Hustle 2.0's advice, and I get ahead of it. I allow the formalities to take their course, and then give my 2.0 Story.

"So I know I have a bit of a different look ..." The woman stops me and says, "Hey, it's no problem, if you could see what's underneath this shirt you'd be surprised." Lesson: we're a lot harder on ourselves than people are out here. It's in this moment I decide that I'm not going to be the one to discriminate against myself. Yes, people will judge, and yes, people will dislike me solely based on my appearance, but I'll be damned if I join that list of haters. I spent many years doing things to earn that judgment, and while that doesn't make it right, the fastest way to put myself back down in that mindset is to be the one who convinces me that the world is never going to accept me.

We finish the interview. The woman says she loves my confidence and energy and that I'm articulate. Then she asks if I'd be willing to come for the second round of interviews. Um, yes! We shake hands, and I'm out the do' fo'sho, feeling pretty good. The second interview is fun. Fourteen of us go into a small room to learn the history of the company and, under observation, do brainstorming and social activities to see how we function in a team. Then we proceed to more individual interviews.

Yes, people will judge, and yes, people will dislike me solely based on my appearance, but I'll be damned if I join that list of haters.

I step into the office with the company's founder. He's pleasant. He asks how I liked the group chat and whether I think the company would be a good addition to my life and goals. Um, YES again! He then asks what my career goals are. We talk about my hope to affect a positive change in the world and the work that I'm doing to get these plans moving forward. Then he tells me he knows I have a history, and that he doesn't believe it will affect my chances of employment with the company. He also keeps it 100 with me and says they're a startup, so he'll need to discuss things with his investor, and he'll reach out after.

This is the part where we can say he knew right there that he wasn't going to hire me. The truth is that we don't know what needs to happen for a company like that to make a decision. We choose the way we want to see things.

I received that phone call ... saying my circumstances are too much for them to hire me. (I'm currently in a pre-release program and am technically still incarcerated, and had told them about this.) He wishes me well and says I had a lot to offer any company. I agree with him. ☺

I don't have legal sales experience, and that was a brand new startup. I'll never know what happened behind closed doors. What I do know is that a marketing company noticed my resume among many more qualified applicants, and my first interview made enough of an impression to go two rounds of interviews. I loved my experience, and even though I didn't get the job, I love that a bunch of college graduates had to compete with me. And most of them didn't get the job either.

On to the next interview, where I'll be smarter, better prepared, on time, more confident, and just as good looking. ☺ Watch out world, this Honey Badger is hungry for a job.

How have you "discriminated against yourself"?

Ceasar describes his feelings about his tattoos and rap sheet. How do you feel about yours?

What story have you told yourself about rejections you experienced?

After seeing how Ceasar handled rejection, what lesson can you incorporate into your future?

CASE STUDY: HONEY BADGER FIGHTS FOR HER RIGHTS

Shelley Winner

Shelley giving a TED Talk

Microsoft gave Shelley an offer. Then they rescinded it.

Shelley Winner had followed in the footsteps of her father to prison, and she sobered up after a long fight with drugs.

Though Shelley had never worked in technology, she knew she loved it and was dead-set on landing a tech job. After getting out of prison, Shelley was connected to Deedee, a mentor. Deedee is a technology executive who cared for Shelley as if she were her own daughter. Deedee helped Shelley navigate the world and even funded a technology training program for her.

Finishing this tech-training program qualified Shelley for a Microsoft job. She is charismatic and has mad sales skills.

Some states now have "ban the box," a law that forbids companies from asking job applicants to check a box on their applications if they have criminal records. The law prevents employers from discriminating against people with criminal histories, so long as the crime isn't related to the job (e.g., a former bank robber won't be hired as a bank teller).

Shelley knew Microsoft had made a mistake in rescinding the offer because of her drug charge, so she fought it. She got the decision reversed, and they rehired her.

Six months later, Shelley was recognized by Microsoft as a "Most Valuable Player." She's been promoted since, becoming the top revenue generator on her team. She was even flown to Seattle headquarters to celebrate her accomplishments.

More companies have decided that they want to hire more people with criminal histories, all because of the outstanding leadership and role modeling of people like Shelley.

How does Shelley's story inspire you to believe in yourself?

SUDOKU

Complete the puzzle by filling in the numbers 1-9 in each row, each column, and each 3x3 grid without repeating a number in any row, column, or 3x3 grid.

	3		4		9			2
	5			3	1			
2					5			4
	6			5		3		8
		1			3	4		
		5					2	6
			9		4	5		
							6	

WORK

Chinese Traditional	gōngzuò
French	travail
German	Arbeit
Portuguese	trabalhos
Spanish	trabajo
Swahili	kazi

When I see people stand fully in their truth, or when I see someone fall down, get back up, and say, “Damn. That really hurt, but this is important to me and I’m going in again”—my gut reaction is, “What a badass.”

- Brené Brown

BURRITO FEO-GUAPO

By Richard Garcia

Makes five burritos

Ingredients:

1 Chata Chilorio shredded beef
1/2 bag of Cactus Annies pork rinds
1 pack of 10 Tortillas
1 Brushy Creek beef summer sausage
1/2 bag of Rice
1 tsp Sevilla Sazon with cilantro and achiote
1/2 bag of Beans
2 Pickles
1 Squeeze cheese (Velveeta)

How to assemble:

- ☐ Put chilorio, pork rinds, and sausage (diced into small pieces) in a bag to marinate and heat up together.
- ☐ Cook rice (add 1 tsp of Sazon) separately in different bowls.
- ☐ Cut up the pickles.
- ☐ Put two tortillas on wax paper and overlap them slightly.
- ☐ Lather beans to your liking.
- ☐ Add rice to your liking.
- ☐ Add a good squirt of squeeze cheese.
- ☐ Add pickles to your liking.
- ☐ Top off with the meat mixture.
- ☐ Roll up burrito with wax paper and eat as is or heat it up for 10 minutes.

DCR
PRISONER

BECOMING THE SOLUTION

Common Ground-Bound

◂ *Illustration by Trenton Dukes*

LEARNING OBJECTIVES

In this crash course, you will ...

- ✓ Evaluate your personal contributions to your predicament and to mass incarceration
- ✓ Get inspired by case studies on a progressive sheriff and on taking steps to reduce criminality
- ✓ Learn to promote and practice peace and positivity with staff and others
- ✓ Recognize that you have a choice when it comes to abstaining from criminal activity
- ✓ Identify how we've segregated ourselves and made enemies out of fellow human beings

In Hustle Guides 1-12, take in-depth courses and gain insight into:

- ✓ Creating your legacy
- ✓ Premeditated positivity: Impact Challenge
- ✓ Toxic masculinity
- ✓ Evolution of the gang, criminal, and institutionalized mindset
- ✓ Improving relationships with authorities

RECOGNIZING THERE'S A PROBLEM

The first step in fixing a problem is recognizing there is one. The relationship between c/o's and us is broken. The misunderstandings and resentment many of us have toward one another fuels the broken connection. When there are riots with officers and they are being assaulted by incarcerated people, there's a problem. When there is no trust between us, there's a problem. When one of us asks a simple question, and an officer snaps out of frustration or assumes we have an angle, there's a problem.

No one's saying we have to be best friends. But couldn't we at least work together to create a more positive environment that we all feel safe in?

I DEHUMANIZED THEM

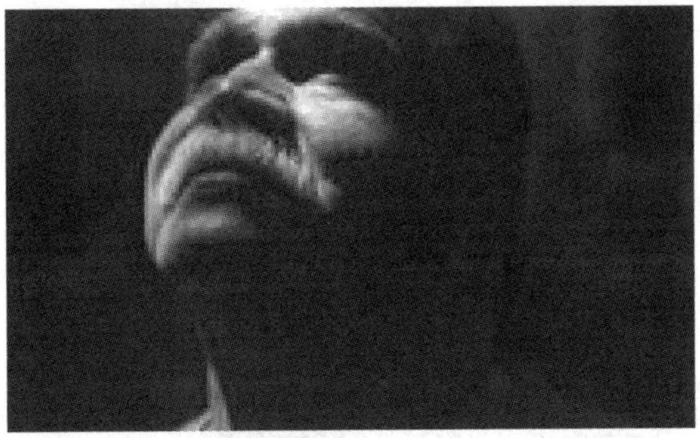

By Alfred Sandoval
aka Sweet Freddy

I painted all cops with the same brush. I assumed all of them were racist bigots who had no humanity, because of the few I had dealt with. I dehumanized them – just like they dehumanized me.

I was wrong.

Once a sergeant apologized to me for making a mistake, and I saw c/o's rag on him for his apology, calling him an "inmate lover." I realized that I just took everyone in uniform to be "bad people," and this sergeant showed me that they all weren't the same.

In the past, my anger toward c/o's led me to stab and assault c/o's who were following orders. Today, I realize they were just doing their jobs.

Today, I don't judge c/o's for doing their jobs; I'm able to separate the bad apples from the decent ones. I treat every one of them with respect; even the ones I don't like. Because it's not about them; it's about me. I'm better for it. I won't let anyone drag me down.

NO JUDGMENT QUIZ: EVALUATING MY CONTRIBUTIONS

	AGREE	DISAGREE
I say good morning and good afternoon to c/o's (even the ones I don't like).	☐	☐
I've been honest with every c/o I encountered this week.	☐	☐
I speak to c/o's the way I want to be spoken to.	☐	☐
I believe all c/o's are the same.	☐	☐
I would never shake hands with a c/o.	☐	☐
I believe all c/o's are against me.	☐	☐
C/o's are corrupt and will set me up if they have the chance.	☐	☐
I have been rude and disrespectful to c/o's.	☐	☐
I'll show a c/o respect only after they show me respect.	☐	☐
I think it's funny when I see someone go off on a c/o.	☐	☐
I believe that a c/o has a very difficult job.	☐	☐
I admire the effort some c/o's put into creating a safe environment.	☐	☐
If the c/o's would just leave me alone, there wouldn't be any problems.	☐	☐
I continue to engage in criminal activity that reinforces stereotypes.	☐	☐

Think about your answers, and then decide whether you're part of the problem or the solution. It's easy to say, "Well they don't say good morning to me, so why would I say good morning to them?" Are you a Honey Badger or a Sloth? A leader or a puppet? When you see something that's broken, can you take the initiative to fix it? We're only responsible for our own character and behavior.

How could you level up?

____

SHOUT OUT TO HONEY BADGER SHERIFF ED GONZALEZ

Ed Gonzalez was elected on November 8, 2016, as the Sheriff of Harris County in Texas. Sheriff Gonzalez started out as a civilian employee and became a police officer in Houston, eventually becoming a sergeant. He served on the elite hostage negotiation team and served in the Homicide Division as an investigator.

The Harris County Sheriff's Office is the third largest Sheriff's Office in the country. Ed leads upwards of 5,000 employees to protect the 4.5 million residents of Harris County.

Ed and his team came to volunteer with Hustle 2.0 at Pelican Bay State Prison for three straight days in 2019. He put his money where his mouth is, making a personal contribution (not from his work budget!) of $1,000 to support our program at Hustle 2.0. The sheriff and his team were true Honey Badgers, keeping their commitments to dance onstage in front of hundreds of Mavericks and allowing themselves to become vulnerable. Ed truly believes in rehabilitation, and those who met him at the function can attest to this. In the SHU, when volunteers shared Love Bombs, he said into the mic to one of our Mavericks, "I love you, brother."

This is what it looks like to challenge the status quo and be the change you want to see in the world. Step your game up, Mavericks!

Sheriff Gonzalez volunteered with Hustle 2.0 for three straight days and contributed $1,000 of his personal salary to support the program!

CREATING PEACE & POSITIVITY

5 Ways to Create Peace with the Authorities

1. Say good morning/evening to them, and watch the walls slowly start crumbling down.
2. View them as individuals; they're humans and want to be treated that way, just like we do.
3. Try smiling instead of frowning (remove that thug mug).
4. Speak to them the way you want to be spoken to.
5. Have empathy when you're not treated properly; realize that negative experiences with other incarcerated people likely influence how they interact with you, and perspectives don't change overnight.

> Resolving things in a peaceful manner: that takes real courage.
>
> \- Jacob Ama

NO JUDGMENT QUIZ: MY VIEWS OF INCARCERATION

	AGREE	DISAGREE
If I could, I'd vote for politicians who are "tough on crime."	☐	☐
I would rather have taxpayer dollars support higher DAs' salaries than improve opportunities for disadvantaged kids.	☐	☐
I believe that the system generally doesn't sentence us to enough time.	☐	☐
Society should incarcerate more people and build more prisons.	☐	☐
My behavior since my incarceration has helped to keep DAs employed.	☐	☐
My behavior since my incarceration has contributed to c/o's overtime.	☐	☐
My behavior before and since my incarceration helps to support tough-on-crime politicians' claims.	☐	☐
Since being incarcerated, I participated in activities that got more time added to my sentence (or reduced the time off I could have earned).	☐	☐
Gangs and gang activity generally lead to violence, more victims, more prisons, more DAs, more c/o's, and more fatherless generations.	☐	☐

How many of us have made choices that give politicians and DAs the fuel and data they need to get reelected as they sell tough-on-crime rhetoric?

THE THINGS WE SAY WE HATE

> *When Mexico sends its people, they're not sending their best. They're sending people that have lots of problems ... They're bringing drugs. They're bringing crime. They're rapists. And some, I assume, are good people.*
>
> - Donald Trump
>
> June 16, 2015, in his speech announcing his candidacy for President of the United States

We hate being dehumanized and being seen and treated as animals.

We say we hate incarceration and want nothing more than freedom.

We hate the lockdowns, having our rights taken from us and violated, the SHU, and the staff training days that keep us locked down.

But do we ever stop to think that *we* are the reason all of this exists? The behavior we perpetuate creates the need for all of this. Consider this:

- If we didn't have riots and stabbings, c/o's wouldn't need training on how to respond to them.
- If we didn't segregate into gangs and use violence, c/o's wouldn't have to separate us from each other or place us in isolation.
- If we didn't engage in criminal activity (selling and using drugs, using cell phones, etc.), c/o's wouldn't get all that overtime writing us up.
- If we didn't stab people, DAs wouldn't have new crimes to prosecute.

How many of us have made choices that give politicians and DAs the fuel and data they need to get reelected as they sell tough-on-crime rhetoric? When they sell "lock 'em up and throw away the key" because we're so violent ... it's like our actions are voting for them; voting for the unions that fund these politicians' campaigns. They base their campaigns on prosecution rates that come from *our activities – not made-up stories*. We're the job security for the DAs that some of us have labeled as "liars."

SQUARING UP

Verb

Disengaging from the criminal identity and embracing a prosocial identity.

> Your actions speak so loudly, I can't hear what you're saying.
>
> – Ralph Waldo Emerson

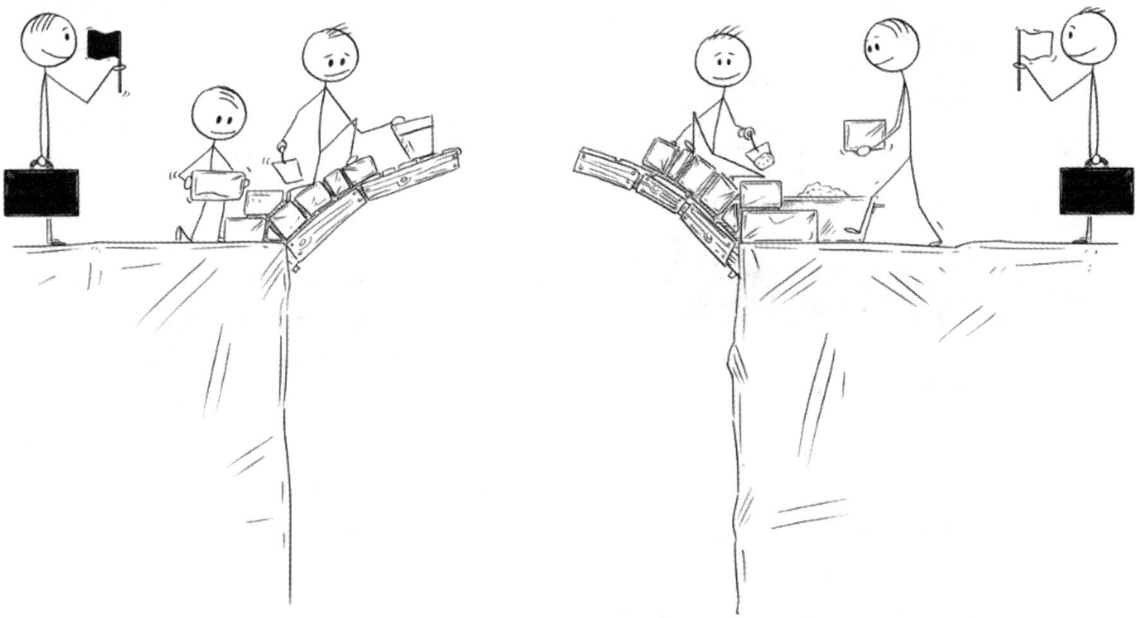

PROGRESSING TOWARD MY FREEDOM

By Little John Perry
aka Buttercup

When you hear "Squaring Up," what are you thinking? Do you think you're being asked to drop your morals? Squaring Up is doing what's right to transform and to go home to your family.

For most of my prison term, I lived the "Don't Care Policy." I had gone so far as to smoke weed in front of c/o's. It used to be difficult for me to make it back to my cell without violence. The old Buttercup wouldn't last a month without going to the hole.

If you want to go home, let your friends know that you no longer have an opinion unless it involves you personally. Stop all criminal behavior to go home.

When you know one of your homeboys wants to go home and is trying to do the right thing, be an accountability partner. Help him mind his own business and stay out of the way. If you're a real friend, tell him to step back and stay away. Remind him of the priorities he's chosen, even on days when he's tempted to backslide.

When I turned 40, wisdom started to kick in. Laws changed that are giving me the opportunity to go home. I know the difference between what's right and wrong, and **once you know the difference, you must make a choice.** The next step is up to you.

A few choices I have made to break some bad habits and criminal behaviors are:

1. I started tucking in my shirt
2. No fighting
3. No weapons

I don't cell up with people who don't care about my freedom or theirs.

I'm a work in progress. For example, I started taking my lines down when leaving the cell, but yes, I still have them. I'm working on this right now. Before the year is up, I plan to do better with giving up more bad habits to make my freedom a reality.

Gang members live by a code, and for some people, the cheese slid off the cracker a long time ago. Those people do not understand or care about you bettering yourself. They only care about the work you put in or about the stories they tell themselves.

ACTION TALKS

By Jacob Ama
aka Sweet Sugarcane

To me, Squaring Up means to be honest with myself as much as possible. That's a strenuous task for most of us, because old habits are hard to break. I know because it's been quite a challenge to overcome obstacles to better myself and make beneficial choices.

It starts with the "small" things. For example, in your work area, when you take tape, glue, paperclips, pens, pencils or stationery and sell it, that's criminal activity—or as we claim, hustling. The problem is that small increments of criminal behavior lead to bigger and more criminal tendencies.

Throughout my transformation, I've adapted to more positive ways as I've taught myself to think in prosocial ways.

My last major disciplinary case was in 2017 for possession and distribution of marijuana. The marijuana was not mine, but I thought I was doing a friend a favor by holding his illegal drugs. Guess what, I got caught with it and all hell broke loose. It was my first time ever being at a Level III yard, and I was one year or so from advancing to a Level II by another override. My stupidity and carelessness cost me a parole date.

I was only mad at myself. I took full responsibility for my actions, and chose to forgive myself. I'm correcting my mistakes by putting in the work to make better choices and not letting negative impulses cloud my judgment. I should have been home, but my careless actions led me to get my priorities in order.

My goal is to transform, and to be found suitable by the parole board. I would like to be reunited with my family and contribute to society.

I believe in the old saying, "Action talks, BS walks." People can say anything, but your actions will solidify your words.

For example, the 4:30 p.m. institutional count is something I never cared about, especially the part about standing up with your bright lights on … I used to think, yeah right! Well guess what, my bright light is on nowadays, and I'm standing straight up to be counted. And that's because one day soon, I'd rather be counted with my family than in a cell.

SUCKA-FREE LIVING

By Kunlyna Tauch
aka Sweet Cheeks

Squaring Up is serious. It's not about whether you get caught or not. It's about really getting rid of "that life." We have been conditioned to this life for so long that we sometimes do not recognize what is criminal or not.

I just started to Square Up. This is a big statement for me to make, and may catch a lot of people by surprise. Since 2015, I have been involved in nearly every program at Pelican Bay, like full-fledged.

But in 2018 I got written up for a tattoo. What it showed was that I was willing to break rules. I totally disregarded the fact that I still had some criminal behaviors. Think of what's involved when you get a tattoo and the artist isn't your cellie. That's a lot of being sneaky and what we would call "wiggling."

That write-up showed me that if I wanted to obtain my freedom, I'll have to be hyper-vigilant of all the rules, even the ones I've considered stupid. Laundry lines, stingers, out of bounds; even feeding the birds. Not just the hot boy stuff, you know what I mean. That write-up shifted my mentality.

Now I talk to my cellie, and we discussed what we are not willing to get a write-up for. We also discussed how we will stay out of talks about "homie business." Putting our two cents in those conversations would be like raising our hands.

Staying sucka-free and earning my freedom is literally a full-time job. No one said that going home from a maximum-security yard would be easy. But if you're hardheaded like me, and are willing to get stubborn about your freedom, you'll rise to the challenge.

If you're hardheaded like me, and are willing to get stubborn about your freedom, you'll rise to the challenge.

MATH WHIZZ

Complete the puzzle by entering the numbers 1 through 9 in each empty white cell. Each number will be used exactly once.

	−		+		=	8
×		×		+		
	+		+		=	8
−		−		−		
	×		+		=	35
=		=		=		
2		6		11		

IMPACT
CHALLENGE
BAG.

PURPOSEFUL LIVING

Mining Fo' Meaning

◂ *Illustration by Trenton Dukes*

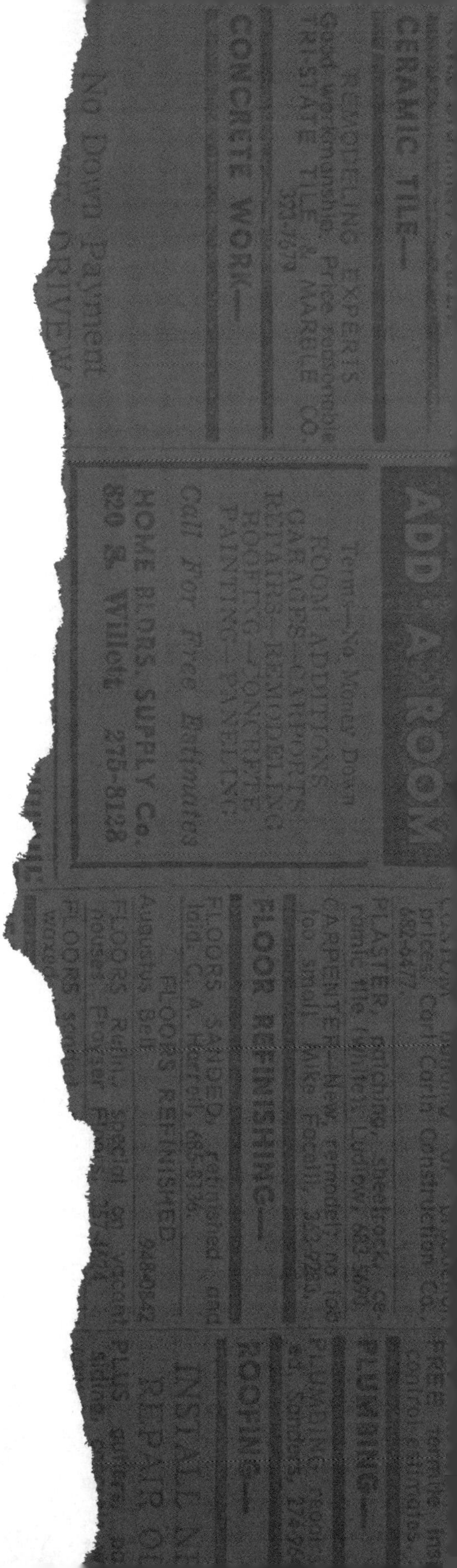

LEARNING OBJECTIVES

In this crash course, you will ...

- ✓ Take a quiz to determine if you're living your purpose, or think you ruined it with bad decisions
- ✓ Analyze case studies on people who found their purpose and are living it while incarcerated
- ✓ Decide the life path you're committed to: dying in shackles, or dying as a free person

In Hustle Guides 1-12, take in-depth courses and gain insight into:

- ✓ Finding your purpose
- ✓ Starting your own nonprofit
- ✓ Implementing your Generous Hustle
- ✓ Money and happiness
- ✓ Healthy living and longevity

> Life is never made unbearable by circumstances, but only by lack of meaning and purpose.
>
> - Viktor Frankl

> I want to live my life in such a way that when I get out of bed in the morning, the devil says, "Aw sh*t, he's up!"
>
> - Steve Maraboli

> Stop letting who you were talk you out of who you're becoming.
>
> - Unknown

NO JUDGMENT QUIZ: AM I LIVING WITH PURPOSE?

	AGREE	DISAGREE
I'm proud of the way I've used my time while incarcerated.	☐	☐
If I weren't here, people would miss the positive impact I make every day.	☐	☐
I feel joy and passion serving others and making a difference.	☐	☐
I know my life's purpose.	☐	☐
I am living out my life's purpose every day.	☐	☐
I believe that living with purpose means I have to change the world.	☐	☐
I've ruined my purpose because I'm incarcerated.	☐	☐
There is nothing special about me that could make a difference.	☐	☐
I want to find my purpose, but don't know where to start.	☐	☐
There is no purpose to life; trying to find one is a waste of time.	☐	☐
Being a good family member can be a purpose in life.	☐	☐
I don't have the resources to live out my purpose.	☐	☐
Living with purpose is only for people who are spiritual or religious.	☐	☐
I thought I found purpose when I joined homies in committing crimes.	☐	☐
I will live with purpose when I'm free; for now, I want to keep my head down.	☐	☐
My purpose in life has changed over the years.	☐	☐
I don't have time to help anyone else.	☐	☐
I don't think I can help anyone else; I can't even help myself.	☐	☐

One thing I've realized about myself through this quiz:

____

> I've learned that people will forget what you said, people will forget what you did, but people will never forget how you made them feel.
>
> - Maya Angelou

> One of the best ways to influence people is to make them feel important.
>
> - Roy T. Bennett

PASSPORT

GENEROUS

Chinese Traditional	kāngǩai
French	généreuse
German	großzügig
Portuguese	generoso
Spanish	generoso
Swahili	mkarimu

DID I RUIN MY PURPOSE?

It's easy to think, "How can I live out my purpose? I've ruined my chance."

Many people in the world think similarly: they've ruined their purpose because of one excuse or another. Sometimes single parents say they're too busy to live purposefully; uneducated people say they need an education first; people who struggle to pay the bills say they need financial stability before they can live their purpose.

The reality is that every one of us can live with purpose if we choose to love and care for others. We have to take off the selfish blinders that say, "I can't." Some will choose to stay self-centered; others will get out of their comfort zones and start today.

Many Mavericks are living their purposes while incarcerated. They found innovative, appropriate ways to serve the incarcerated population, c/o's, and people in the world. They refuse to let incarceration stop them. If you think you've blown your one shot at living out your purpose, read on!

FINDING MY PURPOSE IN PRISON

Timmie was released from Pelican Bay in 2019 and now works as an addiction counselor.

By Timothy Staley
aka Sweet Tim&M

As someone who spent over 15 years in the SHU, I'm here to bear witness that not only is kindness not a weakness, it is one of the greatest strengths I have acquired.

If an entire population spends decades believing something, wouldn't it make us brave to go against the status quo? That's what I did.

In our Impact Challenge, we dared each other to get out of our comfort zones, and yes, maybe embarrass ourselves a bit. It changed the way I treated people, and it changed how they interacted with me. When you add a little kindness into any situation, it can have a ripple effect.

One of my favorite acts of kindness was on my neighbor's birthday. We didn't talk much (he was of another race) ... but I changed that. I got everyone in the pod to make g-bars and we signed a card for him. When he came out of his cell, I still remember the look of shock and gratitude on his face. What I remember even better is the satisfaction I felt from helping out another human, regardless of his race or affiliations. From that point, we continued the tradition for each birthday, and the love and unity we felt was inspiring.

This was in an eight-man pod in the Pelican Bay SHU. If it can be done there, it can be done anywhere. I challenge you to think outside of the box. Who knows, it could change your life ... It certainly changed mine.

We don't have to do all of it alone. We were never meant to.
- Brené Brown

OUR CANCER WALK

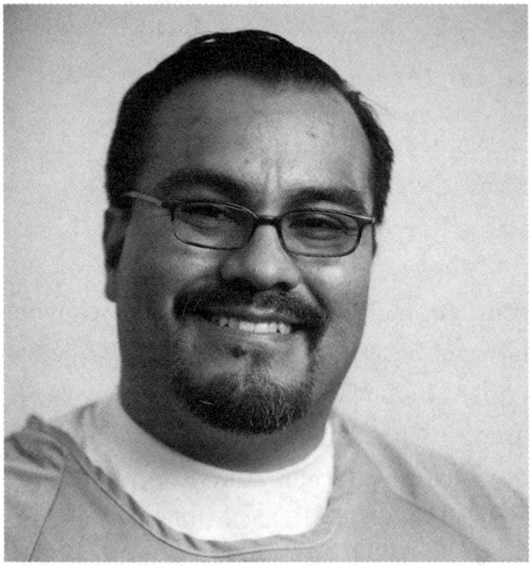

By Abel Torres
aka Fuzzy Koala Bear

Pelican Bay's first benefit walk was born in the Facility B gym during a program function. There, I saw men dropping the thug mugs that they held up for so long. I made the decision to drop my own, and wondered if some staff felt similarly. I took my chances and approached a staff member and made my ask: "What do you think about having a charity walk to benefit those battling cancer?"

I wish I could say the entire process went smoothly. It didn't. Pelican Bay had never had anything close to what I was proposing, but it didn't stop me from following up with staff every chance I got, persistently inquiring about any progress. It took about six months of making a pest out of myself. Finally, we got the news; the warden approved the walk for B Yard.

Before it happened, I had to pass out signed sheets to prove to the National Cancer Society that if they made the effort to haul out to Pelican Bay, it would be worthwhile. Over seven hundred men signed up! Then, more months of silence.

I persisted with my inquiries to staff. I was frustrated and very discouraged at times. It seemed as if someone just wanted to see if they could wait me out and eventually, I'd give up and move on. If this was the case, boy were they wrong!

I needed this walk to happen. In 2013, I lost my son to cancer. He was 15 years old and didn't even know he had cancer until it was too late. Less than two months later, Abel Jr. was dead. I was in the SHU and there was nothing I could say or do to comfort his brother and sister. But this was something I could do in his honor. There was no way I would give up on this.

I am thankful to two staff members who were just as determined as I was. They did everything in their power, and even used their personal time to help us out.

What is one small act of kindness you could perform in the next 24 hours to brighten someone's day?

Solidarity

Illustration by Trenton Dukes

Y E A Q J V J C R E

F I L H B L A L H F V B C T F J

O Z H O C U W W U G C P L N D U L C Q M

Z K J X R J O T K Z G A D J W K K N Y H O K

H I N A W S T D X M P V V C G I M E T Q R W I K U M

K D Z F P G L D V X S P D Z V P F C I C E M Y Y W C I I

V J P Y J J N M M S L M X A E M Q Y Z M H F M P V B G D B D

L R N H D I I N D O X U N E J S N I D T R L Z K X N W Q Q R W N

C R O P D U S T O C T I Z B A E S U K E I D X O T M G I F L V J

Z Z R C H U H Z X M A Y R K V T E U I N U N R Y Q B Z T W N A Z W F

S K E E D S L D V Z J J O E A K Y P V W O R X U G J U E L E R H U M J O

Q N C C T K L V C E R C Z J Q H D B I W K N E Q Y E Y D F Q A P O D K Q

G B D J D R S Q Z A F F K R H E B S I P H Q N Y V B I T V D V M M U S F M W

C F F X A Q F E T E V T G C E S A L J R P S U E S D G N N C D Z S W R U C I

Y C P M X Q V S V W D N E S Y V U E V Q H Y R O O K P F U I N Z J C O I H Z

J W C D F F Z I W R B Q Y U X Y K I S N S V U G E V H D I Q B L U F A S R T D G

J V I B B W I V X W G J I E Q U R E S M P T G Y T D K I L E T R G T N W T K T Y

K K I S I M I W J U P Y Y W T Z R C Q O I U X D Z O A E K X N L Q S H Z C F H Q

S T C K P I R Z P X T D E H W V T X M X L V C P P O L E M E W G H F Y R U V W N

N W D H M V Q S Y F L I U N I T Y B O S B P V V Z C I B L F N G D Q R U I F W B

P H G L X J E H M W S M Z C R Z F J Y E Z Y X B M X U K K W X P V S I N U K F H

O I Q Z D W V H P S Q S E I L R W R S W T L L E D S F J I Q C B Y H O I R P R Y

V C D M P I Q O F Z S R G E X Y A V I S W A S T M H S W X E E Z A N S W N C C O

G U B Q O U A C A E G V N R S M N S E C L R V S O H R Q C C B N Q M M J E H Z V

H X X V W T V R N G Z W N M O I X N A S G Y A N I N Y R A P Z O B F Y W L W A K

W G A H S I T R P K Y K Z X W O E Z Y Q P E X O F S F W Z M R Y G C B M L Z

G K H I L A V O H R Y V Q T H T D M A W Y P C Q H Z F O T W A W K S G U W J

G F W D E F W A C E U E L G V N H Y G B B K S N C A A J O D P D R F E U N T

W V R Z W N A T T A T T X L T V S A L I H T U E O O I X O F G G S Z A N

S G B A X C T R I C G K O G J P D H Y O Q X U R T G Q B O G W C J D N B

Z I F V J K N R O Y D H E F G P F C W X L K K A S M O Z N D Q X Z P

T H I M L H X G T N J G S E Y W L P X B A N X V I I A J D K D G A W

G O F W D U Y F Z I Q R J M W L I E K U W N A G C S N X E X S P

Y Y C D P N E O N L B E Y L T E F T D B Y Z K V O R E L T X

G I I C Z G S D C X D W O I Y R A F W A K N V C P E A O

K R V U M D E U X K T D W V A Y K Z R O E U T N R P

R B D X I D M T B Y K E Y Z Z J T Z S L J O B I

J J A E Y U H L P M S O W W A I C L W T

Q R N K V C L K L C B E J R K T

Y T C F V Q K V M M

COMPASSION
CROP DUST
DIARRHEA
EXPLOSIVE
GREATNESS
GROWTH
HONESTY
HONEY BADGER
INTEGRITY
LEADERSHIP
MOTIVATION
PERSISTENCE
SBD
SERVICE
SHART
SKIDMARK
SLUGGO
TEAMWORK
UNITY
VALUES

YOUR GUARDIAN ANGEL

Don't get tripped up if you don't believe in God or spiritual things. Some of us might not like the idea of guardian angels because we think, "If I had one, where was he when I was a kid??"

Just for a second, imagine you are outside your body; you are the most mature, loving protector and nurturer of your soul.

What do you want for your own future? What would you want your priority and identity to be?

GUARDIAN ANGEL

Noun

A spirit that is believed to watch over and protect a person or place.

LOVE BOMBS FROM MY GUARDIAN ANGEL

Check off things you would tell yourself if your only job in life was to guard, love, and nurture your soul:

- ☐ You are lovable and worthy of love.
- ☐ You matter to this world.
- ☐ Though you've been through so much pain, your future can be redeemable and meaningful.
- ☐ I forgive you.
- ☐ You were meant for more.
- ☐ You are capable of transforming and obtaining peace and fulfillment.
- ☐ Leaving the criminal life isn't easy, but you've got this, and you will reap the rewards that will come from a legal life.

- ☐ You'll never amount to anything.
- ☐ You don't deserve forgiveness, peace, or joy.
- ☐ No one needs you out there anyway.
- ☐ You deserve to die in prison.
- ☐ You're nothing but a criminal and a gang member; stop trying to think otherwise.
- ☐ Your value is dependent on your criminal resume. Go put in more work so you can be somebody.
- ☐ You might as well drop out of this program because it's a waste; a bunch of worthless dreams.

The second column represents how our haters have spoken to us for much of our lives. The problem is that sometimes our biggest hater lives in between our ears.

Who would you be if you spoke to yourself every day as your guardian angel would?

Are you willing to at least try to love yourself the way your guardian angel would?

☐ Yes ☐ No

WERE YOU MEANT FOR MORE?

We believe we're capable of greatness as parents, romantic partners, entrepreneurs, employees, community volunteers, and role models. We have important stories to tell.

Think about what your eulogy could sound like, years or decades from now, if you Squared Up and cut ties with the criminal life. *Check off what your future could realistically involve:*

- ☐ Earning your physical freedom
- ☐ Finishing college
- ☐ Never being incarcerated again
- ☐ Spending quality time with family
- ☐ Enjoying a romantic partner
- ☐ Getting or staying in a good marriage
- ☐ Having kids
- ☐ Being a great parent
- ☐ Being a great grandparent
- ☐ Attending key events (birthday parties, graduations, weddings, funerals)
- ☐ Enjoying good health
- ☐ Holding down a fulfilling career
- ☐ Taking vacations
- ☐ Traveling the country
- ☐ Traveling to other countries
- ☐ Renting your own place
- ☐ Buying a home
- ☐ Giving back/volunteering
- ☐ Being a devoted member of a spiritual community
- ☐ Being a philanthropist
- ☐ Enjoying retirement

What is one thing you can start doing (or stop doing) today to lean into your future?

____

IF YOU DIED TODAY, WHY WOULD YOUR LIFE MATTER?

Yeah, we've posed this question a few times already. Tough question. Especially when most of us have been told our whole lives that we didn't matter.

Our pasts could lead us to painfully conclude that maybe the haters were right. But we get to claim today. Today, we're in a program that matters. Today, we're spreading a movement that matters.

Today, I accept me. I choose to love me. I choose to matter.

One of the best ways to matter is to make a positive difference in people's lives. We're doing that today. And tomorrow. And for the foreseeable future.

> Imagine if you will, being on your death bed – and standing around your bed – the ghosts of the ideas, the dreams, the abilities, the talents given to you by life. And that you for whatever reason, you never acted on those ideas, you never pursued that dream, you never used those talents, we never saw your leadership, you never used your voice, you never wrote that book. And there they are standing around your bed looking at you with large angry eyes saying we came to you, and only you could have given us life! Now we must die with you forever.
>
> The question is – if you die today, what ideas, what dreams, what abilities, what talents, what gifts, would die with you?
>
> – Les Brown

RELEASE·PLANS
SUCCESS
Get Job

REENTRY

Get Out the Do' Fo'Sho'

◂ *Illustration by Trenton Dukes*

LEARNING OBJECTIVES

In this crash course, you will...

- ✓ Learn about preparation and separating yourself from crimeys through a case study
- ✓ Get curious about loved ones' expectations for your release
- ✓ Reconnect with loved ones by completing a 50-question survey together to prepare for reentry

In Hustle Guides 1-12, take in-depth courses and gain insight into:

- ✓ Creating realistic reentry plans
- ✓ Success tips for parole and probation
- ✓ Obtaining essential documents
- ✓ Your release countdown
- ✓ Learning lessons from released graduates

GETTING CURIOUS ABOUT OUR LOVED ONES' EXPECTATIONS

H2.0 families reunite at Pelican Bay

We can't set expectations for anyone but ourselves. Sometimes our families have unrealistic and romanticized expectations of us and of our release. After all, they've been waiting for years for "that day," and romanticized thinking might be keeping their hope alive. You see those tear-jerking reunions on TV and think it will be just like that. That may happen for you, but that is an expectation, and if it doesn't happen, you (or they) might feel let down.

Loved ones' unrealistic expectations create unnecessary pressure, and in turn lead us to fail, or create disappointment, resentment, and distance in the relationships that matter most to us.

It can be helpful to start by asking your loved ones what they expect for your release. If they say "nothing," they're not keeping it 100. They likely haven't thought through all the details of what the coming days with you around will look like … and this is an opportunity for you to open that conversation. If someone cares about you, they likely have positive and negative expectations, fears, hopes, etc.; they're human! It could really help to talk through expectations before your release.

What is one romanticized expectation you or your loved ones have about your release?

SURVEYING YOUR LOVED ONES: 50 REENTRY QUESTIONS

We don't recommend overwhelming your family by sending this entire survey … besides, some of the questions are specific to romantic partners, kids, friends, etc. Know your audience!

Pick three questions to ask a specific individual, by phone or in a letter, and gauge how they like the discussion. If you have kids, engage them in your post-release planning process by asking their opinions as well.

Our Hustle Guides contain a few hundred questions, along with step-by-step guidance, for you and your loved ones. Try on this sampling of important questions!

Circle the three most important questions you will ask a loved one in the next week.

1. On a scale of 1-10, how afraid are you that I'll get arrested again (1 is not scared at all, 10 is extremely scared), and why?
2. What three things excite you the most about my release?
3. What are three activities you most look forward to sharing with me?
4. What are your three biggest fears/concerns/doubts about me coming home?
5. What steps can I take to reconnect with you? What can I start doing now?

6. What three things can I do once I'm home to build and keep your trust?
7. What is one way I could improve my communication with you, starting now, so we can communicate effectively when I'm home?
8. Can you share with me any expectations about my release that could be unrealistic (e.g., "You'll be a millionaire in your first six months out")?
9. What are your expectations about who I am now vs. who I used to be?
10. Where are you expecting me to live (or where in the house will I stay), and how long do you expect me to live there? Do you want me to contribute to rent? How much, and starting how soon?
11. What are some things I could do to help out around the house?
12. Would you be willing to make the house compliant with my parole/probation conditions, and have monthly home inspections from my PO?
13. If any family is involved in gang or criminal activity, are you okay with them not coming to the house?
14. Will you be understanding that I will need quiet space and time to adjust?
15. Would you be willing to go to the Office of Vital Statistics, request, and pay for my birth certificate? *(Biological parents and spouses can do this before your release.)*
16. What kind of activities do you want to do together when I get home?
17. What can I do to respect your space and individualism?
18. How will we help the kids adjust to my presence?
19. How do you expect me to share in parenting responsibilities and decisions?
20. What forms of discipline do you use, and not use, in disciplining the kids?
21. How do you expect me to participate in disciplining our kids?
22. What are your challenges with the children?
23. What are boundaries you want me to observe with co-parenting?
24. How will we share finances?
25. What will we do to prevent getting pregnant before we're ready to be responsible for a new life?
26. What are some dates you'd like to go on together?
27. What are your expectations around faithfulness?
28. Is there anything I should know now that will affect our relationship after I'm out?
29. How can I respect your social life?
30. What are some ground rules we should establish when we get into an argument?
31. What are the best ways I can show you love and support?

32. Do you have any health or dietary issues? Do you want to know about mine?
33. Will you take me shopping and help me purchase clothes?
34. What secondhand stores are around so I can buy affordable clothes?
35. Can I borrow your car once I get a license? How often can I use it? How will you want me to contribute to the costs? Will you add me to your insurance?
36. Are you in a position to help me financially? How much can you afford to spend on me, and for how long, before I'm providing for myself?
37. Do you exercise? How often? Where and how? Will you exercise with me?
38. How has your spiritual life changed since I was incarcerated? What spiritual disciplines will we share?
39. What views, values, and spiritual practices do we want to teach our children?
40. What are your expectations for me when it comes to quality time? What does "quality time" look like for you?
41. Who would you like me to get to know? Is there anyone you will hesitate in introducing me to, or anyone who might not be supportive of you being with me?
42. How would you feel if I went out with friends without you?
43. Will you support me if I feel the need to cut off negative friendships?
44. Who would you like me to avoid spending time with?
45. How will you hold me accountable when I am around people or places that aren't good for me?
46. Can I count on you for direct feedback when you perceive I'm making a mistake or am heading down a path you don't like?
47. Will you help me out when I appear to be antisocial … or too social?
48. What technology do you have available for me to use, or what technology will you purchase for my use?
49. Will you show me where to take tutorials on the internet to learn to use technology? How tech-savvy are you?
50. Is there anything about the way I look or dress that makes you uncomfortable? If so, what would you like me to change?

Who are the three most important people for you to discuss your post-release plans with?

____

HONEY BADGER HOT SNICKERDOODLE SURPRISE

Makes one serving

Ingredients

2 packs of Snickerdoodle cookies
2 packs of Peanut butter
2 packs of Sugar
8 oz of Milk
1 shot of Cinnamon

Instructions

- [ ] Heat up milk in your hot pot.
- [ ] With a cup or the palm of your hand, crush the cookies until they are powder.
- [ ] Place the peanut butter packs in warm water for 5-10 minutes; then roll them around in the palm of your hand until they are soft.
- [ ] When the milk begins to boil, pour half of the milk into your cup and then empty the peanut butter into the cup, stirring until the peanut butter has dissolved.
- [ ] Pour cookies into cup, along with 2 sugar packs and 1 shot of cinnamon, stirring it occasionally.
- [ ] Continue to stir until all ingredients have blended, adding water until the mixture has reached your desired thickness.
- [ ] Ask your cellie if he's going to eat his cookies, get out your pencil and a blank sheet of paper, and start writing SMART goals for reentry. Oh, and enjoy that thick drink.

YOU BE THE JUDGE: IS FREEDOM OVERRATED?

Put yourself in the judge's shoes and reflect on your past three years ... Would you let yourself out? Answer the questions even if you weren't caught.

		TRUE	FALSE
1.	I have not participated in a self-help program (before H2.0).	☐	☐
2.	I was found guilty of a major disciplinary case.	☐	☐
3.	I was in possession of a weapon or weapons stock.	☐	☐
4.	I had clothes lines and curtains hanging up.	☐	☐
5.	I used or sold drugs or alcohol.	☐	☐
6.	I bought alcohol making materials.	☐	☐
7.	I got a fresh tattoo or tatted someone else.	☐	☐
8.	I used an illegal cell phone.	☐	☐
9.	The people I've hung around most discuss gang or criminal activity.	☐	☐
10.	I had contraband that could've gotten me a write-up.	☐	☐
11.	I hung around the poker table (even if I didn't play).	☐	☐
12.	I made money through an illegal hustle.	☐	☐
13.	I skipped school or work.	☐	☐
14.	I skipped a self-help group meeting.	☐	☐
15.	I stole from work (pens, food, cleaning supplies).	☐	☐
16.	I lied to my family about my release date because I got another write-up.	☐	☐
17.	I'm a gang member but won't admit it.	☐	☐
18.	I believe I was just in the wrong place at the wrong time when it comes to my crime.	☐	☐

		TRUE	FALSE
19.	I take classes to rack up certificates but rarely internalize the information; much of it is in-one-ear-and-out-the-other.	☐	☐
20.	If released, I plan to go back to live with family or loved ones who are using drugs or engaging in illegal activities.	☐	☐
21.	I'm still writing to or speaking with homies who are involved in criminal activity on the streets.	☐	☐
22.	I can't really explain the reason why I committed my crime.	☐	☐

KEY:
Especially if these statements are true for you in the past three years, you're proving that you think freedom is overrated. Number of true answers:
1-5: Ask yourself why you care more about these things than your freedom.
6-10: You seem to like it in there.
11+: Must be hard living the Don't Care Policy

Do You Really Want to Reenter Society?

If your goal is to earn and/or keep your freedom and you don't like the score on your self-assessment, what are you going to do about it? Will you make changes starting today … or throw your hands in the air and give up? Look at your options and seriously think about your answer before you make your choice. Check off your answer:

- ☐ I will take the first step today to make a change to earn my freedom.
- ☐ I give up; I'm comfortable spending the rest of my life in prison.

If you're willing to take that first step today, what is it? Stop and write the first step you can take while you're feeling clear about the future you're aiming for:

___

CASE STUDY: FROM THE CELL BLOCKS TO THE SIDEWALKS

By Timothy Staley
aka Sweet Tim&M
Released November 2019 from Pelican Bay

After spending nearly all of my adult life incarcerated, most of it in SHU, I had an epiphany; I don't have to live this way anymore. If I believed in myself, I could succeed where so many times I failed. A crazy thing happened; it worked!

From that point forward, my life changed. I got two years knocked off my sentence due to good behavior credits and acquired tools to help me succeed upon my release.

However, as I was soon to learn, even the best-laid plans can fail. Due to a lockdown at Pelican Bay the day of my release, I was late to the Greyhound station. I missed my prepaid bus home. I had to purchase another ticket to a different town because the next bus to my hometown wasn't for 12 hours (and CDCR didn't want me hanging around town all day). I ended up spending more money and going to a place I didn't want to be.

It was a defining moment in my transformation. It reminded me that no matter how well I am doing or how positive I feel, obstacles will continue to present themselves. It is up to me to decide how I react. In the past, a situation like this would frustrate me and I would react negatively. This time, I recognized the importance of focusing on the solution to the problem, rather than the problem itself. I ended up having a nice trip and enjoyed some beautiful scenery.

I recognized the importance of focusing on the solution to the problem, rather than the problem itself.

The first week after my release, it seemed like all I did was wait in a line or sit in a lobby, filling out paperwork, just to wait in more lines. Sure, I am used to waiting in canteen lines, but it's still frustrating.

The worst was when I waited in line for two hours to get my commercial driver's license at the DMV. I breathed a sigh of relief as I made it to the clerk, but my relief was short-lived. I couldn't even apply for this type of license without my birth certificate and my social security card. I had neither. So, I waited in line for no reason, right?

No, the situation taught me one of the most important lessons thus far: the power of preparation. Over half of the work I do out here is in preparation. It's important to always make to-do lists, then make notations on everything needed for each task.

For example, I had a doctor's appointment on a Friday. On Wednesday, I looked at the doctor's website to see what documents I'd need to bring. I needed my medical insurance card. I didn't have the card yet and wouldn't receive it for a few weeks by mail. I Googled to find out how to get an early copy. I learned I could go to the welfare office and request a temporary printout that the doctor would accept. It worked out.

Which leads me to my next topic: technology! It's amazing how advanced it is out here! It can be overwhelming, but it is a great advantage for us. Google is so useful; we can ask it any question imaginable. For every technology tool, there are free YouTube videos you can watch to learn how to use them.

Another issue that I faced in my transition is deciding who to associate with. This is crucial, because up until now, I have had one type of people that I hung out with my whole life. I have a lot of love for them and the memories shared, no matter how bad some of them were. But now, because I value my freedom, I choose to be selfish when it comes to who I surround myself with. This time, I'm looking out for my future.

From day one, I have had old friends contact me daily, wanting to hang out. I realize that nothing had changed for them. They are doing the same things they did before I went to prison years ago. It only reinforced my commitment to the new path I'm on and my new hustle.

> I choose to be selfish when it comes to who I surround myself with. This time, I'm looking out for my future.

What has helped me significantly is the support system I found upon my release. When people see that you are putting in the positive work, they are more inclined to want to help you. I have the amazing opportunity to follow in the footsteps of two released fellow Honey Badgers: John Jackson and Silverio Strong. They have been a great resource for me. They went through the same journey as I did, they shared ideas, and give advice whenever I need it. It's so important to lean on people early on.

Take advantage of this opportunity. At the end of the day, it all comes down to how you want to live your life and what you want your legacy to be. The more of a chance you give yourself and the more you believe in yourself, the more people are willing to go out of their way to help you succeed. I've learned that I cannot do this on my own. Without the support of others, I am lost. Lucky for us, we have plenty of support, as long as we humble ourselves and put in the necessary footwork to help ourselves. If we do that, we are well on our way.

The more of a chance you give yourself and the more you believe in yourself, the more people are willing to go out of their way to help you succeed.

On a scale of 1-10, how much do you believe in yourself and your resolve to keep your freedom once you're out? Explain why you picked this number.

What could you start (or stop) doing today to believe in yourself a little more?

Which friends or family will you need to cut out of your life to maintain your freedom?

FREEDOM

Chinese Traditional	zìyóu
French	liberté
German	Freiheit
Portuguese	liberdade
Spanish	libertad
Swahili	uhuru

CASE STUDY: BEHIND BARS TO THE BAHAMAS

By Corey McCarthy
Founder & CEO, McCarthy I.E.

I spent seven years, three months, and 10 days in prison in New York. Two words that got me through prison were: endure and overcome.

Right after getting out, I started my business, McCarthy I.E., with nothing but a bike, a duffel bag, and two sheets for drop cloths. I.E. stands for a working example of integrity and efficiency.

In the past seven years, I've grown my company to seven employees, including some who were formerly incarcerated and were refugees. I've remodeled more than 1,000 homes, businesses, and historic landmarks, with annual revenues exceeding $400,000.

I flew to the Bahamas my first day off parole … and sipped on the fruity little mocktails (keeping my sobriety) with the pink umbrellas in 'em.

I now fly all over the country to volunteer my time and share my story in prisons. I serve on the Board of Directors of Peace Prints of Western New York, an organization that helps released people find housing and employment. I also started and run men's groups in Buffalo that promote emotional maturity.

In jail, nearly everybody returns … All you ever hear are excuses and, "I couldn't get a job and my parole officer sent me back."

You never see the guy who doesn't come back … but I wanted you to see me. You can do it too.

What will you do the first day you don't have to answer to a PO?

CRAY

A little old lady was walking down the street dragging two large plastic garbage bags behind her.

One of the bags was ripped and every once in a while, a $20 bill fell out onto the sidewalk.

Noticing this, a policeman stopped her and said, "Ma'am, there are $20 bills falling out of that bag."

"Oh, really? Darn it!" said the little old lady. "I'd better go back and see if I can find them. Thanks for telling me, Officer."

"Well, now, not so fast," said the police officer. "Where did you get all that money? You didn't steal it, did you?"

"Oh, no, no," said the old lady. "You see, my backyard is right next to a golf course. A lot of golfers come and wee wee through a knot hole in my fence, right into my flower garden. It used to really tick me off. Kills the flowers, you know. Then I thought, why not make the best of it?"

"So, now, I stand behind the fence by the knot hole, real quiet, with my hedge clippers. Every time some guy sticks his thing through my fence, I surprise him, grab hold of it and say, 'O.K., buddy! Give me $20 or off it comes!'"

"Well, that seems only fair," said the police officer, laughing. "OK. Good luck! Oh, by the way, what's in the other bag?"
"Not everybody pays," she said.

CRAY

ANGER MANAGEMENT

Unnecessary Roughness

◄ *Illustration by David Vaquera*

LEARNING OBJECTIVES

In this crash course, you will ...

- ✓ Identify the roots of your anger, and think about the last time your anger chose for you
- ✓ Analyze a case study on anger, the costs and consequences of anger, and the violence in your past
- ✓ Learn strategies for not taking the bait

In Hustle Guides 1-12, take in-depth courses and gain insight into:

- ✓ Recognizing the roots of anger
- ✓ Nonviolent communication
- ✓ Conflict resolution
- ✓ Dealing with betrayal and infidelity
- ✓ Dealing with childhood wounds

NO JUDGMENT QUIZ: YOU MAD?

	AGREE	DISAGREE
1. I'm aware of the roots of my anger.	☐	☐
2. I've gotten treatment for my anger problems.	☐	☐
3. I'm always successful in restraining myself from acting out violently.	☐	☐
4. Anger is a choice.	☐	☐
5. Anger is an emotion that cannot be controlled.	☐	☐
6. I never get angry; I merely get my point across.	☐	☐
7. Anger almost always compounds the problem.	☐	☐
8. Anger is a natural and instinctive protection mechanism.	☐	☐
9. I don't get angry; I get even.	☐	☐

When you peel back the onion, what is the greatest source of your anger or resentment in life?

WHEN ANGER CHOOSES FOR US

In Sacramento in June of 2018, a simple mistake of cutting someone off led to a shooting and a suicide.

ABC News reported:

Things escalated quickly. When the cars stopped at the off-ramp, Timothy Mann went to confront Bell even though Nancie Mann and her son both begged him to stay in the car. With both men out of their vehicles, Timothy Mann approached Bell, even though the gun was in plain view, and punched him. Bell shot Mann in the face at point-blank range, and Mann died almost instantly, despite his son's efforts to resuscitate him.

Bell insisted that the shooting was an accident, that he was acting in self-defense. He blamed the victim, Timothy Mann.

"He hit me harder than a mule kick. That's what caused the gun to go off," Bell told one reporter.

But apparently, he couldn't live with the guilt.

Two weeks later, on another Sunday morning, Bell returned to the scene of the crime. He dialed 911 on his mobile phone and identified himself to the dispatcher.

"My name is Donald R. Bell. I was involved in that Hazel incident that happened two weeks ago," he said. "I am going to serve justice on myself."

Bell pulled his white pickup truck to the pile of rocks that marked where he had killed Timothy Mann. This time he pointed the gun at his own head, and pulled the trigger.

Wright, David. "Road Rage Leads to Shooting, Suicide." ABC News, 7 January 2006, https://abcnews.go.com/US/story?id=93070. Accessed 7 September 2018.

When you walk around angry or hateful about the past, who is in control? Are you in control of yourself - or is your anger - or is your betrayer - in control?

According to Jean Lawrence, who wrote *The Root of All Road Rage*:

> *"One study estimates that more than half of all drivers have experienced a surge of road rage at some point, although not all bang into the offender's rear bumper, pull a pistol, or hurl a helpless puppy into oncoming traffic. Still, tens of thousands of accidents happen each year because of aggressive driving, which is also a leading cause of death for young children."*

Have you ever thought about the *root* of road rage?

Isn't it incredibly sad that a human was murdered over something as trivial as a traffic run-in?

Have you seen something similar while incarcerated? Maybe someone got stabbed because they cut in line, or got beat up for saying the wrong thing.

No one can change their past. No one.

When you walk around angry or hateful about the past, who is in control? Are you in control of yourself – or is your anger – or is your betrayer – in control?

Most of us have allowed our anger to control us.

When did your anger recently choose for you? What was the outcome?

How will you become your best self if you keep living in anger or pain from your past?

Violence is the last refuge of the incompetent.

- *Isaac Asimov*

THE COSTS AND CONSEQUENCES OF ANGER

Check off the costs and consequences you've experienced as a result of making decisions out of your past pains, anger, etc.

- ☐ Fighting
- ☐ Getting seriously injured
- ☐ Getting arrested
- ☐ Getting incarcerated
- ☐ Losing freedom
- ☐ Going crazy on someone who didn't deserve it
- ☐ Getting addicted to something
- ☐ Losing privileges over write-ups
- ☐ Getting additional time
- ☐ Going to the hole
- ☐ Losing friendships
- ☐ Losing relationships or closeness with family or loved ones
- ☐ Losing trust in others or myself
- ☐ Losing trust from someone else
- ☐ Living with anxiety
- ☐ Suffering from regrets over the pain I've caused
- ☐ Losing sleep
- ☐ Being mad at myself for acting like an idiot

What other physical or emotional consequences resulted from living in anger or pain? Who would you be and what would your future hold if you stopped being angry?

The saying goes, "hurt people hurt people."

We all want to be freed of emotional pain from the past; but not everyone is willing to do the hard work to obtain freedom.

Freedom is a full-time job. When we're mad, it's often because we're sad underneath. Sometimes mad is easier to deal with than sad.

Some of us have said emotions are for suckas, but realistically, they're something most of us never learned to deal with.

We have traditionally viewed sadness as a weakness. It opens us up to vulnerability. Mad, however, opens us up to violence. When we're mad, we look tough and intimidating. When we let our anger choose for us, we find ourselves in the hole, even angrier than before. We blame the victim, the object of our anger, and tell ourselves, "They had it coming" or, "I had to do what I had to do."

We tell ourselves these lies to feed our anger, and we attempt to starve the sad. But it never goes away. We only get angrier and more violent, creating victim after victim (including ourselves).

THE CONSEQUENCES OF ANGER, PART 1

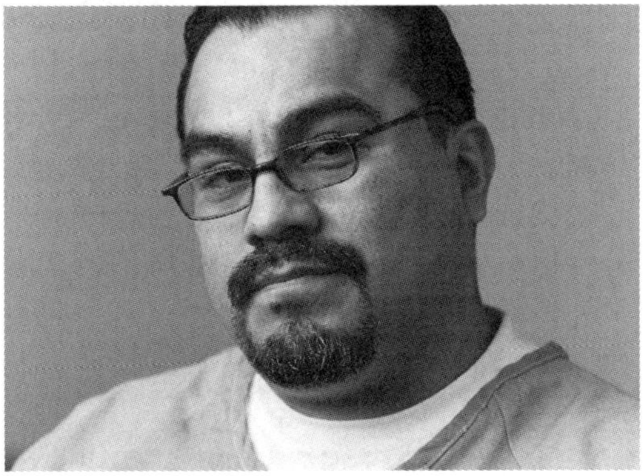

By Abel Torres
aka Fuzzy Koala Bear

For more than a year, my younger brother couldn't keep a job, citing "health reasons." His lack of drive bugged me.

A year later, he says, "I'll just move back in with mom and see what's up after that." I snapped. Pump your brakes, Speed Racer. He was willing to let mom carry his load while he "figured it out"?

> My turning point came the day I realized my anger stemmed from my shame.

I tore into him. I believed I was using a reasonable voice … but later learned I sounded like I was chewing rocks. Everything I felt carried through; I called him every form of lazy and irresponsible.

We stopped speaking. I said I didn't care. I was just as angry as he was. Then I tried to reach out, but it didn't work, so I piled on … I started mocking him to everyone. I chose to be angry and petty. Some older brother I was.

It took a family tragedy for us to speak. When we made up, he explained he wasn't angry, but ashamed because I said all the things he already said to himself. I admitted I was also secretly ashamed of myself.

That's where my real anger originated. I'm the elder brother. I should be taking care of things at home. Instead, I was upset at him for doing what I had been doing all these years ... depending on mom for the little things that make life comfortable.

My turning point came the day I realized my anger stemmed from my shame. I actually admitted this to him, and it's made us closer; more willing to "go there."

Had our family not suffered a death, our pride and anger would probably still have us separated. Anger cost me almost a year with my only brother.

When has pride or anger separated you from loved ones or an opportunity?

THE CONSEQUENCES OF ANGER, PART 2

My wife threw a barbecue for my birthday. It was the first family gathering and celebration in … a long time. My older cousin came over. I thought he wanted to wish me a happy birthday. Nope! He decided it was a good time to get a few things off his chest.

He started in on me about the way I was living and the danger I was putting my family in. My cousin had a point; a year before, my older brother was murdered in front of me.

I hadn't seen my cousin since I was five, and all I could think was, "Is this fool serious?" I remember standing up after he said, "I kept telling you two to stay out of trouble!"

Everything else is a blur. My family tried pulling me off him. I had my arms around his neck after he passed out.

I couldn't believe what I had done to my cousin. I had blacked out. Looking down at him, seeing my hands bruised and bloody, unable to remember how it happened, it seriously scared me.

> I pushed my rage down … until it came out against a member of my family. Who knows where I would have stopped?

I hadn't cried since the day my brother died. I lost myself in anything that could block out the pain anytime my brother came to mind. I pushed my rage down … until it came out against a member of my family.

Not grieving or talking about my loss led to this blowup. I'm thankful there were people to pull me off. Who knows where I would have stopped?

It's been over 21 years, and my cousin and I still haven't spoken. I lost two family members in one year.

When has your anger led you to get carried away?

STRATEGIES FOR NOT TAKING THE BAIT

Check the top three strategies that would stop you from taking the bait.

- [ ] Walk away from confrontation.
- [ ] Sleep on it.
- [ ] Don't make decisions while acting emotionally.
- [ ] Don't try to win an argument; you'll lose in the process of trying to rationalize with a knucklehead.
- [ ] Play the tape forward: if you react, what will the consequences be? How did this end the last time you reacted?
- [ ] Choose forgiveness instead of retaliation.
- [ ] Busy yourself with something positive. Go find a game or pick up a time-consuming hobby, like a 1,000-piece puzzle.
- [ ] Know your triggers.
- [ ] Calm your tone. If you don't, the knucklehead will raise their voice as well. If you end up in a shouting match with a knucklehead, now who's the knucklehead?
- [ ] Mind your own business.
- [ ] Get an education so you won't be dumb enough to take the bait.

What situation tempts you most to act out?

___

When you find yourself in this situation, what's the best strategy for you to not take the bait?

___

BECOMING A MONSTER

Anonymous Author

The betrayal I experienced makes me mad. But if I keep it 100, I'm more sad than mad. I wanted and needed to trust him. I wanted to know I could at least trust *someone* in this world because I've been betrayed by so many others so many times. My own dad left me. It hurts to admit it to myself, but my mom cared more about her boyfriends and her dope than she cared about me.

I thought this homie was different. We'd have taken a bullet for one other. He had been my best friend for five years, the only person I confided in. I can't even count the times I saved him from trouble.

And then he sold me out.

At first, I was in denial, disbelief. When I confirmed it, I cried, in secret. I felt the weight of my sadness and disappointment.

That day, I swore I'd never trust again. I haven't cried since.

I built walls. Thick ones. Sad turned to mad. Now I can turn into a monster in two seconds.

I'm not sure that I even "turn into" a monster anymore. I've become a monster. Watch out if you cross me. Here I am in SHU. I tell myself I'm comfortable here; that life is easier here than on the mainline. Even though I haven't seen my family in 10 years. My daughter stopped writing. I'm lonely as hell. But I tell myself that I belong here. I don't see another future. I like being a criminal; at least it's something I'm good at. It's all I've known for 15 years.

Have you ever felt like a monster or thought that being a criminal was the only thing you'd be good at? When and why did you think this?

When was the most recent time your "sad" turned into "mad"?

H2.O LIB INSTRUCTIONS

Mavs, check out the instructions for the H2.O Lib. The funnier the words you choose to fill in the blanks, the better this turns out. Play this with your cellie. Here's your English lesson for the week.

Adjective	Describes something or somebody, like: dead, hairless, massive, chubby, hot, creepy, sloppy, cheap, naked, dopey, stubby, fugly, clumsy, frisky, ignant, worthless, goofy
Adverb	Tells how something is done. It modifies a verb and usually ends in "ly" like: accidentally, awkwardly, boldly, cautiously, poorly, recklessly
Verb	Describes an action, state, or occurrence, and forms the main part of the predicate of a sentence. Think, "to do something," like: fish, hoop, pound, sleep, shart, cheat, workout, bust down, prone out, resume, suck in, snoop, medicate
Noun	A person, place, or thing, like: moron, stank-breath, cellie, lazy-stick, hot pocket, stash spot, bird bath, burpee, bum, tweaker, homie, fool, dead weight, therapy
Exclamation or silly word	Any sort of funny sound, gasp, grunt, or cry, like: Corn nuts! Gadzooks! Leapin' Lizards! Schnikes!
Plural	Means more than one, like the plural of nut is: nuts

H2O LIB

Ear Hustling in the Vent

The Honey Badger Tongue-lashing his Cellie, Sluggo D. Sloth

You (Honey Badger): What's up __________ (homie's name), I hear that with all these __________ (adjective) laws changing, we can get up out of here sooner. I'm sick of being up in here and wearing this clown suit every day. Instead of lying around like a __________ (adjective) sloth like you, I'm gonna Hustle, __________ (verb), and invest my __________ (noun) in getting' out the do' fo'sho'. What's up with you, I always hear you bumpin' yo' gums about how think you're living that Badger life, but is it all __________ (noun), or are you down to put in the __________ (noun)? Quit playin', you's a bum.

You're really starting to get on my last nerve, Sluggo. When was the last time you even showered, you __________ (animal)? Man, I need a new cellie. You smell like __________ (number) day-old dog farts. You be waking up on fireman status every day; dang your ________________ (body part) stank! I'm cool with the games; I don't wanna have to tell my family that I'm not comin' ________________ (destination) 'cause I got some bunk write-up for being a dirtbag. Being a yard ________________ (noun) ain't what I'm about, time to get on my grind. You in or what?

Sluggo D. Sloth: Or What. The big D in my name stands for Dirtbag, yo. Kick rocks sucka, I got a nap with my name on it. By the way, can I borrow a ________________ (food item), fool? Lying on this bunk all day sho' makes me ________________ (adjective). Hit the light on yo' way out.

INNOCENCE STRIPPED BY FISTS

By Chris Succaw

aka Sweet Butter Pecan

I grew up in an angry place
Where violence was the go-to
More often than not
It was the usual go to.
Innocence stripped by fists
And vile words of degradation
This abuse caused me to grow up
Full of hatred, anger, and frustration.
Growing up I believed that being strong
Was me being violent,
And whenever tested or faced with fear,
Violence was the only way for me to get by it.
Eventually I grew tired
I sought out change
Found the courage to go for it
and let go of the pain.
Let go of the violence.
Let go of the guilt.
Let go of the change.
Let go of the wheel.
Began the process of navigating me to better places.
Healthier living.
More smiling faces.
Sill there remains much work to do
Yet my heart is now open for all the joy to come through.

NO JUDGMENT QUIZ: MY VIOLENT PAST

Reflect on the experiences and beliefs you had growing up. Put a check by the following statements that have been, or still are, true for you.

- [ ] I suffered through the loss of an immediate family member.
- [ ] One of my family members was murdered.
- [ ] I cared about someone who died from gang violence.
- [ ] Violence was committed against me at home.
- [ ] Violence was committed against me on the streets.
- [ ] I committed a violent act against someone else.
- [ ] I joined a gang.
- [ ] The way I was living, I thought there was a good chance I wouldn't make it to age 21.
- [ ] Violence has often been the only form of conflict resolution.
- [ ] I was desensitized to violence at a young age.
- [ ] I'm not even sure how to define violence.
- [ ] I believe that violence is the best way to protect myself.
- [ ] I feel like violence empowers me.
- [ ] I'm violent because of my environment; I have no other choice.
- [ ] I believe violence is necessary.
- [ ] I deeply regret some of my acts of violence.

VIOLENCE

Noun

The intentional use of physical force or power, threatened or actual, against oneself, another person, or against a group or community, which either results in or has a high likelihood of resulting in injury, death, psychological harm, maldevelopment, or deprivation.

CHARACTER DEVELOPMENT

You Ain't Gotta Lie to Kick It

◀ *Illustration by Trenton Dukes*

LEARNING OBJECTIVES

In this crash course, you will ...

- ✓ Complete a case study that leads you to consider forgiving yourself
- ✓ Study the consequences of unforgiveness, what it means to forgive, and how to do it
- ✓ Learn about vulnerability, depression, and healing from abuse
- ✓ Learn about lying to others and yourself, and how romanticized thinking keeps us locked up; take an assessment to discover the type of liar you are
- ✓ Take a quiz to assess your integrity and aspirations when it comes to integrity
- ✓ Learn tips for confession, and take an assessment to determine if you want to come clean
- ✓ Learn to work with accountability partners to reach your goals
- ✓ Understand the difference between values and beliefs, and how these affect your transformation
- ✓ Identify where you got your values from; take a values inventory to determine those that most impacted your life; determine the positive values that you want to embrace for a new future
- ✓ Determine the composition of your identity, and learn how to shift away from a criminal identity

In Hustle Guides 1-12, take in-depth courses and gain insight into:

- ✓ Self-limiting beliefs
- ✓ Accountability and commitments
- ✓ Evaluating your integrity
- ✓ The power of habit
- ✓ Studying personality types

VALUES VS. BELIEFS

The difference between values and beliefs can be confusing. Our values and beliefs both drive our actions, behaviors, and attitudes.

Values are things we think are important. Think: loyalty, equality, integrity, education, effort, and faithfulness.

These are all positive values, and when we think about values, it's natural to think of only the positive ones, because we often aren't aware of the negative values that drive our lives.

Values stem from our beliefs.

Our beliefs come from religion, parents, culture, TV, what we experience, etc. Beliefs are assumptions we make about the world. Beliefs are opinions that we form, and that we believe are so true that they are unmovable at the time.

We can easily form false beliefs, and from them, we can form values that won't serve us (or the world) very well.

VALUES

Noun

1. A person's principles or standards of behavior; one's judgment of what is important in life.
2. Important and lasting beliefs or ideals shared by the members of a culture about what is good or bad and desirable or undesirable. Values have major influence on a person's behavior and attitude and serve as broad guidelines in all situations. Some common business values are fairness, innovation, and community involvement.

BELIEFS

Noun

Assumptions and convictions that are held to be true, by an individual or a group, regarding concepts, events, people, and things.

MY VALUES

Think of your values and beliefs; where did you get them from? *Check all that apply:*

☐ Parents and family
☐ Friends/homies/peers
☐ Neighborhood culture/gangs
☐ Religion or spiritual books
☐ The workplace
☐ Educational institutions
☐ Significant life events and experiences (e.g., deaths, divorce, incarceration, trauma, health issues, etc.)
☐ Music or TV
☐ Media
☐ Politics
☐ Technology
☐ Major historical events (e.g., wars, economic depressions, etc.)

All of our values and beliefs evolve over time. Reflect on the definition of a belief: an acceptance that a statement is true or that something exists.

Many kids would swear on their lives that Santa's real. As they grow up, their beliefs and values evolve. So do ours.

We act on what we think. To evolve and transform, our values have to evolve too.

VALUES AND OUR TRANSFORMATION PROCESS

If we want to transform our hustle and our behavior, it's time we look at the values and beliefs that got us to this place. As adults, we have the opportunity to do some "value remapping" – when we take an objective look at our values, and decide if we want those values to continue to govern the way we behave, communicate, and interact with others.

It takes great humility and courage to do this exercise, and to say, "I inherited that value or belief from my parents, but now I'm going to create and live by new values."

If we asked, "what are the values that you lived out in your past life?" Most of us would claim, "integrity, loyalty, hard work," etc.

Many of us have surely displayed integrity, loyalty, and hard work at times in our lives, but most of us would be dishonest if we said our pasts were characterized by these values. Most of our pasts were dominated by values like greed, entitlement, disregard, disrespect, and worthlessness.

For example, what values led you to use drugs, when you knew they were illegal and harmful to your health?

Many users' answers might be:

- I felt worthless
- I wanted to escape my pain
- I like shortcuts
- I was bored and was seeking excitement
- I wanted to fit in

The values that correlate to these sentiments might include:

Worthlessness
Escapism
Short-sightedness
Boredom
Thrill-seeking
Loneliness

The sooner we take our beer goggles off and are willing to take a look at the negative values that have driven our actions, the sooner we'll get healing and start to transform.

> "If you don't stick to your values when they are being tested, they're not values, they're hobbies.
>
> - Jon Stewart"

YOU TURN: FORMER NEGATIVE VALUES

Put a checkmark next to each value that reared its head at any point in your past (from your childhood, up until today):

- ☐ Greed
- ☐ Envy
- ☐ Jealousy
- ☐ Pride
- ☐ Ambition
- ☐ Power
- ☐ Promiscuity
- ☐ Deception
- ☐ Sexism
- ☐ Racism
- ☐ Rejection
- ☐ Bitterness
- ☐ Disinterest
- ☐ Suspicion
- ☐ Despondency
- ☐ Pessimism
- ☐ Withdrawal
- Disappointment
- ☐ Guilt
- ☐ Poverty Mindset
- ☐ Worry
- ☐ Manipulation
- ☐ Disregard
- ☐ Apathy
- ☐ Entitlement
- ☐ Self-pity
- ☐ Laziness (shortcuts)
- ☐ Boredom
- ☐ Thrill-seeking
- ☐ Acceptance-seeking
- ☐ Escapism (drugs)
- ☐ Hopelessness
- ☐ Misery
- ☐ Sorrow
- ☐ Despair
- ☐ Gloom
- ☐ Ostracism
- ☐ Resignation
- ☐ Condemnation
- ☐ Failure
- ☐ Worthlessness (low self-esteem)
- ☐ Short-sightedness (instant gratification)
- ☐ Disconnectedness
- ☐ Anger
- ☐ Violence
- ☐ Guilt
- ☐ Greed
- ☐ Sadness
- ☐ Loneliness
- ☐ Rigidity
- ☐ Criticism
- ☐ Lethargy
- ☐ Cynicism
- ☐ Frustration
- ☐ Depression
- ☐ Futility
- ☐ Judgment
- ☐ Self-doubt
- ☐ Revenge
- ☐ Fear of ____________
- ☐ Discouragement
- ☐ Hostility
- ☐ Regret
- ☐ Anxiety
- ☐ Humiliation
- ☐ Embarrassment
- ☐ Jealousy
- ☐ Other:
- ☐ ____________
- ☐ ____________
- ☐ ____________
- ☐ ____________
- ☐ ____________
- ☐

Of the values you checked, circle the 10 most pervasive ones from your past (both inside and outside the gates).

CRAY

SLUGGO'S FIVE DRIVING VALUES

1. **Persistence:** I've been on a strictly seafood diet since I got busted. I see food and I eat it.
2. **Honesty:** Im'a be honest (ain't puttin' a 10 on a 2), but when it comes to sloths, I know I'm a catch (I don't know why my penpal picture still ain't hittin' ... these haters be hatin').

3. **Commitment:** Not everyone has the skills to make an 8' lazy stick to change the TV. I ain't gettin' off my bunk. Cellie, get my tray.
4. **Moderation:** I choose to experience success on a very moderate basis. Like, never.

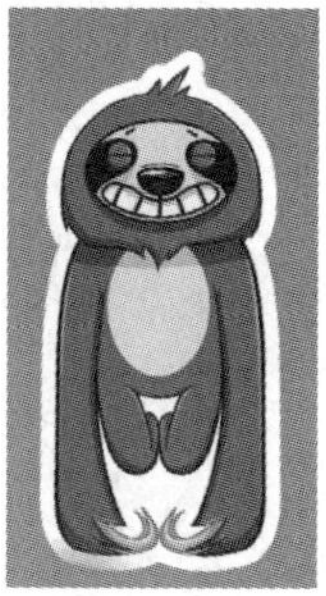

5. **Accountability:** If it's you and me in an elevator, and you smell something, it wasn't me, and I'll have no problem letting the homies know it was you. It ain't snitching; it's called accountability.

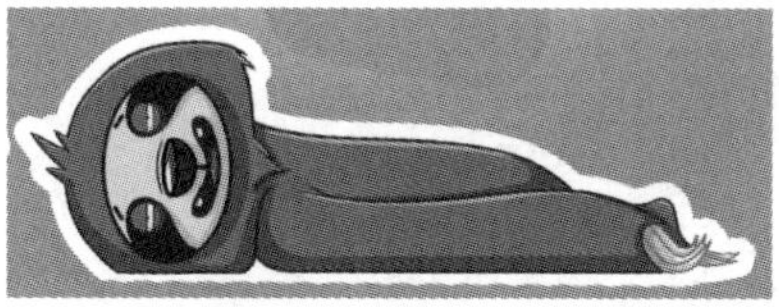

CRAY

MY 2.0 VALUES INVENTORY

Ask yourself these questions as you choose your new 2.0 Values:

- What values do I want to be known for in life?
- When I face hardship, what values do I want guiding my decisions?
- How did I exemplify these values last week? How could I be intentional about exemplifying them this coming week?
- What are the values I respect the most in my role models? When have I seen them exhibit their positive values?
- When interacting with others, what values do I want them to treat me with?
- What values do I want to pass onto my children or youth?
- At my funeral, in the eulogies, what are the values I want to be known for having exemplified?

Determine your 2.0 Values. Narrow the list to <u>no more than 10</u> (circle these) you want to make your 2.0 Driving Values.

- ☐ Accountability
- ☐ Candor
- ☐ Commitment
- ☐ Dependability
- ☐ Dignity
- ☐ Honesty
- ☐ Honor
- ☐ Responsibility
- ☐ Sincerity
- ☐ Transparency
- ☐ Trust
- ☐ Trustworthy
- ☐ Truth
- ☐ Accomplishment
- ☐ Capable
- ☐ Challenge
- ☐ Challenge
- ☐ Competence
- ☐ Credibility
- ☐ Determination
- ☐ Development
- ☐ Drive
- ☐ Effectiveness
- ☐ Empower
- ☐ Endurance
- ☐ Excellence
- ☐ Adaptability
- ☐ Altruism
- ☐ Balance
- ☐ Charity
- ☐ Communication
- ☐ Community
- ☐ Connection
- ☐ Consciousness
- ☐ Contribution
- ☐ Cooperation
- ☐ Courtesy
- ☐ Devotion
- ☐ Equality
- ☐ Ethical
- ☐ Fairness
- ☐ Family
- ☐ Fidelity
- ☐ Friendship
- ☐ Generosity
- ☐ Giving
- ☐ Goodness
- ☐ Harmony
- ☐ Humility
- ☐ Loyalty
- ☐ Maturity
- ☐ Meaning
- ☐ Acceptance
- ☐ Comfort
- ☐ Compassion
- ☐ Contentment
- ☐ Empathy
- ☐ Grace
- ☐ Gratitude
- ☐ Happiness
- ☐ Hope
- ☐ Inspiring
- ☐ Joy
- ☐ Kindness
- ☐ Love
- ☐ Optimism
- ☐ Passion
- ☐ Peace
- ☐ Poise
- ☐ Respect
- ☐ Reverence
- ☐ Satisfaction
- ☐ Serenity
- ☐ Thankful
- ☐ Tranquility
- ☐ Welcoming
- ☐ Creativity
- ☐ Curiosity

- ☐ Greatness
- ☐ Growth
- ☐ Hard work
- ☐ Improvement
- ☐ Influence
- ☐ Intensity
- ☐ Leadership
- ☐ Mastery
- ☐ Motivation
- ☐ Performance
- ☐ Persistence
- ☐ Potential
- ☐ Power
- ☐ Productivity
- ☐ Professionalism
- ☐ Prosperity
- ☐ Recognition
- ☐ Results-oriented
- ☐ Significance
- ☐ Skillfulness
- ☐ Status
- ☐ Success
- ☐ Talent
- ☐ Victory
- ☐ Wealth
- ☐ Winning
- ☐ Ambition
- ☐ Assertiveness
- ☐ Boldness
- ☐ Confidence
- ☐ Dedication
- ☐ Discipline
- ☐ Fortitude
- ☐ Persistence
- ☐ Power
- ☐ Restraint
- ☐ Rigor
- ☐ Self-reliance
- ☐ Temperance
- ☐ Toughness
- ☐ Vigor
- ☐ Will
- ☐ Selfless
- ☐ Sensitivity
- ☐ Service
- ☐ Sharing
- ☐ Spirit
- ☐ Stewardship
- ☐ Support
- ☐ Sustainability
- ☐ Teamwork
- ☐ Tolerance
- ☐ Unity
- ☐ Brilliance
- ☐ Clever
- ☐ Common sense
- ☐ Decisiveness
- ☐ Foresight
- ☐ Insightful
- ☐ Knowledge
- ☐ Learning
- ☐ Logic
- ☐ Openness
- ☐ Realistic
- ☐ Reason
- ☐ Reflective
- ☐ Smart
- ☐ Thoughtful
- ☐ Understanding
- ☐ Vision
- ☐ Wisdom
- ☐ Accuracy
- ☐ Caution
- ☐ Certainty
- ☐ Cleanliness
- ☐ Consistency
- ☐ Control
- ☐ Decisive
- ☐ Economy
- ☐ Justice
- ☐ Lawfulness
- ☐ Moderation
- ☐ Organization
- ☐ Security
- ☐ Stability
- ☐ Structure
- ☐ Thoroughness
- ☐ Timeliness
- ☐ Discovery
- ☐ Exploration
- ☐ Expressive
- ☐ Imagination
- ☐ Innovation
- ☐ Inquisitive
- ☐ Intuitive
- ☐ Openness
- ☐ Originality
- ☐ Uniqueness
- ☐ Wonder
- ☐ Amusement
- ☐ Enthusiasm
- ☐ Experience
- ☐ Fun
- ☐ Playfulness
- ☐ Recreation
- ☐ Spontaneous
- ☐ Surprise
- ☐ Alertness
- ☐ Attentive
- ☐ Awareness
- ☐ Beauty
- ☐ Calm
- ☐ Clear
- ☐ Concentration
- ☐ Focus
- ☐ Silence
- ☐ Simplicity
- ☐ Solitude
- ☐ Independence
- ☐ Individuality
- ☐ Liberty
- ☐ Bravery
- ☐ Conviction
- ☐ Fearlessness
- ☐ Valor
- ☐ Energy
- ☐ Vitality
- ☐ Other:
- ☐ ____________________
- ☐ ____________________
- ☐ ____________________

Adapted from Core Values List by Scott Jeffrey https://scottjeffrey.com/core-values-list/

YOUR IDENTITY

We all have purity and virtuousness in us. When we're kind to our cellie, respectful of a c/o we don't like, or choose to forgive, we are engaging our purity. When we engage meaningfully with education and programs like Hustle 2.0, we're engaging our virtuous sides. Someone who is "pure" is moral and virtuous.

A person's purity refers to living in a wholesome way, abstaining from sin and immorality. A pure soul refers to someone whose intentions are honest and good.

Purity isn't a synonym for "prosocial," but the ideas are similar. When we transform, we become prosocial.

IDENTITY

Noun

The characteristics determining who or what a person or thing is.

PROSOCIAL

Adjective

Relating to or denoting behavior which is positive, helpful, and intended to promote social acceptance and friendship.

VIRTUOUS

Adjective

Having or showing high moral standards.

PURE

Noun

Wholesome and untainted by immorality.

THE COMPOSITION OF YOUR IDENTITY

If an outsider was objectively tasked with assessing your identity, what would they say about you? If they looked at your rap sheet, they might say one thing. If they were family and saw your sincere change over the last few years, would they say something else?

If we analyze our thoughts and behaviors, we can come up with our identity.

Without getting technical, analyze every last corner of your heart. You have both criminality and purity/prosocial thinking behavior in it. Imagine analyzing the composition of your heart today vs. 10 years ago: what percentage was "criminal" vs. "pure"?

Committing crimes or breaking rules is never virtuous or pure. Most of us are still breaking some rules and laws, but since enrolling in Hustle 2.0, most of us have taken steps toward disengaging from criminality and engaging our purity—which results in prosocial behavior.

We all know people whose hearts seem to be 99% criminal, and only 1% pure. We also know a few beautiful souls who seem like their hearts are 99% pure, and 1% criminal. Maybe on the 99% criminal side is a psychopath who murders repeatedly with no empathy or remorse. Maybe on the 99% pure side is a devoted social worker or Mother Theresa.

Of everyone you know, who strikes you as having the most criminal identity?

What about the purest identity?

ASSESS YOUR IDENTITY

Use the two lines below to assess the composition of your heart. Along the spectrum, draw a little heart (♥) to represent your identity.

My Identity 10 Years Ago

99% CRIMINAL — 50% CRIMINAL 50% PURE — 99% PURE

My Identity Today

99% CRIMINAL — 50% CRIMINAL 50% PURE — 99% PURE

Our identity can change over time, and we've got to start somewhere if we want to move toward purity.

If your identity is 51% criminal today and you don't take steps toward purity, your identity will stay rooted in criminality, and you will likely die incarcerated.

If your identity is 51% pure today, you won't obtain or keep your freedom, because nearly half of your thoughts, energy, and actions are still criminal. **However, once you reach 51% purity—the tipping point—it will be easier to get your identity to 52% purity, and then 53%, and so on.**

If you're wondering what percentage you need to earn your freedom and keep it, we don't know. We can say that you must be firmly rooted, for years, in an identity of purity—of prosocial thinking and behavior. Your thoughts can no longer be controlled by criminal thinking, and as a result, your behaviors won't be criminal.

Iron sharpens iron, and together as Honey Badgers, we can continue to move the purity needle.

What single step could you take today to shift your identity just 1% toward purity?

CHOOSING FORGIVENESS

If you choose forgiveness, is forgiveness for you or for the other person?

For you!

Does the other person have to ask for forgiveness for you to choose to forgive?

No.

If you forgive, does it mean you're cool with what they did?

No.

If you forgive, do you have to get back into an unhealthy relationship?

No.

If you forgive, will you forget the pain and immediately stop being sad?

No.

If you don't forgive, who is in control?

They are. Or at least your anger is ... but you're not!

Forgiveness is not about inviting people to hurt you, break your heart, or disappoint you again. You're free to refuse to work with someone or to not engage with someone you can't trust.

If you forgive, do you give yourself the opportunity to transform your hustle and your future?

Yes.

If you forgive, are you giving yourself the possibility of moving forward with peace and purpose, and maybe even joy?

Yes.

Forgiveness is a choice. It's a decision. And it sounds like this: "I forgive me." Or, "I forgive them."

Forgiveness isn't easy … but it can be as simple as saying it.

Repeatedly.

And then maybe one day it will sink in.

Sounds nice, doesn't it? Here's what will likely happen right after you say, "I choose to forgive": your brain will fight you—one minute later, or maybe the next morning, but the fight is coming. The prosecutor in your brain will yell: "Yeah, right! I don't forgive me! I don't forgive them! Being mad is fun! After all, they betrayed me!"

You likely won't feel the warm-fuzzies of forgiveness. You'll likely be super-tempted to revert to unforgiveness. You'll still feel the familiar burn of hate.

When you put someone else on the hook for something that happened yesterday, you're stabbed with the same hook—reliving the pain, losing the chance for connection, and walking away from the future you could be building instead.

Forgiveness allows us to take our attention off the past and put it on the present and the future.

And your brain will keep firing away: "Told you so! You didn't really forgive yourself! You don't deserve it! Stay mad, you hypocrite! Are you going to let them get over on you like that?"

If you choose forgiveness over and over again, and get stubborn about choosing forgiveness, and you surround yourself with a community like this one of Mavericks, a community that doesn't just preach forgiveness but practices it, then maybe one day, your feelings will follow.

Forgiveness allows us to take our attention off the past and put it on the present and the future, where it can do some good.

(If you've chosen to forgive before, you can certainly choose it again, because forgiveness is a recurring process.)

Remember, most of the time, your hate and anger are having zero impact on the other person (unless you're in contact with them). Go ahead and sit around mad and brooding, while they go on with their lives, unaware of the stress and hate you're living with.

If there's a little voice in your head saying that even if you choose forgiveness, it won't be real: fake it till you make it. We dare you to try forgiveness, even if it's just for today. If you want to go back to hating yourself or someone else tomorrow morning, that's your choice.

> If you wait until you feel you deserve forgiveness, or feel like doing it, you will never choose it.

Name one person and one action you will forgive today.

____

FORGIVING MYSELF

By John Jackson
aka Sweet Grandpa

As the oldest of three kids I felt it was my duty to take care of and protect my siblings. At the age of 12, a few years after my mother was murdered (I never knew my father), I chose to live with my aunt instead of with my stepfather, brother, and sister. When I left, I experienced guilt for abandoning my siblings.

The last time I spoke to my brother was in 2003. He told me what I already believed: that I left him and let him down, not only by moving, but through my incarceration.

My brother took his life in 2008. I never cried or grieved for him. Instead, I spent the next 11 years blaming myself for his suicide. I told myself if I had stayed and taken care of him, he'd still be here. If I'd made better choices, I wouldn't be incarcerated, and I could've been there to help him. It hurts me to think he felt so alone that suicide was his only option, the only way to end whatever he was going through.

Blame and guilt consumed me—for decisions I made as a 12 and 17-year-old kid (when I went to prison). I blamed myself for a decision my brother made. I told myself I was a horrible brother and a horrible son to my mother for not taking care of him.

I never considered forgiving myself. I didn't know it was possible. In 2018, I avoided a forgiveness exercise at a Hustle 2.0 event. I spoke to a friend about it briefly but slammed the door. I was terrified.

It took another year before I considered forgiving myself. The one person I trust more than anyone—who had never made me feel uncomfortable before—pushed me to forgive myself.

I don't recall feeling more uncomfortable, or more afraid, of anything in my entire life. The harder she pushed, the more I fought. I gave every excuse. I was shaking just thinking about it. My shame and guilt told me I didn't deserve forgiveness. The voice in my head told me that if she

My shame and guilt told me I
didn't deserve forgiveness.

knew the real me, she would hate me. She'd abandon me. Although common sense told me this wasn't true, shame and guilt convinced me it was.

The next day she simply asked if I wanted to forgive myself. I fearfully said yes. I still fought it, but not as hard. The hardest part was actually saying the words, "I forgive myself." I wanted to say it and mean it, but I knew once I did, the 11 years of guilt and shame that stopped me from grieving for my little brother would be gone. I was afraid to grieve.

When I finally said, "I forgive myself," the words felt disgusting coming out of my mouth ... I still didn't feel worthy of forgiveness. But as soon as I said it, for the first time, I started grieving my brother. I'd never cried so hard and didn't know if I could stop. I forgave myself for being a terrible brother and for abandoning my family, and for being a bad son. I don't know how long I cried.

I didn't sleep much that night. As I grieved my brother, I realized I was not responsible for his suicide; he made his own decisions. Although I made the terrible decisions that led me to prison, I realized I could now make better ones without blaming myself for my brother's suicide.

My decision to forgive took place in 2019. Since then, my brain has fought my decision and told me on numerous occasions that I didn't deserve forgiveness. I chose to follow through with my decision and told myself that I am worthy and deserve the peace and life that comes from forgiveness. I reminded myself that my little brother deserved to be grieved. As my brain kept fighting my decision, I reaffirmed my forgiveness. I've continued making space for more grieving, which has replaced my guilt and shame.

I've become more confident in my ability to make good choices and now see how my unwillingness to forgive myself previously blocked my ability to connect with others ... and how quick I was to disconnect with people—even those I love. I now feel the freedom of not being responsible for everyone else's choices. I've also now started the journey of forgiving myself for other pains I caused to myself and others while incarcerated.

What causes the most guilt and shame in your life?

What possibilities would open up if you forgave yourself?

What did you learn about yourself from John's testimonial?

CONSEQUENCES OF UNFORGIVENESS

Think of the feelings and consequences you've experienced over your unforgiveness (of yourself or someone else). *Check all the feelings you've experienced:*

- [ ] Hatred
- [ ] Vengeance
- [ ] Depression
- [ ] Suicidal thoughts
- [ ] Health issues
- [ ] Fear
- [ ] Despair
- [ ] Jealousy
- [ ] Embarrassment
- [ ] Loneliness
- [ ] Getting incarcerated
- [ ] Aggression
- [ ] Bringing anger and bitterness into new relationships and experiences
- [ ] Frustration
- [ ] Addiction
- [ ] Grief
- [ ] Envy
- [ ] Restlessness
- [ ] Disconnection
- [ ] Feeling like a hypocrite spiritually
- [ ] An inability to enjoy the present because you're consumed by the past
- [ ] Alienation and losing connection with people
- [ ] Resentment
- [ ] Revenge
- [ ] Disgust
- [ ] Anxiety
- [ ] Sleeplessness
- [ ] Sadness
- [ ] Shame
- [ ] Violence
- [ ] Guilt
- [ ] Doubt
- [ ] Betrayal
- [ ] Humiliation
- [ ] Worthlessness
- [ ] Fatigue
- [ ] Feeling a lack of purpose or hope in life

Any other feelings or consequences from your unforgiveness?

How are those feelings working out?

Imagine carrying these feelings is like carrying a 10-pound bowling ball in your chest, weighing you down at every step. Do you want to hold on tight to that big ball of hate that's conquering your heart? Do you love walking around angry, with your thug mug on every day?

I am amazed by how many individuals mess up every new day with yesterday. They insist on bringing into today the failures of yesterday and in so doing, they pollute a potentially wonderful day.

- Gary Chapman

EMBRACING VULNERABILITY

Abuse and depression are two things that we don't usually speak much about when we're incarcerated, but both have affected nearly all of us, so we're opening up the dialogue.

DEALING WITH DEPRESSION

By Cecil Sagapolu
aka Sweet Candy

There's a lot of depression in prison. With the right support, we can get through it.

I've been depressed several times, especially when I couldn't see my kids growing up. Now my daughter is 22 and my son is 20. To get through my depression, I read, wrote poems to reflect on my feelings, and kept working out (sometimes excessively). I still go through depressing moments frequently, especially when I miss my kids' events. When I feel depressed, I create space to express my feelings.

Vulnerability allows me to get things off my chest in a healthy way; it relieves some of the issues I've bottled up over the years.

Vulnerability is a strength; it leaves room for others who feel weak to find comfort in you. When we open up, other people open up, too.

I feel like vulnerability shows how secure you are. I think most people lack confidence in themselves and worry about how others view them.

> I feel like vulnerability shows how secure you are.

Sharing with a safe person can lighten your load. You don't have to carry the weight by yourself. Then maybe you'll stop feeling so alone.

What's a productive way for you to express your feelings the next time you feel depressed or disappointed?

A DIALOGUE ABOUT ABUSE

By Alfred Sandoval
aka Sweet Freddy

I was discriminated against as a kid because I didn't speak English. I was beaten and had ruler marks across my face from my teachers. I was abused.

A lot of us are angry because of the abuse we experienced as children. Anger leads to living with hate and not caring about anything.

I've heard that up to 60% of men in prison have been molested. A lot of men are afraid to talk about abuse. It can feel like taking away their manhood. So they hide.

Hiding our pain leads to another mask, another thug mug. When youngsters cover their faces with tattoos, I think they're hiding in shame.

If we want to heal, we need to talk about the abuse.

Broaching the conversation is tough. Vulnerability can be viewed as a weakness, and how do we know who to trust? But don't make excuses and delay the healing dialogue. There will always be people who will make fun of you if you share vulnerability, so find someone who is emotionally mature.

I want us to start a dialogue around abuse. Ask your trusted friends about their childhoods. When I did, I realized how much we've all suffered – not just from abuse, but from discrimination and hate, too.

When I came off of death row, I was full of hate. I was fighting with the c/o's every day. A friend told me that he saw nothing but darkness in my eyes; just hate and demons.

Then I met my wife. We talked for hours. She called it peeling the onion. She said, "You do have a belly button; you just don't know it." She opened up my heart.

Everyone I know in prison has lost a family member or experienced trauma.

The longer it takes to open up, the more that "it" (whatever "it" is) will set you back. The sooner you deal with it and heal, the sooner you'll understand your self-sabotaging decisions (like drinking or using drugs). You'll feel freer … and you'll save a lot of money. ☺

How have you masked your feelings about abuse?

SELF-ASSESSMENT: THE PERSON I WANT TO BE

I want ...	**TRUE**	**FALSE**
1. To be considered trustworthy by others.	☐	☐
2. To feel trustworthy.	☐	☐
3. To be considered an honorable person.	☐	☐
4. My kids/family to believe me.	☐	☐
5. The parole board/my PO to show me trust.	☐	☐
6. To feel good about myself.	☐	☐
7. To believe in myself.	☐	☐
8. To feel more connected to people.	☐	☐
9. Others to be able to count on me.	☐	☐
10. My yes to mean yes, and my no to mean no.	☐	☐

What is one thing you could do to improve your integrity?

____

LYING TO YOURSELF

Self-deception is when we invent a lie for our own sakes, and/or are motivated to hold onto a belief that is untrue. We get something from telling ourselves this lie, e.g., increased confidence, escaped accountability, or comfort.

Think back to the lies we told about our crimes. Most of us lied to the cops when we got busted in hopes of beating the case ... and stuck with it. We told our lawyer, the homies, our families, and anyone who would listen. Which of your lies have you come to embrace as "truth"?

Looking back on what actually happened can be one of the most difficult things you will ever do.

We tell lies about what happened in our crimes because we don't want to face the consequences, look like monsters, change the perceptions we've shown others, or ... because it might be embarrassing.

Decide what you want more:

☐ To hold on to your lie and romanticized story

Or

☐ Your freedom

Because you can't have both.

> I am not the product of my circumstances. I am the product of my decisions.
>
> - Stephen Covey

SELF-ASSESSMENT: WHAT TYPE OF LIAR ARE YOU?

For each question, circle the statement that best describes you.

1.

   A. I sometimes bend the truth to avoid hurting someone's feelings.
   B. I'm not in the habit of lying, but I lie occasionally.
   C. Lying is my default response to questions.
   D. Lying is part of my life strategy.

2.

   A. I rarely lie, and when I do, it's not harmful.
   B. When I lie, I feel guilty afterwards.
   C. I generally feel uncomfortable telling the truth.
   D. I don't feel shame or remorse when I lie, even if my lie hurts someone.

3.

   A. I think small lies can sometimes be beneficial.
   B. I usually fess up and ask for forgiveness after telling a lie.
   C. I started lying as a kid and now it's a habit.
   D. I lie whenever it's necessary to get my way.

4.

   A. Sometimes I only tell part of the truth, but I don't think of that as lying.
   B. Telling lies is something I'd like to change about myself.
   C. I lie even when I don't have anything to lose by telling the truth.
   D. I enjoy the power that lying gives me.

KEY: If you answered mostly ...
A's: You may be White Liar.
B's: You may be an Occasional Liar.
C's: You may be a Compulsive Liar.
D's: You may be a Sociopathic/Pathological Liar.

THE PHYSICAL TIMELINE OF A LIE

When you tell a lie, your body reacts immediately. These are things you have no control over ... the only thing you *do* have control over is whether you lie or tell the truth. Below is a timeline of the effects, from the first minute to three days after a lie.

00:01:00	The stress of telling a lie triggers your nervous system to release stress hormones like cortisol and testosterone. These hormones trigger your fight or flight response. If the lie is big, or puts you in danger, you may experience an adrenaline rush. You may sweat, your pupils dilate, and your heart rate and blood pressure increase.
00:05:00	Your brain struggles to hold in working memory the differences between what you know to be true and the lie. As a result of this extra brain work, your decision-making ability is compromised. You may find yourself telling additional lies to try to keep up with the first. You stop thinking as clearly and critically.
00:10:00	You may start to feel angry, especially towards the person you lied to. Your body's visceral reaction to stress causes you to be on the offensive and lash out.
00:30:00	The stress hormones released when you lied have gone, and as you calm down you may feel worried or remorseful for your lie. You may try to feel better by being extra sweet to the person you lied to, or by demonizing him or her as someone not deserving of the truth.
24:00:00	One day later, your brain forms a negative association towards the person you lied to. We tend to avoid people and situations that make us uncomfortable, so you may find yourself feeling resentful, distant, or cold towards the person. If you are a seasoned, habitual liar, you are "living the lie." Rather than feeling bad about it, you've committed to your lie and may lose touch with the truth.
72:00:00	Three days after lying, your body may still suffer the physical toll of your deception. Living with the stress of lies can cause chronic anxiety. Heightened levels of stress hormones like cortisol compromise both your ability to think clearly and your immune system. The stress causes you to sleep worse, which in turn weakens your immune system. You are more susceptible to illness.

Sources: https://www.psychologytoday.com/us/blog/stronger-the-broken-places/201903/the-cost-lie
https://boss.blogs.nytimes.com/2014/03/11/the-surprisingly-large-cost-of-telling-small-lies/

INTEGRITY CHECK

The sooner you have the courage to get honest, the sooner you will experience freedom (emotional, psychological, spiritual, and even physical). The truth is, we *all* lie, and most of us tell some form of a lie every single day. Are you brave enough to get honest about your lies, and to stop lying by making claims that you "always" keep it 100?

In the past month …	**AGREE**	**DISAGREE**
1. I told the truth to every c/o I interacted with.	☐	☐
2. I've been honest about my addictions or vices, and my related behaviors, with everyone I've discussed them with (e.g., the homies, in groups, loved ones).	☐	☐
3. I was 100% honest with all of my friends and family about how I'm feeling (e.g., when someone asks how I'm doing, I don't paint a false image).	☐	☐
4. I was honest about my workout (e.g., telling someone how many reps I did, not taking shortcuts or cheating).	☐	☐
5. I've been honest with the homies or others about the relationships I'm in (or am not in), e.g., how many people I'm writing.	☐	☐

> A half-truth is a whole lie.
>
> – Yiddish Proverb

NO JUDGMENT QUIZ: DO YOU WANT TO COME CLEAN?

Consider a thing or two you have been dishonest about that has weighed heavily on your mind.

If I come clean ...

	TRUE	FALSE
I will experience freedom from being honest.	☐	☐
I will have a clean conscience.	☐	☐
I will have more respect for myself.	☐	☐
I will sleep better at night.	☐	☐
I will have better relationships with others.	☐	☐
I will have a better chance of earning and keeping my freedom.	☐	☐
I will be more trustworthy.	☐	☐
I am more likely to be accepted for who I am.	☐	☐
I will start the journey of forgiving myself or won't feel as much self-hate.	☐	☐
I will gain the peace that comes from people knowing the real me.	☐	☐

What conclusion can you draw from your answers to this quiz?

____

CONFESSION

Almost everyone has done at least one thing that would lead to shame or crisis if it was discovered.

The higher we rise, the farther we have to fall. The farther we fall, the more it hurts. This can create a need to bury the skeletons deeper in the closet. Because if they're ever found, they could cost us everything we've built.

The more we bury, the more we feel like a fraud and the more we disrespect ourselves. The more we disrespect ourselves, the more likely we are to make self-sabotaging decisions.

Shame thrives in secrecy.

If you've been lying for a long time (to yourself and/or others), it may take more than one or two confessions to come clean. You have to deconstruct the house of lies and teach yourself new habits.

5 Tips for Confession

1. Confess to yourself before anyone else. That might seem obvious (or unnecessary). But if you deceive, deny, or minimize mistakes when you tell yourself what happened, you won't succeed in confessing to anyone else. Try writing out your confession.
2. Confessing to a therapist, chaplain, or trusted friend can be a great next step.
3. Keep the circle of the confession to the circle of the sin. This means you don't need to confess to everyone you run into. Ask yourself, who did your lie hurt? If you lied to a homie, coming clean with just that person might be sufficient, unless your lie hurt others too.
4. Be complete with the confessions so you're not lying or minimizing the truth (which could lead to losing credibility a second time).
5. Avoid oversharing. When nosy people dig for sensational details, tell them it's not their business, thank you very much. Sharing details is often counterproductive. When someone starts digging, ask yourself (and maybe even the person), "Does this person really need to know this? Why? What is their motive for asking? If they know the answer, will it help or hurt them?"

A confession is important. But the apology is what matters when you're working to restore broken trust. A confession is *not the same* as an apology. In H2.0's 12-book series, we have an entire course on how to give a meaningful apology, which is key to restoring relationships.

MY INTEGRITY: EVALUATION AND PLAN

Who is it time to sit down with for a heart-to-heart?

Check the box that represents how you feel about your integrity with the following people:

	Living a Big Fat Lie; a long way to go	Room for improve-ment	Proud of my integrity	Not applicable
My cellie	☐	☐	☐	☐
My family	☐	☐	☐	☐
My kids	☐	☐	☐	☐
The homies in here	☐	☐	☐	☐
The homies on the streets	☐	☐	☐	☐
Other friends	☐	☐	☐	☐
My coworkers/supervisors	☐	☐	☐	☐
With God/my higher power	☐	☐	☐	☐
C/o's	☐	☐	☐	☐
My romantic partners(s)	☐	☐	☐	☐
My penpals	☐	☐	☐	☐
My religious leader/mentor	☐	☐	☐	☐
With myself	☐	☐	☐	☐

Commitment is an act, not a word.

- Jean-Paul Sartre

My Integrity Priority Plan

I'm making a commitment to myself to take these action steps to have more respect for myself and the other person:

By this date	The person I will get more honest with	The specific step I will take to get more honest	My desired outcome of this step is

My Pledge to Myself

I promise to take these three steps by the dates I wrote above. ______________________

(signature)

IF YOU'RE SERIOUS ABOUT YOUR WORD, SHARE YOUR COMMITMENTS WITH AN ACCOUNTABILITY PARTNER.

SAMPLE QUESTIONS FOR ACCOUNTABILITY PARTNERS

Want to make progress with a goal? Get an accountability partner and meet weekly to discuss at least three of these questions.

1. What was your biggest priority last week?
2. Did you accomplish it? If not, what did you prioritize over this priority?
3. What is the greatest obstacle you are currently facing?
4. What was your personal highlight from the past week?
5. In the past week, when did you lie or hide the truth?
6. How are you taking care of yourself physically through exercise, rest, and eating?
7. How are you investing in your closest relationships, e.g., your spouse, children, cellie, best friends?
8. How have you been unforgiving, bitter, or angry towards someone this week?
9. How have you intentionally hurt someone this week?
10. How have your actions mirrored your words this week?
11. How have your actions failed to mirror your words this week?
12. What actions do you regret from this past week?
13. What needs to happen for the upcoming week to be successful?
14. How do you define success?
15. What specific goal would you like me to hold you accountable to this next week?

Who could you ask to be your accountability partner?

HUSTLE GUIDE
HOT SHOT

By Jason Romero

aka Sweet Cherry

Stay up and stay focused on studying The Preseason with this Hot Shot of caffeine!

Makes one serving

Ingredients:

2 spoons of Hot cocoa
1 fat shot of Coffee
1 pack of Sugar
1 Candy bar (2 if you're a fatty)

Instructions:

- [ ] Boil water in hot pot.
- [ ] Add cocoa, coffee, and sugar pack into your cup.
- [ ] Smash candy bar on the ground; open it up and pour into a cup.
- [ ] Add boiling hot water to cup, stirring occasionally.
- [ ] Stir mixture thoroughly until chocolate and coffee are dissolved.
- [ ] Get crackin' on the next crash course!

T R A N S F O R M A T I O N U

S U I

O T C O N S E Q U E N C E W H

N I U C L

I B E H E F F E C T S P O F T

A W D Y W L Y

P Q D J T N L Y U P W J L R X

J P G L R F U Q Q

F N P T B G R B R V V W L Q N

Q O S L Q I F Q E Z S

H I E W L X E J N A S M C H P

O S M S R P F E N O U R Q

N S P D T M V A R J O D E H Q

E A A N P I O F S C I E P U B

Y P T E A B M H X F T E W D O

B M H M S C X J X C R O T Q

A O Y A T Z V Q H I A F W T T

D C Q W V G H P N R N B

G W H L U E V J W N X L V R S

E Y C V X Q M T M B

R X V P X Q L Q W X O C Q S P

P P F F U Q A P

G F G M V P S D E A T K U I M

N M O K Q A

I P U U U O N N Q P G P O U U

L A S X

A X G E D U T I N G A M K Q K

E H

H R E S P O N S I B I L I T Y

ACTIONS
AMENDS
COMPASSION
CONSEQUENCE
EFFECTS
EMPATHY
FREEDOM
HEALING
HONEY BADGER
MAGNITUDE
PAIN
PAST
RESPONSIBILITY
TRANSFORMATION

VICTIM AWARENESS

Ripple Effect

LEARNING OBJECTIVES

In this crash course, you will ...

- ✓ Assess your knowledge about victim awareness
- ✓ Evaluate a case study to see what it looks like to take responsibility for your actions
- ✓ Learn about restorative justice
- ✓ Identify the victims of your crimes; understand the ripple effect of your crimes
- ✓ Apply concepts about victim awareness through a case study on selling drugs

In Hustle Guides 1-12, take in-depth courses and gain insight into:

- ✓ How to give a meaningful apology
- ✓ Making a plan for living amends
- ✓ Emotional suicide/learning to feel again
- ✓ Domestic violence
- ✓ Sexual violence

RIPPLE EFFECT

Imagine dropping a stone into a still pond. As it falls in the water, there's a central point where the water is impacted. Then quickly, ripples expand outward until the ripples from this stone have affected every part of the pond. All of this from one stone.

Our actions are like this stone. They can have a far-reaching impact on the lives of others. When we commit crimes, the impact can be long-lasting and easily go unnoticed by us.

Victim awareness is about examining the ripples that are created by our actions in the lives of others.

To earn and keep our freedom, we must first gain sincere awareness, empathy, and compassion, while taking the steps to prevent making future victims.

What is Restorative Justice (RJ)?

Hustle 2.0 offers multiple courses in victim awareness, empathy, learning to feel again, and making amends in our 12-book series. We cover important perspectives and activities that are traditionally found in RJ programs.

Restorative Justice is a system in which volunteers and professionals help incarcerated people to rehabilitate, and sometimes to reconcile with their victims, so they can re-establish a connection with society and their community. Four common parts of RJ include:

- Open Discussion: meeting with victims
- Group Activities: shared activities between victims and the incarcerated
- Legal Awareness: understanding the consequences of actions
- Educational Programs: school and rehabilitation

NO JUDGMENT QUIZ: VICTIM AWARENESS

	AGREE	DISAGREE
1. Victim awareness is punishing yourself for the pain that you've caused others.	☐	☐
2. I have reservations about owning up to my past.	☐	☐
3. Thinking about the pain I've caused the victims of my crimes is something I'm scared to do.	☐	☐
4. I don't see how taking ownership for my actions will help. What's done is done.	☐	☐
5. I don't believe I'm worthy of forgiveness.	☐	☐
6. I've taken full responsibility for the pain my actions have caused.	☐	☐
7. I've made a list of every individual who was victimized by every one of my crimes.	☐	☐
8. I've written apology letters to *all* of the victims of my crimes (and sent the letters when allowed/appropriate).	☐	☐
9. I've read stories of victims of crimes similar to mine.	☐	☐
10. I'm seeking to make amends in some way to those I have harmed.	☐	☐
11. I feel deep remorse over the hurtful things I've done to people.	☐	☐
12. I believe that victim awareness is essential to the rehabilitation process.	☐	☐

QUIZ: IDENTIFY THE VICTIMS OF YOUR CRIMES

Check Yes/No for all who qualify as a victim of your crimes.

	YES	NO
1. The immediate victim(s) of the crime	☐	☐
2. That victim's parents	☐	☐
3. That victim's siblings	☐	☐
4. That victim's children	☐	☐
5. That victim's extended family, e.g., cousins, nieces, nephews, grandparents	☐	☐
6. That victim's friends	☐	☐
7. Your parents	☐	☐
8. Your siblings	☐	☐
9. Your children	☐	☐
10. Your extended family, e.g., cousins, nieces, nephews, grandparents	☐	☐
11. Your friends	☐	☐
12. Your community	☐	☐
13. Taxpayers	☐	☐
14. First responders (e.g., police, EMS, firefighters, 911 operators, witnesses to the crime)	☐	☐

Answer Key: The correct answer to all the questions is YES, unless the people don't exist (e.g., you don't have children)

Each of these people are victims in some way. It is easy to dismiss victims when we didn't see the impact directly, but the effect on their lives is real and deserves to be acknowledged.

NO MORE EXCUSES

By Thabiti Salim Wilson

aka Fudgy

I used to hug the block and slang crack rock,
Patrol the set with marks and glocks,
No care for who I hurt or harmed,
As long as my pockets were fat and my turf was armed

I loved the notoriety I had,
I was feared, and respected,
How could that be bad?
I did what I wanted, put in work on my enemy
I didn't see no wrong,
It was only natural to me

It was the lifestyle, it was all I knew
I was taught to bang the red and hate the blue
To get my money by any means
Pistol in hand chasing the greens

This mindset led me to a prison cell
If heaven is the streets, then this is hell

And still I didn't change my ways
I made excuses for why I misbehaved
Justification for actions taken
Then realization now I am awakened

I now see there was no right in my wrong
The criminal mind is dead and gone

It hasn't been easy; the work is hard
I'd have it no other way as I walk the yard
Head held high because my future is bright
No need for excuses now that I'm living right

CASE STUDY: SELLING HEROIN

Carlos is a drug dealer who thinks that selling drugs is a victimless crime. He sells to adults who make a conscious decision to buy from him. He thinks, "If I don't sell to this person, someone else will, so it might as well be me who gets the money."

Every week Carlos sells to a drug addict named Joseph who spends half his check on heroin. Carlos thinks, "No victims here."

Joseph's addiction becomes worse and he neglects his children's needs more and more. They don't have clothes or supplies for school; they can't afford the school lunch, so they go without. Eventually Joseph loses his job and is unable to pay the rent and they lose their house. Now his kids are homeless, and they have no idea why. They have never done drugs but are negatively impacted by the choices of both their father and of Carlos, who sells drugs to his father.

Sound familiar? It's easy for us to rationalize our behaviors and choices. We hear this "someone's gotta do it" mentality every day – about selling drugs, stabbings, stealing, etc. We're quick to complain about our circumstances … but when will we start taking responsibility for our actions?

It's not hard to see that Joseph's kids are victims. Why would we want to be contributors to the victimization of innocent children, when we claim to be protectors of them?

When was the most recent time – while incarcerated or outside – you caused injury to someone's daddy or mommy?

When was the last time you took action against someone's father, brother, or son … and their loved ones waited for someone who would never show up?

> If you're not part of the solution, you're part of the problem.

When was the most recent time – while incarcerated or outside – you caused injury to someone's daddy or mommy?

When was the last time you took action against someone's father, brother, or son … and their loved ones waited for someone who would never show up?

SELF-REFLECTION: VICTIM AWARENESS

Think back to a crime you committed that led to remorse or shame. Summarize what happened.

____

Who was hurt (the victim) through your crime? Describe the negative impact. If you don't know the victim's name or the impact, imagine it and write what you think the impact could have been.

Victim's name: ____________________

Impact on the victim: ____

____

Victim's name: ____________________

Impact on the victim: ____

____

Victim's name: ____________________

Impact on the victim: ____

____

When you think of the pain you created, what negative feelings and consequences do you experience (e.g., shame, self-hate, regret, anxiety ...)?

____

People are hard to hate up close.

– Brené Brown

SUDOKU

Complete the puzzle by filling in the numbers 1-9 in each row, each column, and each 3x3 grid without repeating a number in any row, column, or 3x3 grid.

						8	5	1
5	8	6					3	
		3						9
	6	1	7					
	9		1				4	7
7				3	5	9		
				5		1		
	2		6					8
6		8			9			3

OWNING IT

By Darryl Baca
aka Sweet Owl

The victim of my crime was Antonio Gutierrez. He was in a rival gang. He was 20 years old when I killed him in retaliation, because my car got shot up. He wasn't the one who did it, and I knew it. I was seeking revenge against his homeboys.

I think about Antonio all the time. I think about the senseless way I took his precious life over something material: a car. I deprived him of being a father and an uncle. I didn't allow him to live, to experience life.

I regularly think about Antonio's mother, Ms. Gutierrez. I think about the pain and heartache I've caused her, and how my choice affected her. I wonder, was she ever able to move on and live a normal life? Or has she been in constant mourning?

I took Antonio's life on March 7, 1981. I would think that every March 7th, Ms. Gutierrez goes through an agonizing day of tears and pain, going to the cemetery. She never deserved this. No one does.

My sister lost her son to gang violence. To this day, she mourns. She still has that hate and anger over gangs. Every anniversary of her son's death, she goes to her son's grave. She married her husband on the same day her son was born to commemorate her son's life. She always talks about her son's life and murder. Once when she wrote to me about his life, she said, "Even though he's not here, at least my son didn't take someone else's life."

That stuck with me because that's what I did. Understanding the pain I've caused has allowed me the opportunity to have a different impact. I am better than this.

If I were standing at the pearly gates, St. Peter might have said something like this about the old me:

> *"Darryl was a naturally kind person at heart, but he was evil when you crossed him. He could be your worst nightmare. He would assault you, rob you, and leave you alone in self-pity. He didn't care and didn't know how to care."*

I lived that way for decades; 32 years of living in a world of abandonment and hopelessness. I didn't care about anyone or myself.

My hopelessness led to recklessness. I changed lives, permanently, for the worse. I did and had things done to people, that caused them to lose their minds. Some probably still haven't recovered because of my actions. I had a way to make people feel worthless. I was able to ostracize people, even from those they grew up with and cared about.

I made a lot of terrible decisions dealing with staff too. When they were respectful with me, I was respectful back. But when they weren't, I allowed myself to take the bait. I was disrespectful and argumentative. I didn't care about cell extractions and I didn't care about consequences or myself.

My brother was shot by the cops. He survived … yet because of this experience and many others, I concluded that cops were all one-and-the-same: my enemy. I came to see that my negative way of thinking, and my actions, led to hatred and animosity.

Once I educated myself, I learned new perspectives. Things started to have value and meaning.

Today, I regularly extend my hand to officers, because I choose to show them a gesture of respect. Not all of them accept my handshake, but that won't stop me from trying.

Today, I regularly extend my hand to officers, because I choose to show them a gesture of respect. Not all of them accept my handshake, but that won't stop me from trying.

Can I Get A
COURTESY FLUSH!
D5-123

PERSEVERING

2 Legit 2 Quit

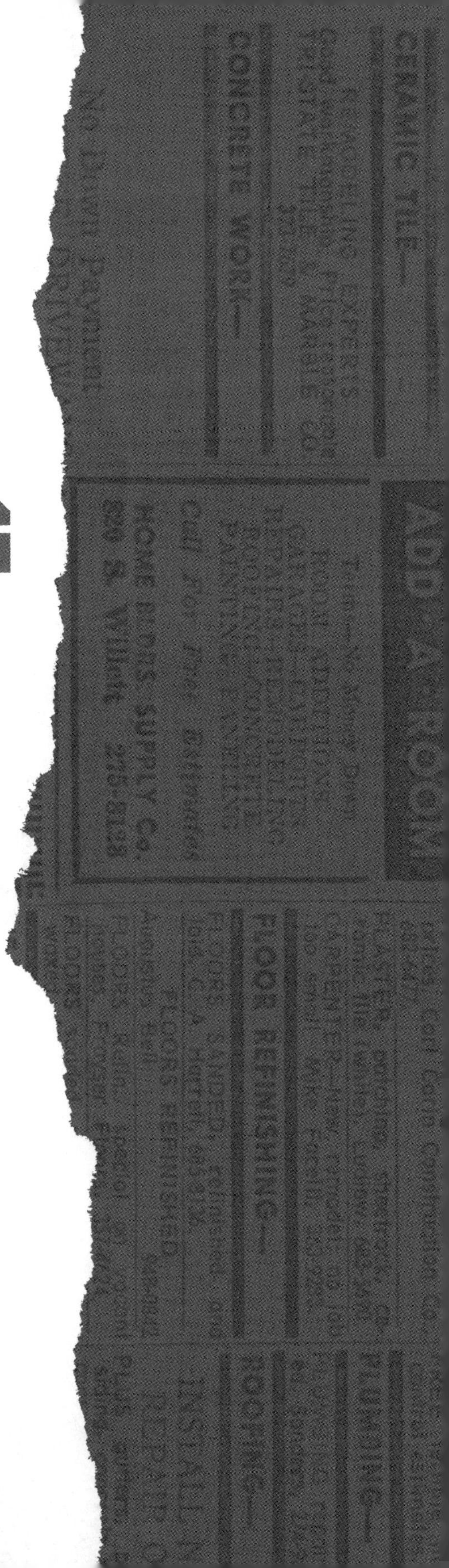

◄ *Illustration by Trenton Dukes*

LEARNING OBJECTIVES

In this crash course, you will ...

- ✓ Continue to affirm yourself through the hard times
- ✓ Get inspired by two case studies on persevering through seemingly insurmountable obstacles
- ✓ Learn tips on maintaining hope from those who survived 30+ years in isolation
- ✓ Learn how important grit is to overcoming obstacles, rate your grit, and learn to grow your grit

In Hustle Guides 1-12, take in-depth courses and gain insight into:

- ✓ Resilient grieving
- ✓ Addiction and recovery
- ✓ Relapse prevention plans
- ✓ Depression and suicide
- ✓ Coping skills

25 WAYS TO MAINTAIN HOPE IN A HOPELESS PLACE

Check off three new things you can start doing to become a more Hopeful Honey Badger!

- [ ] Engage in a faith. Pray, study, and go to church.
- [ ] Meditate at least 10 minutes each day.
- [ ] Surround yourself with positive influences and friends. Get a positive cellie.
- [ ] Be quick to reach out for support when things go haywire.
- [ ] Maintain relationships with family and loved ones. Stop running from them.
- [ ] Get a hobby. Draw, read, or write poetry.
- [ ] Find a positive mentor.
- [ ] Become a mentor.
- [ ] Never lose your sense of humor. Laugh. It's good for you.
- [ ] Give yourself positive words of affirmation (Love Bombs!) every day.
- [ ] Begin a workout regimen and stick to it.
- [ ] Set a short-term goal.
- [ ] Get a job that gives you purpose.
- [ ] Find a purpose that makes you want to wake up every day.
- [ ] Forgive yourself. Stop beating yourself up and emotionally shackling yourself to the past.
- [ ] Forgive your enemies and see how much mindshare frees up for positivity. Get the hate out of your heart.
- [ ] Be kind to someone you don't know.
- [ ] Eat healthy. You are what you eat.
- [ ] Talk to someone you can trust, or to a therapist. Yes, a therapist.
- [ ] Get a penpal and write letters.
- [ ] Become a legal beagle and help others fight for their freedom.
- [ ] Read up on the changing laws and how even lifers go home. You could be next. Prepare, and help short-timers prepare.
- [ ] Learn a new language.
- [ ] Educate yourself. Enroll in college, earn your GED, or join a self-help group. Read. A lot.
- [ ] Realize you have a choice on how you view each day. You want to wake up hating and complaining? That's a choice. Your bed doesn't have a wrong side; get up and make the most of every moment.

Dear Life,
When I asked if my day could get worse, it was a rhetorical question ...

Not a challenge.

ATTEMPTS TO BREAK THE HUMAN SPIRIT

By Arturo Castellanos
aka Sweet Tamale

The SHU was designed to break the human spirit.

Imagine being told you'd be locked in the SHU until you died of old age, went crazy, debriefed (informed), or paroled. This was a reality for many of us.

Between 1990 and 1995, CDCR did not have a facility that could handle people with serious mental problems. So CDCR housed them in the Pelican Bay SHU. There were two to five of them in each unit, and they would bang on the metal 24/7. They would sometimes throw and smear feces on themselves and on the cell. We were literally locked up in an insane asylum.

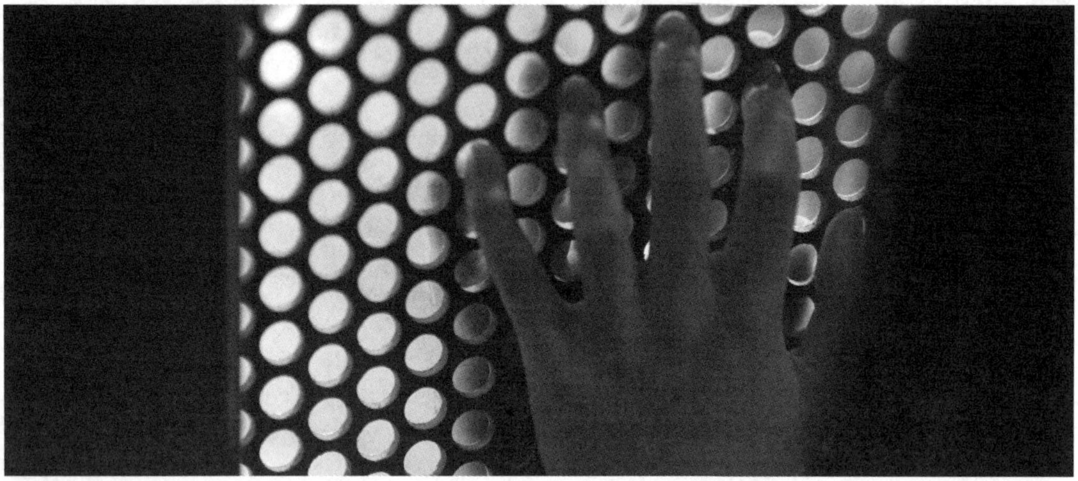

> The difference between those who broke and those who didn't was attitude. The negative guys broke.
> – Arturo Castellanos

In 1995, they were moved to mental units. After that, the SHU became so quiet you could hear a pin drop. We had to get used to all the banging; then we had to get used to it being so quiet.

There were some respectful staff members who inspired hope in us; hope that someday things would change, and that the ugliness would be exposed.

I saw the SHU break some strong people. The difference between those who broke and those who didn't was attitude. The negative ones broke. The positive ones refused to be broken, mentally or otherwise, whether we had a date or not. We kept hope alive by engaging in activities. The SHU taught me how to survive any situation.

DON'T LET YOUR TIME DO YOU

By Kunlyna Tauch

aka Sweet Cheeks

Momma always told me I was
hard-headed
Headed down the wrong road
She knew
Knew I wasn't one to heed advice
It was the vice
Of the streets that I listened to

With sticky fingertips, I missed
dinners at home
With the fam throughout my adoles-
cent phase
I phased out – 'cause being broke
was played out
I stayed up late nights learning the
tricks of the trade
Hard life when you're knocked down,
a hard knock life
24 hours a day
On a 6-month lockdown
Down and out playas get played
Ballas get knocked down a size
Stuck in the cell getting treated like a
"knock" now

Hitting books
Hitting water bags
Getting money in a new way
Weighing your options preparing for
street life
Preparing for new days

Went legit
But the hustle is still real
New way to hustle
That's Hustle 2.0: Two times
But the struggle is still real
Putting in work like them old days
When I used to do dirt
Parole prep!
Spent too much time watching my fam-
ily hurt
Time to put my family first

Ready for the challenge
That's my next step!
Doing time is a mindstate
Don't let your time do you!
Your freedom is worth the hustle
Time to bring out that Maverick in you

GRIT

Noun

1. Courage and resolve; strength of character
2. Passion and perseverance for long-term goals

RESILIENCE

Noun

1. The capacity to recover quickly from difficulties; toughness
2. The ability of a substance or object to spring back into shape; elasticity

SELF-ASSESSMENT: GOT GRIT?

	STRONGLY DISAGREE	DISAGREE	NEUTRAL	AGREE	STRONGLY AGREE
1. I face challenges every day and overcome them.	☐	☐	☐	☐	☐
2. Setbacks don't discourage me.	☐	☐	☐	☐	☐
3. I am a hard worker.	☐	☐	☐	☐	☐
4. I finish what I start.	☐	☐	☐	☐	☐
5. I've achieved a goal that took years to complete.	☐	☐	☐	☐	☐
6. I am diligent.	☐	☐	☐	☐	☐
7. When I work out, I finish strong.	☐	☐	☐	☐	☐
8. I am disciplined.	☐	☐	☐	☐	☐

Key: The more you answered "strongly agree," the more grit you've got.

WHAT IS GRIT?

Angela Duckworth wrote a book about the importance of grit.

> Why do some people succeed and others fail? Grit is one of the greatest determinants of success and whether we hit our goals. It's far more important than talent.
>
> – Angela Duckworth

She wrote, "Grit is passion and perseverance for an important goal. It's the hallmark of high achievers in every domain." Angela also found scientific evidence that grit can grow.

Here's what *grit* isn't:

It ain't talent … or how badly you want to make parole the month before your hearing. It's about having what researchers call "an ultimate concern" – something you care about so much that it gives order and meaning to almost everything you do. Grit is holding onto your goal with everything you've got, even when you fail or get shot down.

If your "ultimate concern" truly is going home, you will experience disappointment if you go to board and get a three-year denial, but your disappointment won't lead you to drinking alcohol or stopping programming.

Ms. Duckworth believes that in the end, grit matters much more than talent or luck. People with grit, who demonstrate self-control and conscientiousness, are the ones who come out ahead.

Adapted from Source https://angeladuckworth.com/qa/

In which area of your life have you demonstrated the most grit?

Look at your priorities and activities. Can you truthfully claim that obtaining (and keeping) your freedom is your "ultimate concern"?

THE GRIT OF A HONEY BADGER

By Gabriel Arce

Hook:

It's the grit of a Honey Badger
That kept me going throughout all the pain; all the laughter
We're in the game man; a difference where it really matters
Stepping up to the plate like designated batters
[Repeat 4x]

Verse 1:

With no exceptions
No longer are we walkin' the wrong direction
I'm boutta bring to your attention
How we caught it on time like an interception
It was a difficult process but I came a long way
From almost giving up, not wanting to live another day
Surrounded by so much negativity it was hard
Growin up in a city where all of my role models were armed
With no direction or guidance, all I knew was defiance
But now I'm rollin' with that H2.0; that's my new alliance
I transformed my thinking, transformed my hustle
Transformed like Bumble Bee and now I'm ready to rumble
Through all that I went through, it gave me the grit
To persevere them obstacles, never callin' it quits
Equipped now with the skills of real leadership
I'm gonna stand any storm, no matter how bad it gets

It took a long time; so many failed attempts
But I kept a positive mind when hope was hard to accept
Now each day I wake up, I'm grateful for another breath
I'ma continue with resilience, moving forward with every step
[Hook: Repeat Here]

Verse 2:
They tried to throw you off when they told you that
Education is for fools and prison's where it's really at
I'm just tryna open up your eyes as I'm rhyming
Hopefully you see the truth and don't remain blinded

Divided by groups
Now we stand for reunitement
And we ain't gonna stop
Till we completed our assignment

I "stepped to the line," addressing my hurt and pain
Reflecting on past decisions and my mistakes
In spite of the bad weather I once felt everyday
I came to realize that I grew bcuz the rain

I forgive where forgiveness was unlikely expected
Now when I look into the mirror I can smile at my reflection
Hustle-Two-Point-O we got the grit of a legend
And we're here to make a positive difference with no exceptions

GROW YOUR GRIT

Step 1: Define what grit or mental toughness means for you.

Be clear about your goal and what success looks like, e.g.,:

- Busting down with your cellie for a month straight without missing a day
- Committing to eating sweets only twice a week

Step 2: Build grit with small wins.

We can make the mistake of thinking that grit is how we respond to stressful situations, but what about everyday circumstances that make us want to quit?

Just like when we work out and build stamina, we need to do the same thing to build grit. Grit needs to be worked to grow.

Instead of skipping that last set of your workout, hit it like it's the first one. Prove to yourself you have what it takes to do more, rather than just rolling off your bunk like Sluggo.

Step 3: Build strong habits (and stop depending on motivation).

Grit isn't about getting off your bunk in the morning and feeling inspired or magically courageous to do something you didn't want to do when you went to sleep last night. It's about building daily habits that allow you to stick to a schedule and overcome challenges and distractions, over and over and over again.

The H2.0 Homies who survived decades in the SHU weren't necessarily more courageous or more talented ... but every survivor was mentally tough and gritty. They made habits of being positive and of not giving up. They did what they were supposed to do on a consistent basis, and their small daily wins and habits built their grit.

> Success is not final, failure is not fatal: it is the courage to continue that counts.
>
> – Winston Churchill

Coffee

N	S	R	I	E	S	P	R	D	E
W	U	G	N	O	S	S	E	R	C
O	G	C	D	O	C	H	A	O	A
R	A	U	E	M	B	C	O	B	F
B	R	P	R	A	E	A	N	U	A
P	E	R	C	N	S	P	I	S	T
T	A	L	O	A	R	P	C	E	A
O	A	C	I	B	A	U	C	T	I
R	R	A	G	C	A	F	F	H	P
N	O	S	U	E	N	I	E	I	O

ARABICA
BEANS
BROWN SUGAR
CAFFEINE
CAPPUCCINO
CUP
DECAF
ESPRESSO
ETHIOPIA
GRINDER
MOCHA
NO SUGAR
PERCOLATOR
ROBUSTA

THE FIRE INSIDE ME

By Darryl Baca
aka Sweet Owl

> The fire inside me burned brighter than all the fires around me.

Earning my AA Degree in Social and Behavioral Science is one of my greatest academic accomplishments. Given my background, I am very proud of what I achieved. I wasn't a good student as a child and didn't like reading. From ages nine to 10, I was forced to read at the dining room table.

I was housed in the Pelican Bay SHU for 32 consecutive years. College was new in the SHU, so there was no consistency when delivering books and materials. This made it difficult to meet deadlines, and we incurred penalties for lateness. We faced resistance from some c/o's who paid for their kids to attend college and saw us getting a free education.

I've always had a strong desire to learn something new and different, so despite the setbacks and threats of being kicked out, I wasn't about to give up. My education was finally something positive. It gave my life meaning, and I was a passionate, disciplined student.

After decades in the SHU—and not breaking—grit was embedded in every fiber of my being. It's who I am: a survivor. I adapted to every SHU environment; Tracy, New Folsom, Corcoran, and Pelican Bay. I endured because "the fire inside me burned brighter than all the fires around me."

We all have the inner strength to survive and adapt to our surroundings. We are predispositioned to survive. As Honey Badgers, we are born with a survival instinct gene.

I never give up on or quit anything positive in my life, whether it's a goal I'm trying to achieve, family and friends, or relationships. It's important to never tap out on things that mean the most—especially relationships. Relationships are the most difficult thing to hold onto. They require time, energy and commitment.

There are people who try to prevent you from being the best person you want to be. Those are the people and things you give up. But giving up or quitting on something positive? That is a reflection of your character.

Humans are creatures of habit. If you quit when things get tough, it gets that much easier to quit the next time. On the other hand, if you force yourself to push through it, the grit begins to grow in you.

- Travis Bradberry

WOULD YOU RATHER ...

Meditate for 10 minutes every day

Or ...

Have a cellie who's so fat they snore while they're awake

LOVE BOMBS

Shade in the hearts (♥) of the five Love Bombs your soul needs to hear most:

- ♡ I respect myself for having courage and strength.
- ♡ There is strength in my vulnerability.
- ♡ I'm ready to believe in myself, in change, and in a positive future.
- ♡ I'm ready to dream big.
- ♡ The pain from my past does not control or define me.
- ♡ When I embrace the pain from my past, I'm being courageous.
- ♡ I can't change my past, but I am choosing to learn from it.
- ♡ I'm choosing to break free from the shackles of shame.
- ♡ I am capable of healing old wounds.
- ♡ My story has value.
- ♡ My life has value.
- ♡ Honey Badgers never quit.
- ♡ I have character and insight today because I've learned from my past.
- ♡ I'm in Hustle 2.0 because I'm committed to becoming a 2.0 version of me.
- ♡ I've failed and am still standing.
- ♡ I know I can do this.
- ♡ I'm committed to my freedom.
- ♡ There are no limits to what I can accomplish.
- ♡ I am confident.
- ♡ My peers see me as a leader.
- ♡ I'm comfortable with my vulnerabilities.
- ♡ I am worthy.
- ♡ I am proud of how far I've come.
- ♡ I belong.
- ♡ I am brave.
- ♡ I have the capacity to love.
- ♡ I will manifest greatness.
- ♡ People love to be around me.
- ♡ I'm a Honey Badger!!
- ♡ Khrya-ya-ya-ya!

DO
THE
HUSTLE

$
HONEY
Badgers
HUSTLE
2.0

READING, MANDOS, AND SURVEY

The Last Mile

◀ *Illustration by Mr. Romo*

RECOMMENDED READING

Title/Author	Description
Atomic Habits by James Clear	Learn to form good habits, break bad ones, and master the tiny behaviors that lead to remarkable results.
Necessary Endings by Henry Cloud	Learn to give up relationships that are holding you back so you don't repeat misery.
Lying by Sam Harris	Learn to simplify your life by merely telling the truth in situations where others lie.
Never Split the Difference by Chris Voss	Learn to negotiate as if your life depended on it, whether it's buying a car, negotiating a salary, or deliberating with your partner.
How to Talk So Kids Will Listen & Listen So Kids Will Talk by Adele Faber	Learn to effectively communicate with your child and solve common parenting problems.
Daring Greatly by Brené Brown	Learn how having the courage to be vulnerable transforms the way we live, love, parent, and lead.
Get Out of Your Own Way by Mark Goulston	Transform 40 common self-defeating behaviors, including procrastination, envy, obsession, anger, self-pity, guilt, and rebellion.
The Four Agreements by Don Miguel Ruiz	Learn a code of conduct that can transform your life into a new experience of freedom, true happiness, and love.
Extreme Ownership: How U.S. Navy SEALs Lead and Win by Jocko Willink	Two U.S. Navy SEAL officers who led the most highly decorated special operations unit of the Iraq War teach leadership principles that apply to business and life.
How To Get A Date Worth Keeping by Henry Cloud	You're attracted to the wrong kind, while the right kind lack the "chemistry." Learn this step-by-step program to getting the dates you want.

Title/Author	Description
The Courage to Be Disliked by Ichirou Kishimi	Your past trauma doesn't need to affect your happiness now. Learn the importance of liking yourself and accepting that most people won't like you.
The Wisdom of The Enneagram by Russ Hudson and Don Richard Riso	Based on nine personality types, this tool for transformation helps you overcome barriers, realize your gifts and strengths, and discover your deepest direction in life.
Zero to One by Peter Thiel	Legendary entrepreneur Peter Thiel presents how to ask the questions that lead you to find value in unexpected places.
The Book of Forgiving by Desmond Tutu and Mpho Tutu	Learn the art of forgiveness from the Nobel Peace Prize winner and realize we are all capable of healing and transformation.
How to Talk to Anyone by Leil Lowndes	Learn a more skillful way of dealing with people that leads to love and respect.
The 7 Habits of Highly Effective People by Stephen Covey	Learn to solve personal and professional problems.
The Lean Startup by Eric Ries	Rather than wasting time creating elaborate business plans, learn a way to test your vision and adapt before it's too late.
The Five Love Languages by Gary Chapman	Learn to speak and understand your mate's love language, and you will love and truly feel loved in return.
The Five Languages of Apology by Gary Chapman	Heal relationships with the five languages of apology: 1) Expressing regret, 2) Accepting responsibility, 3) Making restitution, 4) Genuinely repenting, and 5) Requesting forgiveness.

MANDOS

It's time to test your knowledge to see how much game you've soaked up in The Preseason! For the next 50 questions, circle the best answer to each question and bubble your answers on your Bubble Sheet on page 346. To receive that shiny new certificate from Hustle 2.0, you will need to score at least 80% on the Mandos. You've got this, Honey Badger!

1. Behavior, which is positive, helpful, and intended to promote social acceptance and friendship, is called:
   - A. Being prosocial
   - B. Social optimism
   - C. Positive social media
   - D. Positive realism

2. Placing the blame on others and pretending to be innocent is an example of which criminal thinking error?
   - A. Playing the victim
   - B. Doing God's work
   - C. Viewing yourself as a good person
   - D. Testifying in court

3. One day after having told a lie, what happens?
   - A. Your nose starts to grow like Pinocchio
   - B. Your mind struggles to hold the lie in working memory
   - C. Your brain has formed a negative association towards the person you lied to
   - D. Your guilty conscience prepares you to confess and ask for forgiveness

4. One way to grow your grit, which is key to success, is to:
   - A. Build strong habits
   - B. Grow your talent
   - C. Roll up your sleeves and get your hands dirty
   - D. Get used to failing

5. When a follower makes a bad decision called by a leader, the follower often:
   - A. Files a charge against the corrupt leader
   - B. Stops following the leader
   - C. Asks for a suitable punishment
   - D. Looks at themselves as the victim

6. Sound advice when making a confession is:
   - A. Confess only for the behavior you were caught for
   - B. Publicly confess so everyone knows you're taking ownership
   - C. Speak with a confident voice so you sound credible
   - D. Don't minimize the truth

7. What did 75% of hiring and HR professionals report about the cost of hiring people with criminal histories?
   A. The cost of hiring people with criminal histories is higher than hiring those without one
   B. The cost is equal to or less than hiring people without criminal histories
   C. People with a criminal history pose a significant risk to the company
   D. People with criminal histories outperform average entry-level employees

8. When providing references to an employer:
   A. List them at the bottom of your resume
   B. Write "References available upon request" and wait until they ask for them
   C. List them on a separate sheet and have them ready at the interview
   D. Include c/o's you worked for in jail or prison if it's the only employment you had

9. From where does the term Maverick originate?
   A. Texas Ranger and sidekick Sam Maverick
   B. Mark Cuban, owner of the Dallas Mavericks
   C. Texas Rancher Sam Maverick
   D. The movie Top Gun

10. The first step in solving a problem is:
    A. Apologizing
    B. Seeking a qualified mediator
    C. Recognizing there is one
    D. Hitting rock bottom

11. Restorative justice often involves:
    A. Paying restitution to victims
    B. Procedural justice training for officers
    C. Officer accountability
    D. Reconciling with victims

12. What percentage of Mandos do you have to answer correctly to earn a certificate?
    A. 50%
    B. 75%
    C. 80%
    D. 100%

13. Why was Fuzzy Koala Bear so motivated to make the cancer walk happen?
    A. He wanted everyone to walk a few laps after canteen
    B. He lost his son to cancer in 2013
    C. He wanted to do something newspaper-worthy
    D. He found out he had cancer
14. The resume format that leads many employers to assume you're hiding something is:
    A. Chronological
    B. Functional
    C. Ideological
    D. Pedagogical
15. By choosing to engage in criminal activity while incarcerated, what choice is being made?
    A. Spending more time in an environment we claim to hate, rather than being with those we love
    B. Getting free chocolate milk
    C. Making the right decision; talking about change
    D. Giving c/o's exactly what they're putting out there
16. The sheriff featured in The Preseason:
    A. Personally arrested one of the Mavs in H2.0
    B. Danced in front of Mavericks and donated $1,000 to H2.0
    C. Has 7,000 employees
    D. Served in the Homicide Division as an interrogator
17. At $14.25/hour, what are your lost wages if you've been incarcerated for 10 years?
    A. $9.99 + tax
    B. $208K
    C. $296K
    D. $593K
18. For many employers, the following is more important than your resume:
    A. LinkedIn
    B. Facebook
    C. The recruiter's profile
    D. JobHunter.com profile
19. What is a way to create peace with the authorities?
    A. Imagine you are all brothers from another mother
    B. Tell them to read the cupcaking crash course to step their game up
    C. Don't recidivate
    D. Say good morning/evening to them

20. According to Nkongoli, a survivor of the Rwandan genocide, you're already dead when you are:
    A. Able to commit murder
    B. Resigned and oppressed
    C. A victim of genocide
    D. Living in hatred

21. An industry that is less likely to hire someone with a criminal history is:
    A. Aviation
    B. Hospitality
    C. Web design
    D. Finance

22. Which criminal thinking error leads someone to reject feedback and to lie by leaving facts out intentionally?
    A. Closed channel thinking
    B. Playing the victim
    C. Ownership attitude
    D. Denial

23. If you wait until you deserve forgiveness or until you feel like forgiving, what will probably happen?
    A. You will work harder for it
    B. You will only have to choose forgiveness once
    C. You will likely never choose forgiveness
    D. You will forget about the offense

24. If you analyzed the annual income of gang members and the org structure of gangs, most of them would resemble the income and structure of:
    A. A private investment firm, where the partners make billions
    B. A union, where workers get paid more when they put in more years
    C. A communist economy, where everyone gets paid the same
    D. McDonald's, with 99% of workers averaging $7/hour or less

25. If a Honey Badger sells tacos and burritos to other incarcerated people, this is an example of:
    A. Prosocial thinking
    B. Using entrepreneurial skills
    C. How sharing is caring
    D. Culinary expertise

26. According to Dr. Mollica, why might it be easier for young people to be manipulated?
    A. They are easily brainwashed
    B. Facebook controls them
    C. They want attention and love
    D. Because of their idealistic nature

27. Why does Dr. Mollica consider young males to be the most dangerous people on the planet?
    A. They easily respond to authority and want approval
    B. They are the largest population
    C. They have the greatest potential
    D. They play

28. Studies show that the following percentage of people are uncomfortable in a group setting:
    A. 10%
    B. 25%
    C. 50%
    D. 90%

29. An example of a character trait is:
    A. A strong credit score
    B. Generosity
    C. An educational accomplishment, like college
    D. Being physically fit

30. What is the best way to tell your story to a potential employer?
    A. Speak about criminal charges the employer is likely to understand
    B. Tell your 2.0 story at the beginning of an interview
    C. Wait until they run the background check; then answer questions directly
    D. Include it in bullet points in the experience section of your resume

31. What is the most powerful drug for the mind?
    A. Anger
    B. Hope
    C. Love
    D. Nicotine

32. Cecil shares that he still goes through depression. What does he do when he is depressed?
    A. Creates space to express his feelings
    B. Doesn't talk about it
    C. Gets into a fight
    D. Sings "Let It Go"

33. The state-sanctioned killings of Tutsi people were generally referred to as what by the people committing the crimes?

   A. Playing a video game
   B. Work
   C. Spring cleaning
   D. Doing what I gotta do

34. Forgiving someone means:

   A. You get back into a healthy relationship with the person you forgave
   B. Your pain and sadness will go away once you've truly forgiven
   C. You allow yourself to transform your future
   D. You are inviting the person to hurt you again

35. Having grit is about having what?

   A. An ultimate concern that gives order and meaning to everything you do
   B. "Built Ford Tough" character
   C. Falling back into old ways when you get bad news
   D. Double-ups at breakfast

36. When we're mad, underneath, we're often actually:

   A. Nervous
   B. Sad
   C. Anxious
   D. Gassy

37. A tip for being a great conversationalist is to:

   A. Stay in the moment
   B. Think of what you'll say or ask next
   C. Speak just slightly more than you listen
   D. Always refer to the other person as "Mr." or "Ms."

38. Squaring Up is:

   A. Succeeding in keeping 100% of the laws and rules
   B. Being a boring conversationalist
   C. Peacefully confronting your opponent
   D. Disengaging from the criminal identity and embracing a prosocial identity

39. The best way to achieve a large goal is to:

   A. Make sure you're highly motivated before committing to it
   B. Think about the large goal for at least one week before committing
   C. Hit rock bottom before deciding to aim big
   D. Achieve many small goals

40. What is one of the most important lessons Timothy Staley has learned so far?

    A. To keep in touch with old friends
    B. The power of preparation
    C. Learn to use Google
    D. He can do it on his own

41. When a company or gang leader is open-minded, he/she:

    A. Asks for and uses feedback
    B. Risks compromising his/her morals
    C. Risks compromising the company's values
    D. Doesn't have the backbone of a good leader

42. According to Arturo Castellanos, what kept the SHU from breaking him and others?

    A. The silence
    B. The gassings
    C. Respectful c/o's
    D. A positive attitude

43. What is the definition of values?

    A. Your principles or standards of behavior
    B. Low prices at the dollar store
    C. The promo items you get in your quarterly package
    D. Assumptions and convictions that are held to be true

44. What acts of kindness did Timothy Staley perform in the SHU?

    A. Gave his cellie an Atomic Wedgie every morning
    B. Made g-bars and birthday cards
    C. Organized a Cancer Walk
    D. Talked about his problems with one person every day

45. Which SMART goals step may require you to develop new skills?

    A. Relevant experience
    B. Attainable
    C. Skills assessment
    D. Measurable

46. What does "upfront disclosure" mean in a job interview?

    A. Wearing skinny jeans that disclose everything upfront
    B. Oversharing personal information
    C. Disclosing in detail why you're the best candidate
    D. Telling your story on your own terms with honesty and vulnerability

47. What book helps readers avoid repeating misery?

   A. Beating a Dead Horse: You Know What You Need To Do So Stop Talking About It
   B. Crucial Conversations: Tools for Talking When the Stakes Are High
   C. Necessary Endings
   D. Boundaries: When to Say Yes, How to Say No To Take Control of Your Life

48. Of the four deliverables to earn a certificate from Hustle 2.0, which is optional?

   A. Scoring 80% on your Mandos
   B. Survey, parts 1 and 2
   C. Call to action
   D. None, all four are all required to earn a certificate

49. If you enroll in Hustle 2.0's 12-book program, you can major in which of the following?

   A. Entrepreneurship and Team-building
   B. Employment and Business Etiquette
   C. Reentry and Entrepreneurship
   D. Cracking jokes and sipping Cokes

50. The part of The Preseason that you have permission to make copies of is:

   A. The Hustle 2.0 Preseason Application and Mail Order Form
   B. The Rundown
   C. The Call to Action
   D. Nothing – it's all copyrighted

SURVEY, PART I

Note that circling your answers on here isn't enough –
you must transfer your answers to the Bubble Sheet to get a certificate!

51. How much more time do you realistically expect to be incarcerated on this sentence?

    A. Less than 6 months
    B. 6 months to 1 year
    C. 1-2 years
    D. 3-10 years
    E. 10+ Years

52. What was your primary reason for *starting* The Preseason?

    A. I was bored/looking for something to do, and it was available
    B. I'm a regular programmer
    C. I thought Hustle 2.0 sounded cool, and/or I saw others doing it
    D. I wanted to earn a certificate or to impress my family
    E. I want to transform or learn/grow

53. What was your primary reason for *completing* The Preseason?

    A. I had nothing better to do
    B. I wanted a certificate
    C. I authentically want to learn and transform
    D. I found the program to be relevant and fun
    E. I like the challenge

54. What best describes the value you received from The Preseason?

    A. I have more hope for a better future
    B. I believe in myself and my confidence increased
    C. I learned practical skills that will improve my chances of success
    D. I am better equipped to keep my freedom
    E. H2.0 furthered my transformation

55. If you could access more Hustle 2.0 programming, you would:

   A. Sign up for The Combine (4 books in 4 months)
   B. Sign up for the Full Program (12 books in 12 months)
   C. Not sign up for more because you're getting out soon
   D. Not sign up for more because you don't want to invest more time in H2.0
   E. Not sign up for more because you didn't care for The Preseason

56. If you could access more Hustle 2.0 programming, the Major that interests you most is:

   A. Entrepreneurship
   B. Employment Readiness
   C. Leadership and Management
   D. Healthy Relationships
   E. Reentry Planning

57. To access more Hustle 2.0 programming, you would:

   A. Be interested to learn how my family or I could purchase more H2.0
   B. Be interested to learn how to recruit a sponsor to purchase more H2.0
   C. Be interested only if my family or I don't have to purchase it
   D. Not be interested because I don't want to continue H2.0
   E. Not be interested because I don't think H2.0 is worth anyone paying for it

58. If Hustle 2.0 could offer you a Parole Board Readiness program with tips for the interview with the parole board, getting the most out of a lawyer, preparing your file, living amends, addressing gang involvement, addressing victims' protests, etc., would you:

   A. Be interested in this program because I will go to a parole board that will determine my suitability for release
   B. Be interested in this program because I want to learn these tips, even if I don't go to a parole board
   C. Not be interested because I won't be evaluated by a parole board
   D. Not be interested in this program because I don't want more Hustle 2.0
   E. Not be interested because I will be released soon

59. The Preseason is more relevant to my needs than other programs offered at my facility.

A. Strongly disagree | B. Disagree | C. Neutral | D. Agree | E. Strongly agree

60. The Preseason has taught me more practical skills than other programs offered at my facility.

A. Strongly disagree | B. Disagree | C. Neutral | D. Agree | E. Strongly agree

61. The Preseason has contributed to my knowledge, skills, and personal development.

A. Strongly disagree | B. Disagree | C. Neutral | D. Agree | E. Strongly agree

62. I am more interested in entrepreneurship and starting a business after my release because of my participation in The Preseason.

A. Strongly disagree | B. Disagree | C. Neutral | D. Agree | E. Strongly agree

63. My confidence has improved because of my participation in The Preseason.

A. Strongly disagree | B. Disagree | C. Neutral | D. Agree | E. Strongly agree

64. I got more value out of The Preseason than I was expecting.

A. Strongly disagree | B. Disagree | C. Neutral | D. Agree | E. Strongly agree

65. The Preseason is the best program I've taken while incarcerated.

A. Strongly disagree | B. Disagree | C. Neutral | D. Agree | E. Strongly agree

66. The Preseason is the coolest program I've taken while incarcerated.

A. Strongly disagree B. Disagree C. Neutral D. Agree E. Strongly agree

67. The Preseason gives me hope for the future.

A. Strongly disagree B. Disagree C. Neutral D. Agree E. Strongly agree

68. As a result of completing The Preseason, I set some new goals for a positive future.

A. Strongly disagree B. Disagree C. Neutral D. Agree E. Strongly agree

69. The Preseason is the most rigorous program I've completed.

A. Strongly disagree B. Disagree C. Neutral D. Agree E. Strongly agree

70. The Preseason is the first time I've completed a program by choice.

A. Strongly disagree B. Disagree C. Neutral D. Agree E. Strongly agree

RECRUITING HONEY BADGERS

Pluggin' 'Em In

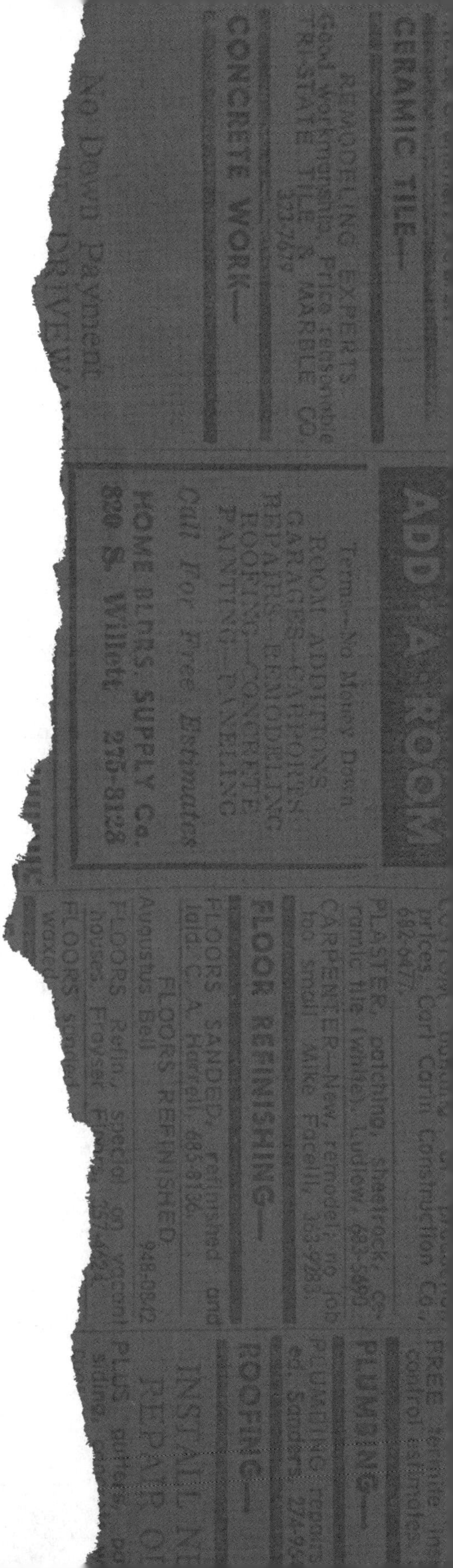

EACH ONE, TEACH ONE

If this book belongs to you, don't complete this section (instead, complete the four deliverables at the end of the book to earn your certificate!). The Mail Order Form and The Preseason Application are only for new recruits. You have our permission to make copies of the Form and Application and distribute them to people with Maverick/Honey Badger potential. People with criminal histories who have been released are welcome to participate.

Know someone who wants (or needs ...) The Preseason? They have two options:

1. **Mail Order Form**
   They (or their loved ones) can purchase The Preseason—this is the only guaranteed way to get the program. Someone who buys the program should not submit The Preseason Application.

OR

2. **The Preseason Application**
   They can apply for a scholarship for The Preseason. Scholarships are funded by external sponsors and are highly competitive. They are not guaranteed, and obtaining one can take time. H2.0 is an equal opportunity scholarship provider, but we do screen out sloths.

Completed Mail Order Forms and Preseason Applications can be submitted via email to info@hustle20.com or via snail mail to:

Hustle 2.0
500 Westover Dr #15672
Sanford, NC 27330

The Preseason can also be purchased on our website at: www.hustle20.com

HUSTLE 2.0

ORDER FORM FOR THE PRESEASON

Shipping To (Envío Para):

Inmate Name (Nombre del recluso) ____________________

Inmate # (Número de Preso) ____________________

Institution Name (Institucion) ____________________

Dorm / Housing (Dormitorio / Cuarto) ____________________

Institution Address (Direccion) ____________________

PO Box # ____________________

City (Ciudad) ____________________ State (Estado) ____________________

Zip (Código Postal) ____________________

From (De):

☐ New Customer (Nuevo Cliente) ☐ Existing Customer (Cliente Existente)

Sender's Name (Nombre) ____________________

Email (we will send your receipt here) ____________________

Address (Direccion) ____________________

Phone # (Teléfono) ____________________

City (Ciudad) ____________________ State (Estado) ____________________

Zip (Código Postal) ____________________

Select Payment Method (Seleccione un método de pago):

☐ Check, Money Order (make payable to "Hustle 2.0") ☐ Visa ☐ Master Card ☐ American Express

on back of your credit card

Credit Card Number (Número de tarjeta)

Expiration Date (Fecha de vencimiento)

3- or 4-Digit Security Code (Código de seguridad)

Cardholder's Name (Nombre del dueño de tarjeta) ____________________

Phone # (Teléfono) ____________________

Cardholder's Address (Direccion del dueño de tarjeta) ____________________ City (Ciudad) ____________________ State (Estado) ____________________ Zip (Código Postal) ____________________

Cardholder's Signature (Firma del dueño de tarjeta) ____________________

Date (Fecha) ____________________

Complete Your Order:

H2.0 Program	**Quantity**	**Price**	**Total Price**
The Preseason		x $50.00	=
		Sales Tax	Included
		Shipping & Handling	+$7.95
		TOTAL	=

Mail your order form to:

Hustle 2.0, PBC
500 Westover Dr #15672
Sanford, NC 27330

Or place your order at **www.Hustle20.com**

HUSTLE 2.0 PRESEASON APPLICATION

Please write legibly!

Applicant's Information:

________________ ________________ ________________

FIRST NAME MIDDLE NAME LAST NAME

________________ ________________

NAME OF INSTITUTION INMATE NUMBER

Your Full Mailing Address:

____

____

____

To qualify for a scholarship, Hustle 2.0 needs your permission to post your questionnaire and photo on its website, social media, or other marketing materials. We do this to advertise your application to potential scholarship sponsors.

I give Hustle 2.0 permission to publish my answers to the "Why I Want To Be A Certified Hustler" questionnaire and to publish a photo of me if I included one. I understand that I am not guaranteed a spot in Hustle 2.0; I will only receive the program if a sponsor provides a scholarship to the program.

________________ ________________ __________

PRINT FULL NAME SIGNATURE DATE

Mail your completed application and questionnaire to:

Hustle 2.0
500 Westover Dr. #15672
Sanford, NC 27330

Optional: Including a photo of yourself with your application can help secure a sponsor for your scholarship more quickly. The best photos are of you smiling or looking professional (note that we don't return pictures).

WHY I WANT TO BECOME A CERTIFIED HUSTLER

My name is ____________ (FIRST NAME) ____________ (LAST NAME) and I'm ______ (AGE) years old. I'm at ____________ (FACILITY NAME) in ____________ (CITY), ____________ (STATE) serving a ____________ (# YEARS/MONTHS) sentence. Over my life, I've done a total of ____________ (# YEARS/MONTHS) behind bars, and the first time I was arrested, I was ______ (AGE) years old.

I want a second chance because ______________________________

____

I want to start pursuing my dream of ______________________________

____

A difficult obstacle I've overcome in my life is ______________________________

____

I'm proud of myself for ______________________________

____

Three positive things about me are:

1) ______________________________

2) ______________________________

3) ______________________________

If I lived up to my full potential, my contribution to this world could be:

____

Here's what this opportunity with Hustle 2.0 would mean for me and my future:

____

Thank you for considering me!

____

(YOUR SIGNATURE)

Illustration by Trenton Dukes

HUSTLE 2.0

CONGRATULATIONS!
THIS CERTIFICATE IS AWARDED TO

Abel Torres

FOR COMPLETING HUSTLE 2.0'S
PRESEASON PROGRAM

WE HONOR YOUR COURAGE AND COMMITMENT.
WE BELIEVE IN YOU AND YOUR SECOND CHANCE!

August 2020

Charles Hoke, Co-founder & CEO

CERTIFICATE REQUIREMENTS

Earnin' Yo' Stripes

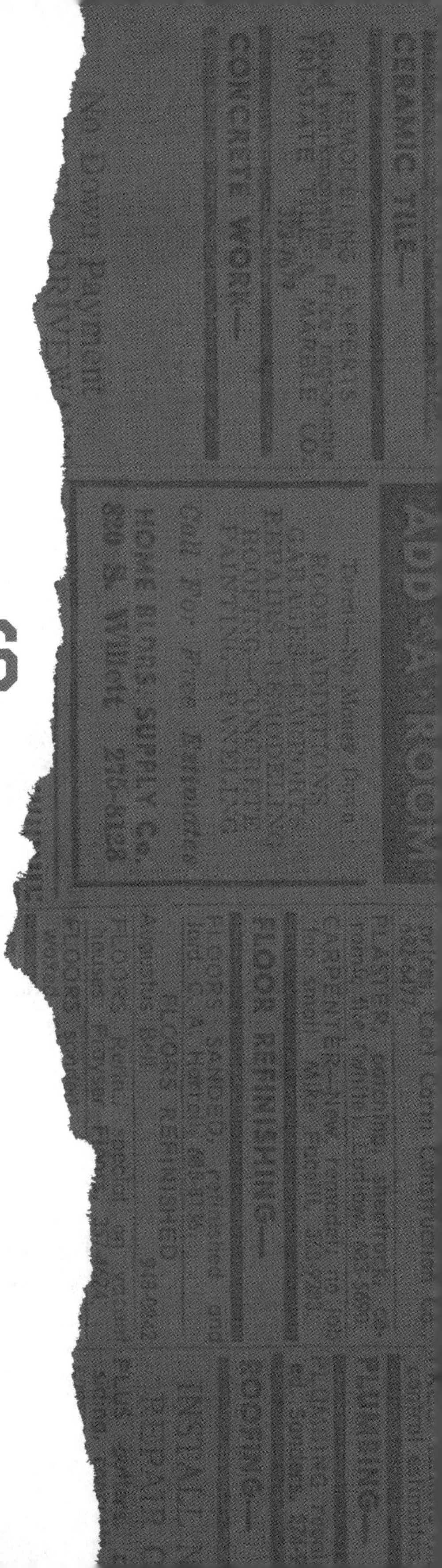

THANK YOU!

We thank you from the bottom of our Honey Badger hearts for completing The Preseason. We hope the time you invested was worth missing those re-runs of Cops on TV. ☺ We believe in you, Honey Badger!!! If it wasn't obvious, we packed The Preseason with testimonials and wisdom from men and women who, without knowing you, care deeply about your success. This is for us, by us! It's our honor to do some of your time with you. We know you can live up to your full potential. Many of us have done it and are still doing it today. We believe in you!

> After examining the higher-quality research studies, we found that, on average, incarcerated people who participated in correctional education programs had 43 percent lower odds of recidivating than those who did not.
>
> *Source: Evaluating the Effectiveness of Correctional Education by Rand Corporation*

CERTIFY YOUR HUSTLE

Earn a legit certificate with a gold seal to add to your file or send to your family to make them proud!

Certificate Requirements

You must mail us all four completed deliverables to earn your certificate.

Deliverable #1: Contact Info
Deliverable #2: Bubble Sheet
Deliverable #3: Survey, Part II
Deliverable #4: Call to Action

What's a MIC?

MIC stands for: Maverick Identification Code. Your MIC is just your birthday formatted as MMDDYY. For example, if your birthday is August 1, 1965, then your MIC is 080165. Let's break that down further:

1. The first 2 digits represent your month of birth.

Jan = 01	*Apr = 04*	*Jul = 07*	*Oct = 10*
Feb = 02	*May = 05*	*Aug = 08*	*Nov = 11*
Mar = 03	*Jun = 06*	*Sep = 09*	*Dec = 12*

2. The middle 2 digits represent your day of birth (01-31).
3. The last 2 digits represent the last two numbers of your year of birth (e.g., if you were born in 1965, write 65; if you were born in 2002, write 02).

Combine these 6 digits to form your MIC here:

___ ___ ___ ___ ___ ___

Month Day Year

Now go enter your MIC at the top of your Bubble Sheet!

Illustration by Trenton Dukes

MAIL EVERYTHING FROM THIS POINT FORWARD TO H2.0!

Deliverable #1: Contact Info

Write this in your best handwriting so we get your certificate right!

Name You Want Printed on Certificate:

______________________ ______________________ ______________________

FIRST MIDDLE (OPTIONAL) LAST

Offender ID: ______________ Your Correctional Facility: ______________________

Your Mailing Address (include your name, inmate ID, housing/cell, and facility name and address):

____

____

____

____

We will print one certificate. We can either send it to you, or to someone of your choice. What's your preference? Only check one box.

☐ Send it to me

Or

☐ Send it to someone who cares about me (include their full name and mailing address):

____

____

____

____

Mail all four completed deliverables to:
Hustle 2.0, PBC
500 Westover Dr #15672
Sanford, NC 27330

Deliverable #2: Bubble Sheet

Using a pencil or blue or black pen, transfer your Mando answers (questions 1 to 50) and Survey, Part 1 answers (questions 51 to 70) to the Bubble Sheet. Shade each bubble in completely. Don't get sloppy if you want that certificate!

Write and bubble in your six-digit MIC (i.e., your birthday formatted as MMDDYY)

M	M	D	D	Y	Y
0	0	0	0	0	0
1	1	1	1	1	1
2	2	2	2	2	2
3	3	3	3	3	3
4	4	4	4	4	4
5	5	5	5	5	5
6	6	6	6	6	6
7	7	7	7	7	7
8	8	8	8	8	8
9	9	9	9	9	9

1.	A B C D	21.	A B C D	41.	A B C D ⊗	61.	A B C D E
2.	A B C D	22.	A B C D	42.	A B C D ⊗	62.	A B C D E
3.	A B C D	23.	A B C D	43.	A B C D ⊗	63.	A B C D E
4.	A B C D	24.	A B C D	44.	A B C D ⊗	64.	A B C D E
5.	A B C D	25.	A B C D	45.	A B C D ⊗	65.	A B C D E
6.	A B C D	26.	A B C D	46.	A B C D ⊗	66.	A B C D E
7.	A B C D	27.	A B C D	47.	A B C D ⊗	67.	A B C D E
8.	A B C D	28.	A B C D	48.	A B C D ⊗	68.	A B C D E
9.	A B C D	29.	A B C D	49.	A B C D ⊗	69.	A B C D E
10.	A B C D	30.	A B C D	50.	A B C D ⊗	70.	A B C D E
11.	A B C D	31.	A B C D	51.	A B C D E		
12.	A B C D	32.	A B C D	52.	A B C D E		
13.	A B C D	33.	A B C D	53.	A B C D E		
14.	A B C D	34.	A B C D	54.	A B C D E		
15.	A B C D	35.	A B C D	55.	A B C D E		
16.	A B C D	36.	A B C D	56.	A B C D E		
17.	A B C D	37.	A B C D	57.	A B C D E		
18.	A B C D	38.	A B C D	58.	A B C D E		
19.	A B C D	39.	A B C D	59.	A B C D E		
20.	A B C D	40.	A B C D	60.	A B C D E		

Form Identifier — DO NOT MARK

Deliverable #3: Survey, Part II

On a scale of 1 to 10, how likely would you be to recommend Hustle 2.0 to an incarcerated person who is into programming? Circle your answer.

1	2	3	4	5	6	7	8	9	10
I wouldn't recommend it									*I'm for sure recommending H2.0!*

Please provide feedback about The Preseason content, humor, art, testimonials, relatability, tone, applicability to your life, etc.

____

____

How did you relate (or not relate) to the testimonials and case studies of currently and formerly incarcerated people?

____

____

How could we improve The Preseason?

____

____

____

If you're hoping for more Hustle 2.0 training, what do you most want to get out of it? If you're not interested in more Hustle 2.0 training, why not?

____

____

____

Deliverable #4: Call to Action

Whenever possible, Hustle 2.0 partners with correctional systems, corporations, faith-based organizations, volunteer groups, and nonprofits to purchase H2.0 programs for Mavericks.

If more H2.0 is made available to you, would you want to participate in *(check only one):*

☐ The Combine (4 books over 4 months)
☐ The Full Program with the majors (12 books over 12 months)
☐ The Parole Board Readiness Program
☐ I don't want to complete more H2.0 programming

Imagine a sponsor is considering providing you with a scholarship for more H2.0 programming. In up to 3 sentences, shoot your best shot: write why this opportunity matters and why you will take it seriously if they fund your H2.0 scholarship:

___

___

___

___

If a funding partner is *not* available, would you like to learn how you or your loved ones could purchase more H2.0 programming? ☐ **Yes** ☐ **No**

THANK YOU!